To: Carol & Jim
Happy Trails!
Glenn Maynard

Strapped into
an American Dream

Glenn Maynard

 **Strategic Book Publishing**

Photos by Tracy Wishneski Maynard Thielman. Copyright © 1992-
1993 Tracy Wishneski Maynard Thielman. Used by permission.

Author photo by Amber Gray.

Strategic Book Publishing
An imprint of Strategic Book Group
P.O. Box 333
Durham CT 06422
 http://www.StrategicBookGroup.com

ISBN: 978-1-60976-030-4

Book Design: Bruce Salender

Printed in the United States of America

Dedication

This book is dedicated to the Oprah Winfrey Book of the Month Club, and to all of the armchair travelers who can only read about chucking it all and hitting the road. Buckle up.

Special Thanks

to my family for their assistance and support of this journey, especially my brother, Frank Maynard, owner of New England Kitchen & Bath, who turned the RV's bright orange interior into a modern interior. Thanks to Tracy Thielman and her parents, Bill Wishneski and Judith Fenton, for all of their help and support. Thanks to all of the people along the way who provided food and shelter and running water. Thanks to Glenn F. Russell, Jr., Esq. for his legal assistance. Finally, thanks to Elizabeth Page, who fought on my behalf to convince her publishing company that they should publish my story.

Contents

Chapter One

Memories of childhood shape a life. I have fond memories when stretching my mind back for a ride to my earliest years. I used to dream about being a major league baseball star. Some children dream of being in Hollywood, or becoming policemen or firemen. Most of these dreams fizzle with age, but we can fondly look back at the precariousness of such impressionable minds and wonder if it's possible to recapture those glory days.

My dreams faded with age, my baseball aspirations swallowed by statistics. However, some children are consumed by fantastic visions, obsessively shadowing them until they're captured. These children become overpowered by such fantasies, which eventually merge with their lives. I was married to such a girl for five years. Her name was Tracy.

A monkey traveling around the country in a purple van existed as a childhood fantasy so authentic that Tracy never brushed it aside, nor did she grow out of it. Her childhood dissolved, but there remained the dream of traveling around the country in the purple van with the monkey. This purple metallic van contained a bed and a kitchen. The monkey would awaken Tracy every morning for breakfast, which was when they'd plan their day. They had the freedom to travel where and when they chose. Even though this was merely a little girl's fantasy, she never forgot it.

The year was 1991 when Tracy and I landed in Florida, which was our first vacation together. Her cousin Dave and his wife Cindy played host in Jacksonville and presented us with our own wing to settle into. The following day they invited us to bathe in their outdoor whirlpool on a seventy-degree February day while they peddled away on bikes.

While reclining in the rough waters, a brilliant winter sun shining on our faces, we agreed that there had to be another way to live. Tracy began reading the real estate section of the local paper. We were encouraged by the fact that the cost of housing was considerably less than the numbers we were used to seeing and went off on a tangent, discussing our options. One such option had us working Connecticut wages to pay for a small mortgage in Florida. Well, it made perfect sense in that soothing whirlpool. It was merely an alternative, and it opened our minds. This type of thinking drove us to seek more in our lives.

That afternoon, we realized that our options could be endless. Settling on our present situation wouldn't suffice. But at dinner that evening, it appeared that Tracy had taken this too far. Dave and Cindy had placed a nice spread on the table, and we began to get delirious.

"I've always wanted to go to Washington," Tracy insisted.

"Me too," I agreed, "and I really want to see Colorado."

Pictures of massive mountains filled my head, triggering a smile at the thought. Prior to Florida, and aside from a 1984 trip to the Bahamas, I hadn't been out of New England. I had always wondered what it would be like to motor along the roadways through different states, answering to no one. The mere thought of it felt so wild and free.

"I've always wanted to see the Grand Canyon," Tracy continued. "And Mount Rushmore...definitely Mount Rushmore." She had experienced California and Colorado in her younger days, via family getaways, but her image of the west was unfocused, due to how young she had been during these visits.

"I'd do anything to get to California," I said.

Dave and Cindy glanced back and forth at us, as if viewing a tennis match. Our emotions soared, even though these ideas exceeded our means, or seemingly so, before Tracy took a giant step forward.

"Let's quit our jobs and see all the states," she decided. "We'll take a year." Her high cheekbones jerked higher, her smile brightened the room, and her blue eyes mixed joy with joke, although I couldn't confirm the latter ingredient.

"Yeah," I exclaimed, but with unconvinced excitement. "Let's do it."

Dave and Cindy chuckled. I had trouble believing we could migrate across the country to California, never mind all the states, but what a thrill to merely discuss our dreams.

The following evening, Dave and Cindy invited us to a fine restaurant on the water, where my horizons broadened the moment I stuck a chunk of breaded alligator between my jaws. Normally, if it didn't resemble a burger, I would thumb my nose at it. But as we rode home, Tracy spoke of the dream with renewed excitement. However, talk is cheap, and I decided the fun was over when a dose of reality splashed me in the face. This had gone far enough.

"No way," I said. "That's impossible. We can't afford that. What are we going to do, stay in a motel every night?"

"We'll get an RV," she answered.

"Get a what?"

"A recreational vehicle; a motorhome. It has a bed, a kitchen, and a bathroom."

"I can't drive something that big," I admitted. "That's why I drive a Sprint."

"They come in all sizes," she insisted. "My father's friend, Gil, has a bed, a kitchen, and a bathroom in his van. We don't have to get something that's outrageous to drive."

I began mulling it over, but additional doubts surfaced. I started deflating, but curiosity kept me hyped. "How much do these things cost? We can't afford something like that."

Tracy always accused me of making assertions about situations I knew nothing about. I didn't think we could afford anything so involved, so I went with that argument.

"We can buy a used RV in the newspaper," she said. "It doesn't have to be brand new."

"But what about insurance? It'll cost a fortune to insure, and then we wouldn't be able to afford health insurance."

Tracy turned her head away for a moment in disbelief or thought, but faced me again after her short retreat. "There are temporary health plans," she continued, "and maybe our group plans can be continued for a while after we leave our jobs. Information is free, so we should at least look into it."

I simply couldn't fathom quitting the security of our jobs and traveling for an entire year. This was ludicrous, and not having a paycheck every two weeks fueled my fire. We were in debt. Only wealthy or retired people could pull this off. We could not do this. We had no money, and we'd need lots of it. Who were we?

Then I envisioned trudging into work the following Monday. I tensed while thinking about it, but with the shape of the economy, I thought I should be satisfied with just having a job. That's when a shock wave jolted me, and I realized that maybe I wasn't as fortunate as I had believed. Managers reminded us that we should consider ourselves lucky to have jobs. People struggle all year at jobs they despise for a week or two of vacation, which breezes by more rapidly than the work week. Tracy and I constituted living proof.

I moved onto the possibility of quitting that job and taking off; chucking it all, hitting the road, and becoming radical. The thought alone was certainly an adrenaline rush. However, it would entail further convincing from this girl who had a childhood fantasy to fulfill.

Chapter Two

Florida had clearly altered our minds. Our ten day vacation evolved into an about-face in our approach to life. We scrutinized our lives, drawing up a list of what we wanted out of life. What would it take to make us love life? Too many people settle into their lives, striving for nothing more than routine. They may not be happy, but a false sense of security appeases them, and we now found ourselves in this category.

Our routine seemed simpler than trying something new. We were so wrapped in routine that no time remained for things that made us happy. Nor was there time for the real "US" to break from the shell and express our true nature. This pattern could dominate our lives if ignored. We could donate our lives to one company until retirement, never getting the opportunity to see or do what we want, only planning for "someday."

We are all mortals, and no one knows when our time is up. Will I live to be ninety years old, or will I perish tomorrow? We don't think about it because it's morbid, and nothing will happen to us...ever. But if tomorrow is my fateful day, what happens to the activities saved for retirement? Am I satisfied with my life thus far? If not, then I'd better start fulfilling it before nothing is accomplished and time runs out.

Aha. This was what we couldn't afford. Life is too short to wait for someday, because that day usually never comes. Could we afford not to take this trip? I came face-to-face with that question, and the answer quickly became available.

I'm a teenager again in my second life. The switch-over occurred in 1980, while I opened my glazed eyes and noticed my brother, Frank, standing above. He had mentioned a car accident, but I had no recollection of it. Frank retained most of the mystery so he wouldn't upset me. However, my doses of medication skewed what I needed to comprehend, and Frank was more surprised to see my eyes than I was to see his.

As details emerged, I learned that the metal tent straddling my body prevented the sheets from tampering with my third degree burns. I had been pinned underneath the car, and the catalytic converter singed my skin for over an hour. The brace around my neck was not for whiplash. My neck was broken. Once curiosity eased in, I wondered why I wasn't dead or paralyzed. However, I eventually learned that I had come one-eighth of an inch from being a paraplegic.

No remedy existed for my broken ribs, broken pelvis, broken hand or dislocated shoulder. If the car hadn't landed on its tires after being upended and colliding into a tree fourteen feet from the ground, then treatment wouldn't have been necessary for my burns or for my neck.

I casually asked my brother about Charlie, Mike, Joe, and Brock; my four friends who were in the car. It was supposed to have been just a night out at the movies. Where were they? He sugar-coated his explanation when the truth was that they had been tossed out of the car like rag dolls. Brock had actually landed in a tree, Joe and Mike were wandering around on the highway in a daze, and Charlie remained in the car bouncing around like a pinball. Through all this horrific chaos, they had thankfully survived with only minor injuries.

The rest of the details came piecemeal. I would spend evenings rehashing stories. One such story regarded the night of the accident, when my family bonded by holding hands in a circle of prayer while occupying the waiting room. My parents, Carole and Frank, took hold of their other five children, and prayed to keep the family at eight. Karen, Lee, Gladie, Kathy, and Frank, Jr. prayed for their brother to rejoin them.

They closed their eyes and raised their hopes. Their prayers worked, because moments later my brother fought his way past hospital staff, determined to see his younger brother as alive as his hopes. My eyelashes parted for the first time, and I stole a groggy glimpse of the world. The doctors reiterated my good fortune; I was a miracle survivor.

Three skin-graft operations hospitalized me for two months. The burns created constant agony as all layers of skin, plus flesh the size of a football, had melted from my backside. The burns were truly deep, like my thoughts.

Lowered by stretcher into a medicated and boiling whirlpool three times daily for three weeks, I could only perceive the world as inhumane when my wound was submerged. I clenched the metal bars overhead. I gritted my teeth ferociously and perilously and begged for mercy. I squeezed so hard that I left impressions of my hands on the metal as I strained to alleviate the trauma.

I tensed prior to the moment my wound clashed with water. I felt steam rising, and then the next stage: I wailed. People appeared from all over the hospital, peeking into the room. Several nurses around the whirlpool anchored me from all angles, mumbling words of compassion to make it all better. But it never was, and helpless tears rolled down my cheeks, adding to the water in the pool until the torture subsided twenty minutes later.

During three days in critical condition, drifting in and out of consciousness, doctors believed I had a fifty-fifty chance of survival. There are no guarantees in life, and I remember those agonizing thoughts about the other fifty percent. I had two months of lying on my right side to think about it...day after day and night after night.

Although I left the hospital craving a fulfilling life, I began taking life for granted again during the ten years following the accident. I didn't particularly like myself for this. The strong, determined thoughts that had filled my mind during my stay in the hospital were gradually overcome with routine.

I couldn't afford to fear what could go wrong on this trip. If I feared experience, I'd have none, and that would be drastic. If we seized this opportunity, then we could handle anything. If we put it off, then it would slip through our fingers forever. We were sure of it.

I kept thinking about the accident. I kept thinking about how precious life is. I kept thinking about the pain. I kept thinking about how foolish it would be to follow a path just because that's what everyone else does, and because that's the thing to do. I respected life too much to be pushed along with the herd. I had met a girl who shared a common denominator with me, and I had a burning desire to fulfill our dream.

Chapter Three

Once I warmed up to the idea, knowing that anything is possible, my horizons widened. Our focus became an obsession, but turning fantasy into reality became a complex mental game. Too many times I asked myself who we were fooling, once a rush came over me as if to rouse me from this dream. Tracy repressed similar emotions.

Convincing ourselves to unload all of our energy into this goal became critical. We had to decide whether or not to take the trip. Groundbreaking ceremonies could wait no longer, and large plans require large steps.

Visions of my brother standing over my hospital bed continued, as did flashbacks of swerving the car three times before hearing that explosive crash, which erased the picture. I read them as messages that life is too short to spend waiting; a persuasive ingredient.

We chose to depart in May of 1992, having fifteen months to prepare. Although our relationship was good, it wasn't solid. Having dated for just over a year up to this point, we felt that our lives had been designed to cross paths and lead us to travel. We determined that a true relationship is never perfect, but that this journey could bond us.

Expanding our plans as we progressed, we decided to make this not only a journey, but our honeymoon. April twenty-fifth was the wedding date we chose by counting back one week per state from Louisiana to coincide with Mardi Gras. We couldn't come up with a better way to begin a marriage, and we believed that our imperfections would work themselves out. Besides, every couple has their moments. How could we go wrong? We would always have an awesome adventure under our belts. However we ended up, we felt as though we were still fated to cross paths and share what most people only dream about.

Our enormous anticipation of our future blinded wedding anxieties. The plans that we concocted to travel through America dwarfed even our wedding. One of life's most significant events took a backseat, even while it unfolded. That's how potent our plans for America had become, and nothing could contend with such a force.

Chapter Four

Our foremost travel considerations included a mode of transportation, its size, and the components within. We needed a unit large enough to store a year's supply of belongings. We needed a bathroom, kitchenette, stove, oven, refrigerator, table, and bed. It had to be in excellent mechanical order because any breakdown would be critical and costly.

Two months of scanning newspaper ads and visiting dealers to see what was available turned up no ideal vehicle within our price range. All of the RVs that private RV owners showed us were all too big, too expensive, or just plain ugly. Although we initially pondered a popup, it seemed only suitable for a weekend excursion. Wind or rain would be miserable, and cranking it up and down at each stop wouldn't be pleasant for an entire year. We investigated Class B fully loaded vans, but time and research narrowed our vehicle to a motorhome not too big to drive and not too small to call our home for a year.

As our dedicated search progressed, Tracy's father, Bill, clipped an RV ad with no picture from the local paper. Two weeks following our engagement, we bought this twenty-two foot 1978 Dodge Rockwood. Its new engine had logged just three hundred miles, which became our determining factor. Bill told the owner that the RV had to be in top mechanical order since I was "as me-chanically-inclined as a box of Cheerios."

My vast knowledge of the automobile extends no further than gas, oil, and wiper fluid. I admit it. However, mechanics are out there, and we contacted mechanically inclined friends of ours to give it a once-over before we made the investment. One mechanic lay underneath the RV and banged on the gas tanks while the oth-ers swarmed over the major parts, whatever they may be.

After our test drive with the panel of inspectors strapped to the kitchen table, the owner returned to his house and awaited our de-cision. When I asked for a show of hands for those in favor, Tracy and I were taken aback by the unanimous vote; all four hands raised toward the roof.

I later pulled my father aside for a personal opinion.

"So, what do you think?" I asked.

He surveyed the interior of the camper thoughtfully before re-sponding. "Could use some tweeters," he replied as he studied what he believed to be inadequate speakers.

The RV parked in our driveway served as both a daily re-minder of our sincerity and proof that nothing could stop us. It wasn't just an RV. It was an object that nullified that deep-rooted uncertainty plaguing us since Florida. It was the first major step that edged fantasy toward reality.

We now owned an RV, but the color of orange dominated the interior. The orange stripes against the white siding of the exterior didn't bother us much because they were minor. However, it felt as if we were walking into McDonald's; the gaudy orange of the shag carpet, curtains, tables, counters, and wallpaper. All of this was no less horrifying than the eight-track cassette deck protruding from the dashboard.

We were faced with two options: we could completely over-haul the interior, or play eight-track cassettes and wear bell bottom jeans to relive this era. We opted for renovation, but without the hands of family and friends, we would have been driven to paint the RV purple and bring a monkey along.

Chapter Five

We made numerous overwhelming decisions in such a short period of time, and rarely did we have a moment to ponder their impact. Sometimes reality raided our sleep. A surge flashed through our minds like a bolt of lightning regarding the very idea of just going.

We imagined living on the road, not knowing where we'd sleep at night. We had wildlife concerns; animals that would be foreign to us. Tornadoes whirling around Kansas also whirled around my head. We needed a storage area in which to put our belongings. As the wedding drew near, we wondered if we'd be leaving with money. Both of our cars were still very much in our ownership, and nobody seemed to want to change that.

As time passed, the lagging economy lagged some more, and the threat of layoffs loomed for both of us. It was critical for us to escape this stranglehold, but this escape didn't come without the fear associated with being unemployed. Soon, we would be quitting our jobs and strapping ourselves into an American dream.

Tracy also found herself stuck in the undesirable position of a stressful work environment, which held back her inspiration to express herself through art. She had no time to perfect her gift, creating only distress and frustration. Something she despised prevented her from performing what she loved. For her, breaking away became an act of passion and an opportunity to fulfill that childhood fantasy.

May 3, 1992

I choked up when Tracy and her father embraced, then wished each other luck in the year ahead. It jolted me into realizing that we weren't merely taking a drive to the store, or going on a week's vacation. I paused until the end; a long hug for a long separation. This meaningful hug came from the man who did plenty to help us attain this dream. Bill knew what this trip meant to us, persevering until he was confident we'd be safe and comfortable.

I averted my emotions until their showing of affection split. My emotions battled for control while Bill approached me for a firm handshake. He not only wanted the best for his daughter and me, but I'm sure he'd spent a few nights wondering what the hell we would do if our camper suffered a breakdown in Death Valley or some other faraway and deserted place. I know it had crossed our minds a couple hundred times.

Tracy grabbed her little Miniature Schnauzer, Molly, who weighs in at ten pounds before haircuts, and placed her into the camper. She leaped up the steps and into the driver's seat, then bounded over to the passenger's seat to look outside, and waited for us to join her.

Inside the back window, a black sign with bold red letters read, "Beware of Dog." Below the window could be interpreted as another warning to some: a "Just Married" sign written by Tracy's aunt in black marker on a brown paper bag, plastered by three pounds of Scotch tape.

We anxiously boarded the camper and took our seats. I drove, and Molly sat on Tracy's lap as we backed out of Bill's driveway in Bristol, Connecticut, stopping in the road amongst family, friends, and neighbors who stepped out their front doors to wave goodbye.

As cameras flashed, I shifted into drive, inching our twenty-two foot house away from the home in which Tracy had grown up. She glanced back at it for perhaps the final time, because this little house went to the market.

While barging through to the stop sign ahead, the side view mirror revealed a small crowd gathered in the street. That part was behind us. However, we still had one more stop at my parent's house in Glastonbury. The overwhelming joy that we had been anticipating for fifteen months was absent. We thought it would slap us once we were officially on the road, having left Glastonbury.

My brother, Frank, had planned a going away party with family and friends to see us off. It was like any ordinary gathering at the house. However, it was hard for me to comprehend that we would be falling off this part of the earth; the only part which familiar faces inhabited. After gathering everyone together in the front yard, we said our goodbyes while scanning the vehicle we hoped would do us proud. In all the excitement, we actually left to go cross-country with thirty-three dollars tucked into my wallet. We forgot about visiting the bank, and it was Sunday.

Then we found ourselves strapped into an American dream with the engine running. It seemed like a different vehicle now that it had full cabinets and a cool refrigerator. Now it was our home. Tracy and I couldn't have been closer to the trip than at this moment. I glanced at Tracy. She returned my glance with a look of nervous elation. Time would not stand still.

The RV crept around the cul-de-sac in front of my parent's house on Arrowhead Drive, not once, but twice, before passing our last crowd. My two little nephews, Matthew and Nicky, opened and closed their little raised hands, repeating after their mothers. "Have a nice car ride!" They were unsure of what was happening, yet made a large impression on us. I gazed at them, trying to imagine what they would look like when we returned.

We pulled away from everyone and everything, officially on our journey. Everything came down to this moment as we passed twenty or so waving hands. Fifteen months for this. The day was grandiose, but the moment even larger, and now our future would unravel before us.

We felt different the moment we pulled away. Our lives changed considerably as we drove down the street. We felt free, on the road to adventure. Maybe sometime soon we'd feel it, sending shock waves through us, like we expected.

"This is it," said Tracy, a contagious smile wrapping around her face.

Bursting with passion, we rolled onto the first highway of the trip, unable to fathom the enormity of our present situation. We were just easing forward, further along in time and space. Soon we'd be lost, footloose, rolling along aimlessly.

Our first destination was Misquamicut Beach in Westerly, Rhode Island, where we could treasure a few days relaxing from a taxing fifteen months of preparation. Tracy's Aunt Joan and Uncle Jerry had invited us to park our camper in the dirt driveway of their unfinished cottage. As anxious as I was to start heading west, the layover sounded inviting.

The sun headed west, as if urging us to follow, but we only admired the way it cast a pink tint on the clouds as we arrived at our parking spot. After plugging into the cottage, assisted by what little light remained, we were set for the duration of our stay.

Soon after arriving, Joan and Jerry joined us and we all sat at the dinette in our new home, sipping champagne and orange juice. Tracy clinked her glass against mine. We paused long enough to cherish the moment, then clinked the two other glasses. Raising these vessels up high, we toasted to our new life.

When they left, it gave us time to reflect on what was behind us and what could possibly lie ahead. The ideal plan would move us through the northern states for the spring and summer and the southern states for the fall and winter. However, this spring happened to be freezing. The temperatures were not conducive to bathing suits. In fact, we began our first full day on the beach wearing winter coats.

May 6, 1992

We encountered an endurance test while adapting to camper life. This was an adjustment period of sink-or-swim challenges. It all began when Tracy turned on the water for a shower. The hot water heater was not working, forcing us to boil water in order to take baths. We dumped the hot water into a dishpan, added cold water from the tap, and prepared for a warm bath. Since the shower adapter in the bathroom dribbled, we had to forget showers for the year.

Naturally, this disturbed us. The bathroom was barely large enough for us to make a complete turn without bumping our heads or elbows. After placing the toilet lid down, we put the dishpan of water on it, closed the shower curtain sectioning off the bathroom, and grabbed a plastic cup. We then had to dive into the pan head first, saturating our heads, then use cups of water to rinse the soap and shampoo.

The late winter afflicted me with a cold. My nose ran faster than my patience. Having run out of potable water and drinking water, I was forced to build up saliva in order to take a vitamin C pill. If nothing else, I thought this would make for a fine "when I was your age..." story.

We planned to visit Charleston Beach. Driving away from Misquamicut, we heard a clamor on the rooftop as we passed under overhanging trees. I pulled over to the shoulder, climbed the ladder in the rear, and found the antenna twisted and leaning against the top of the air conditioner, visibly destroyed.

We had no television, no showers, and no hot water to go with my cold. Shortly thereafter, Tracy began to sniffle and cough. With me trying to control my sheer dismay from this awful start and Tracy trying to work in a little optimism and humor, we moved further down the road until the RV suddenly died.

The winding noise we heard while turning the key indicated a problem with the battery, so we jumped the main battery with the RV battery. It fired up immediately, enabling us to carry on for another mile before it stalled again.

Repeating the process worked a second time, but not a third, as we blocked traffic at a stoplight. A pickup truck eased my rage by pulling up to the front and offering to give us a jumpstart. He had noticed the "Just Married" sign, quickly started the RV, and we backtracked to the cottage and hoped to get towed to a service center.

AAA advised us that they service RV's in every state but Rhode Island. However, our persistence earned us a phone number to Arlington RV Supercenter. They told us they could tow the camper, but wouldn't be able to work on it for another week because everyone brought their campers out for the spring, which had created a backlog. However, they advised us to come down and they'd get to us as soon as possible. Furthermore, they invited us to stay there overnight with full hookups at no charge until the RV was fixed.

When the tow truck arrived, Tracy and I sat in the front seat with a driver who wanted to join our travels. He asked many questions, swiveling his head from the road to his copilots as we bore down on long stretches of interstate.

"What are you getting for mileage on that thing?" he asked

I shot a glance back to the camper on the flatbed before responding. "Right now at least one hundred miles per gallon!"

May 7, 1992

Molly barked convulsively when mechanics tinkered with her camper, forcing us to remove her to the waiting room. She's very high-strung and barks at anything that moves. We only had to wait three hours for the RV. Our hot water heater and battery were fixed, our water supply was full, and our credit card was maxed out.

We traded Charleston for Newport. Tracy had heard enticing descriptions of Cliff Walk and wanted to see it for herself. We had the vehicle. We had the time.

Springtime found me sheltered in a green down jacket and Tracy in a couple of sweaters tucked under her brown leather coat. We meandered down the paved path alongside the cliff top. Waves crashed and echoed far below against the rocks jutting from the water. Waves also broke further out in the menacing ocean and on the arched beach to our left, which we were overlooking.

Traveling further down the road brought us to a slanted wall of basketball-sized rocks leading down into the ocean. Algae-covered rocks sat at the base of the cliff, and others emerged further into the ocean as waves receded.

It was blustery and chilly. Fighting frigid ocean breezes wasn't enjoyable enough for us to stay. But as we returned to the camper, we noticed a young couple preparing a hang glider at the highest part of the cliff.

We exchanged greetings while passing by. The man scurried around the glider, making alterations for the jump, while the woman waited to assist. Never having seen a hang gliding operation, we rushed ahead for a seat on cement stairs. Although our distance could have disqualified us as key witnesses, we had our camcorder ready to film liftoff.

The man repeatedly glanced our way from his bent over position during his mad rush. He'd snap his head back and forth, making us wonder if we offended him with our camera. Then he waved us over, so we strolled his way.

Ross was his name, a rosy-cheeked man with dirty-blonde curly hair and a mustache. The girl helping him was his friend. His light brown retriever continuously circled the kite, wagging its tail in anticipation of the jump.

Ross protected his head with a tightly strapped blue helmet as he worked, screaming over the deafening wind. Whoooosh. Whoooosh. Wave after wave of wind attempted to disable them. Everything had to be repeated.

"Can you guys give me a hand in getting this ready to fly?"

I screamed, "yes" in response, chafing my windpipe.

The wind continued to push the operation off balance. Ross then began to shout orders. He entered the kite, attached the straps hanging behind him and held onto two black bars in front of him to create an overall look of having entangled himself in a tripod. His pace continued to be fast and furious. Perfect wind comes infrequently.

His friend stood on the edge of the cliff and held the kite back with two thick wires, one in each hand. Ross directed me to hold the wire coming down the left side. Tracy held the one on the right. The sweeping, jolting wind forced us near the edge, but Ross assured us that we were safe.

The shifting wind quickened, and jumping off this cliff appeared suicidal. I eyed Tracy, her long blonde hair blinding her as her bent knees helped her hold to the ground. She looked as queasy about our recruitment as I, but we couldn't back out. Tracy's eyes finally met mine, but her face offered no indication of her feelings, not even a facial expression.

21

Ross dismissed Tracy as the time neared, screaming inaudibly, which his friend interpreted as a cue to let go and hustle away. He repeated his command for the novices. "Clear! Clear!"

A split-second after I dove to the side, Ross scrambled, jumped off the cliff, and rode the wind up, up and away. He instantly towered above us, yelling "Thank you! Thank you!"

We cheered his accomplishment as he headed out into the ocean instead of to the beach, where I thought his destination would have been. That's where my destination would have been. Emotion poured from the kite, raining down upon the three of us. "Wahoo! Wahoo," he screamed.

Tracy and I admired Ross as he rode the surges of wind higher and higher. We thought that we had our freedom, but then we saw Ross turn into a bird. He had been hang gliding for ten years, wanting to jump from Cliff Walk for five. Tracy and I had helped him soar.

Since he planned to land on the beach, we made our way there with his dog flopping about, wondering when his master was coming down. On the beach, we watched Ross flying far over the ocean before turning around and heading toward us.

The hang glider thumped down on the beach directly in front of our camper, and the dog shot off like a bullet, jumping all over Ross as he descended from the clouds. The biting wind clung to our skin. Ross needed time to pack up, so we moved onward. Even though Ross alone soared with the kite, I believe we all got a little high.

Rhode Island is a pea compared to most states. This marked the end of state number one, and although we had serious doubts as to the feasibility of the trip after a breakdown on day three, we now had clear visions of Massachusetts.

May 10, 1992

After pushing through our namesake town of Maynard, we moved from Massachusetts up to New Hampshire. This marked our third state in seven days. Our mood reached another level due to the change of landscape in northern Massachusetts. It happened in a snap. The spirit of the trip shined while starting into the hills, where Tracy took the helm for the first time and cruised into higher elevation as we carved our path north. The sun reflected off oncoming traffic as we reflected on our new life on the road.

The rippled hills, inflating gradually enough for a bicycle pump to do the job, subtly emerged as small mountains neatly tucked away in the distance like charcoal paint dabs. Route 202 was the winding road that ventured in and around these mountains, which continued to grow with each mile. Every turn introduced a new mountain. A steady chain welcomed us to the state that would die if it did not live free, and how free it felt to sail through these natural wonders.

Once through the capital of Concord, we hopped onto Interstate 93 heading north after I accepted the steering wheel in this tag-team effort. After six hours of driving, we needed a place to settle for the night. Unfortunately, New Hampshire didn't participate in our book of free campgrounds. Being on the road for a year with about seven thousand dollars and a couple unsold automobiles, we had to do everything in our power not to drop money into campgrounds or we'd be home rather early.

My eyes began to play tricks, and our standards started to decline. A green triangle on the map indicated a rest area, and we pulled in not a second too soon. The sign on the bulletin board warned that New Hampshire law prohibited rests that exceeded four hours, making me wonder why the natives don't resemble zombies.

I would stand corrected upon meeting the groundskeeper. I watched him pull down the flag for the night, then approached him to ask about staying here anyway. I pointed to the rig and asked him, "Would it be all right if we stayed here overnight in that camper?"

The burly groundskeeper stared at me with his permanently bulging mouth and severely weathered face before managing, "People...stay here...all...the time."

Here stood a native who must not have rested more than the four hours designated by state law. His words were separated by gaps. "I'm...the one...who...allows...them to," he continued, proud of this power to grant requests such as mine. "It would be...fine...if you...stayed the night."

Few cars occupied the rest area, and it didn't look too troublesome this far north, so we jumped at his permission.

"Great, thank you," I said, as the man continued to stare as if awaiting a tip. "We just got married and are traveling cross-country for a year."

Mr. Groundsman blew over my statement with citations from the bible and slowly, carefully, spoke about how great marriage can be.

When I arose in the early morning, I strolled into the rest area's information booth to learn that the town was Canterbury and met a uniformed older man who stood behind a counter. While conversing, the man appeared troubled when I referred to our camper outside.

"You were parked here all night, weren't you?"

"Yes. The man working here last night gave us permission."

He turned his head and pursed his lips. "He always does that, and has no business doing so. I don't know about that guy. He's getting old...and senile," he said, pointing his right index finger to his head.

He went on to warn me about the dangers of rest areas. "I hate to see people camp in the rest areas. There has been one murder here, and I don't want to hear about another. You have to be very careful where you stay. You know, there are twenty-four hour areas in some parts of the country, and police patrol those lots constantly. You're better off in those areas."

The previous night, we had been too tired to care where we parked for the night. We had figured that New Hampshire was too laid back for murder, but we were dead wrong. Crime happens anytime, to anyone, anywhere, but if we dwelled on that, it would sap the thrill right out of the trip. We stored his tip and moved onward.

Heading to Franconia Notch to see The Old Man of the Mountain, we found Highway 93 to be a peaceful interstate. There were few cars on this road, which entertained us through mounds of forest and into the White Mountains. One sign warned of moose crossing, while another read, "Brake for Moose. It could save your life." Clouds congregated by the mountaintops as the threat of rain loomed. We saw no moose, but I was determined to catch a glimpse of one.

Franconia Notch is a glacier-carved gorge in the White Mountains, snuggled between the Kinsman and Franconia ranges. The Old Man of the Mountain ignored us our entire visit, showing only his profile. This forty-foot high head formed by glacial action thousands of years ago is twelve hundred feet above Profile Lake, where his features mirror all from the mountainside. Five separate ledges form the head.

Tracy mixed New Hampshire Mountain stream water into her paint, then sat and painted the Old Man. Her first chance for creativity arrived as the sun greeted us from above, the peacefulness of the state soothing us. The warmth of the sun felt soft on my skin, and Tracy's contentment shined back from within. The time that elapsed seemed trivial, at best.

Apple Hill campground in Bethlehem provided us with a much needed dump station and some shuteye. I wandered into the office as Tracy attempted to pick up the sugar that had spilled from the cabinet onto the dinette, sprinkling her pile of clean clothes. Camper life was proving its inconveniences in a mad way.

The campground owner stood on the front porch as I approached. The middle-aged lady had short, dark hair and a scratchy voice. However, she was as pleasant as could be. "How can I help you?" she scratched.

Since we had rolled into the campground to camp, she invited me in to sign a contract at her sugar-free dining room table. While chatting, our campground fee was whittled down from seventeen dollars to thirteen dollars because of our honeymoon. Now she had proved to be an even more pleasant lady. I asked her where we could track down moose.

"We have moose right here in the campground," she began. "We also have a bear with two cubs. They're friendly, though Mother can get nasty while protecting her cubs."

Tracy entered the office after dodging the two little old and shaggy dogs that pestered all visitors. Part two of the story continued as Tracy inconspicuously shook the dogs from her leg and took a seat inside. The lady related the rest of the story of the three bears, giggling hysterically the whole time.

"There's a mobile home park about a quarter-mile down the road. One day, the owner of the park called to tell me that my bear was visiting. I told her that it wasn't my bear, but we sure got a laugh out of it."

After completing the deal, she followed us out to the camper, wished us a great trip, and ended with this message: "I wish you all the happiness in the world, and just enough unhappiness to know the difference."

May 12, 1992

While camping in the White Mountains, I arose early in the morning to do some writing outside with the birds. The birds didn't write, but they helped provide the perfect setting for progress. This forest offered a large boulder for my chair, allowing me to sit for a while and absorb the harmony of the birds and the stream. I watched the sun rub its eyes, casting shadows on nature's woodwork and highlighting the greens and browns. Chipmunks scurried about, forest trees towered above, and density blocked any hope of distant views. This arena elevated me through the morning.

The camper was cluttered, and Tracy and I were exhausted from travel. Unfortunately, the campground rates in New Hampshire separated us from relaxation. Constant movement, that's what life on the road becomes. We felt like fugitives. Although there were no free campgrounds where we were headed in Maine, a four dollar fee enticed us to the town of West Bethel.

Welcome to Maine: the way life should be. Crocker pond was the exact location of this campground, keeping us within the White Mountain National Forest, but on Maine's turf. I guided the RV down a paved road through the forest, which turned into a dirt road after a while, then changed back to pavement, then back to dirt. The lazy miles made us wonder if we'd ever get there, creeping around narrow corners, hoping that a hot rod would not be arcing into us.

The end of the road, which showed us to the campground, seemed vertical. The camper strained and chugged to the top as we enjoyed the view of the treetops. At the peak, the bulletin board informed us that the campground was closed this time of year, but invited us to camp for free. Could this be the break we craved?

Pulling into a site, we discovered that somebody else had actually made the trek as well. Man's best friend accompanied him, and I lured him over with a question.

"Any animals out in this neck of the woods?" I asked, sitting inside the RV with the engine humming.

"Haven't seen any," he said, drifting to the camper and kicking up leaves on the way.

After a brief exchange, we learned that he went by the name of Tommy. He had been living in Portland, Maine, for eight months after being uprooted from New York City. He concluded our brief exchange with an invitation to come to his campfire later on for some drinks.

"I kinda wanted to be alone this weekend," he admitted, "but you guys are all right. You can stay."

We started reorganizing the mess, preparing ourselves for the party. It shocked us to hear another vehicle pull into this place. It was a van. When it passed, the man driving said without quite yelling, "Happy Honeymoon."

My impatience at a Laundromat earlier in the day had left us with a half-dried laundry pile, so what a perfect time to try out our clothesline attachment for our RV. Tracy dug through our storage area, extracted the line, and we worked together to attach it from the RV to a tree.

However, a free campground meant we needed groceries for three days of rest and relaxation at Crocker Pond. When I backed out of the site, the clothesline snapped and our clothes were strewn all over Maine.

Tracy and I accepted Tommy's offer, spending the warm evening in front of his campfire. His tan Labrador struggled to get up and down with arthritis. Molly couldn't visit with us since another dog roamed in her world. However, we could hear her barking three sites away.

"Molly," screamed Tracy. "Quiet."

"Did you say Molly?" asked Tommy with a puzzled look on his face. "Is your dog's name Molly?"

"Yes," she said.

"That's my dog's name," exclaimed Tommy, pointing to his Molly. And there we camped, Molly, Molly, Tommy, Tracy and I.

As the evening progressed and the chill pushed its way in, we discovered that the few hours had taken their toll and our discussions involved sports, religion, weddings, love, music, camping, and more. Our Rum and coke cocktails helped the conversation flow, but it was more than that. We immediately connected with Tommy, who made us want to hear his life story and tell him ours.

"So you two just quit your jobs?" Tommy asked, rubbing the warmth of the fire into his hands.

"We didn't just quit our jobs," Tracy answered. "We carefully planned this trip for fifteen months. It wasn't just a careless decision." She shrugged her shoulders and spoke with her hands, a sign that she was enthralled.

Tommy shook his head while retaining eye contact with the snapping fire, which began to shoot higher flames from the log he had just added. "I don't know if I'd have the guts to do that," he admitted.

"What would you be afraid of?" asked Tracy, leaning into the blaze for an immediate response, which did not come.

Tommy continued to stare into his fire for answers and came up empty, but his eventual reply was a popular one. "I don't know," he said.

Tracy's eyes had bounded from the fire to Tommy several times as his answer was in the works, and seemed to have an answer to his even before he said a word. "What I find amazing about people's reactions is that they would love to do it... travel, see the country, but they're afraid to do it, and they don't know why. If we've learned anything...it's if you want something bad enough, then why not get it? If you don't get it, then you must not want it bad enough." The topic ended with that deep thought.

Tommy listened to every word intently, nodding to indicate his understanding, until Tracy asked about his profession. He related stories of lives lost as he worked as a physician's assistant and how deeply it affected him. "Having a life slip away is my worst fear," he said, "but the satisfaction associated with saving lives is what drove me into the field, and it's what keeps me there."

His love for his work was obvious. It wasn't just a job, but rather something that provided him with deep satisfaction, which Tracy and I admired. He cared for and about people, which made his company all the more welcome. We listened to him intently, since he spoke about life in such a positive light, and we wanted his reflections to shine on us.

Driving rain interrupted our discussions, so we invited Tommy into the camper while his Molly sat in the truck. We spent another couple of hours drinking and learning, learning and drinking. The smell of smoke on our clothes permeated the camper, but the rain did not follow us in.

It was 4:00 A.M. before Tommy returned to the woods. Twenty hours prior, Tommy had been a stranger. When we put the night to sleep, we had all had a hand in regurgitating our life stories. Staring into an encompassing fire induces people to confide in others. Campfires are hypnotic and therapeutic.

We set up a reunion with Tommy the following night. This included guitars and a kerosene lamp shooting off light from the center of the picnic table. A fire raged in the trash can that stuck about a foot out of the ground. Campfire smoke billowed into the air. Tommy entered the picture with his guitar and a harmonica attached to his face.

Flipping through our music book, we agreed on John Denver's "Take me home." I had never played it, but I knew the notes. Since Tracy hadn't fiddled with guitars much, she helped with the vocals, and Tommy's strumming carried us through nicely.

Tommy stood at the end of the table. Tracy stood nearby with her empty hands in her pockets on this frigid night, determining how the song should be sung. I stood to the side, leaning in with my foot on the bench. After a series of practice strokes, silence gave way to the squawking and chirping of the wilderness.

Our two guitars soon drowned out the sounds of nature. The one in Tommy's hands played more effortlessly than mine, accompanied by our three sets of vocals trying to harmonize. The sound was fine, and we couldn't help but smile at this dry run, which followed a ten minute warm-up. This magical moment filled the circle of light created by fire and lamp, dramatized by the surrounding darkness.

When the song ended, Tommy played on with both guitar and harmonica culminating in a grand finale, and no other tune sounded as smooth for the duration of the concert. It didn't matter if our greatest effort sounded poor to the creatures and their habitat. Their setting pumped blissfulness into our veins. It felt so wonderful, so natural.

May 15, 1992

We glanced at Crocker Pond a final time while gently teetering back down the bumpy dirt road. Back and forth, side to side, our weary bodies swayed with the flow. Our holding tank restricted us to one shower each in the three days, so our video camera filmed only scenery on this day. We greeted some days feeling special and some days feeling fatigued. But imprinted on our minds on this particular morning was what had occurred the night before. We continued to sway down the road.

"That's exactly what I pictured this trip would be like," Tracy said. "Playing guitar around a campfire. It was so great." She chuckled with her reminiscing.

I looked over at Tracy, surprised that her spirits were so much higher than our present condition. I smiled at her. She continued to stare at the road ahead, discussing our chance meeting with Tommy and Molly in the middle of a forest in Maine.

We hoped the rest of our trip would include encounters similar to this, but nothing was certain. Driving down this dirt road, we didn't know what was around the bend any more than what was around the coast. Our job was to push on and find out for ourselves. Now that we had a taste, we craved more.

Heading into Maine was a dream for us. We had no expectations, and found that it sharply contrasted to New Hampshire. There was flat land and water most of the way to Kennebunkport, through Acadia National Park, and even heading north toward Quebec. Not a lot transpired in Maine. Away from the rockiness of the rugged coast, Maine was flat, drab, and plain. With all of the moose warnings, we still had to venture to the zoo to see one, and it was lying with its front legs tucked into its body the entire time. Even the moose seemed to agree with my first impression of Maine.

Mile after mile we drove, up and through inland Maine. It was still barren, but it was a tranquil drive with no competing vehicles. Mobile homes dominated the state. Every once in a while a house passed us by, but never a castle. Towns were named after countries such as Norway and Poland, and residents appeared to be working out of their homes; minuscule businesses with signs painted on plywood.

One sign indicated a tag sale, and a couple of bicycles brought us to an abrupt halt. Picture a twenty-two foot motorhome skidding briefly on sandy pavement as it passes by. We needed a bike to replace the one we destroyed backing out of a driveway. A sign on the three-speed asked for forty-five dollars, but I offered thirty-five dollars to the large, old gray-bearded man possessing few teeth, and he accepted with a slow nod.

"Thanks," said Tracy. "We lost a bike in our travels through the forty-eight states, Canada and Mexico."

"Mexico, Maine?" asked the man, as he slowly rocked back and forth on a rocking chair, chancing his weight. "I always wanted to go there."

"No," said Tracy. "Mexico...the country."

We handed the man the cash, secured our new transportation to the back of the camper, and plowed on.

May 20, 1992

The weariness of traveling flat land, day after day, took its toll on us. Seeking a day off, we looked toward our free campground book for permission. The town of Beddington, about forty miles east of Bangor, granted our wish. Having seen enough of Maine, we needed time to reorganize and figure out what Quebec had to offer. Great news came our way during a phone call home, when we learned that our bank account had swelled from the sale of Tracy's car. It seemed impossible for our moods to deflate on such a day, knowing that $6,700 would take us much deeper into this country.

We rode on. What was once flat, drab land transformed into paradise. We smiled wide. We sang to the music on the radio. We bounced in our seats. We knew that this was just the beginning. We could see much further now. Yet, even as our camper moved on through solitude, the further we drove, the less there was to see. But we had plenty. We had health and happiness. We had each other. And we had enough money to continue this American dream indefinitely.

Pine trees densely lining both sides of Route 193 created a more pleasing Maine. Houses and cars were few and far between. A series of small blue bee huts, hundreds of them, appeared to our left. Then we passed burned fields. It looked as though a crop had burned to the soil. We could only guess at the goings-on out here. However, Maine represented foreign land to us. This was the backwoods of Maine. We had heard that reference plenty, and now came the opportunity for us to attach personal experience to it.

Looking for CCC Road, we passed a forest Ranger Station and turned around to ask for directions. It had occurred to us that we were moving nowhere at great speeds. There's a sense you get while nearing civilization. You know that even the slightest of towns are forthcoming because there is always a house just ahead, or something as obvious as a water tower.

No sense came to us in Maine, and it seemed that no sense would. We saw one Fire truck parked next to a small white house, so we decided to knock on the door. With no response, we decided to knock on the door again.

"Just a minute," yelled a woman from inside as if she had had to repeat herself. A tall, elderly lady in a white robe which matched her hair swung the door open and greeted us with a smile.

I asked her if she knew the whereabouts of Stacy Pond or Deer Lake, and she opened the storm door enough to slide outside with Tracy, myself, and the millions upon millions of bugs. A dirt road ran along the side of the house. That was where she directed us, so it was a good thing we stopped or we could have ended up in Mexico.

"This is road 30,000," she said. "Take it about ten miles into the forest."

The road strayed even further from civilization, but it was a place to park and rest. She informed us that the burned fields are blueberry fields burned every year after picking to kill off the weeds.

I needed to know one last thing. "Would you recommend Stacey Pond or Deer Lake?" I asked.

"Stacy Pond," she responded. "Deer Lake seems to be a rough area, and I don't know if that's what you want."

The gravel road would have been quicker as a footpath. Dust kicked up behind us, lingering for miles. Trees and swamps shaded the scene at dusk as we hoped for a sight of wildlife, but we only slowed for a small animal wobbling across the road, resembling the porcupine we had seen at the zoo. The journey filled the camper with dust, pouring into every pore and onto every internal inch, until we spotted a trailer up ahead.

Pulling up to the bulletin board did not provide us with an answer as to our whereabouts. We focused on the trailer away from the small circle grounds that rested on cinder blocks. We looked around at this small clearing in the forest, tossed between the possibility of it being what we wanted and the likelihood that it was not. I knew what Tracy was thinking, and I knew that she knew of my thoughts, but neither of us spoke.

Just then, a middle-aged lady confidently strolled up to our RV looking as if she was the one to ask.

"Where exactly are we?" I asked, almost laughing.

"This is Stacy Pond."

"I was looking for Stacy. Where can I park?"

She looked at the trailer, then over to the popup beside her car. With two sites filled, a third site proved to be a chore for her to find without our imposing on a neighbor.

"Let me ask Frank if you can park next to him."

Two elderly men came to answer her knock.

"Frank," she began loudly, "can they park next to you?"

"Sure," said Frank, stepping out of the trailer as cautiously as he could and revealing what remained of the white topping on his head.

I asked this lady if she was in charge, but she told me that she was just camping, and pointed to the popup. She wouldn't touch my question about the duration of her stay, brushing past it to say she'd "been here a while." Her world included a car, a popup, and an outhouse.

When she returned home, Frank remained outside.

"How long have you been here?" I asked

"Oh, a couple of weeks."

"Are you from Maine?"

"Oh yes. I just come out here for a couple of weeks a year with my brother. I'm eighty-two years old and my brother's eighty-three." Frank then stepped a stride closer to me and whispered, "My brother's got cancer. He's got it bad. I take him out here when I go."

The bugs ended our conversation on this sweltering night, pushing Frank and I our separate ways. Popup-lady stayed inside all alone, occasionally making the long, miserable trek to the ladies room, which reassured us of our decision to go with the RV. I passed through the RV door and slammed it behind me before insects could move to the light. I hated to break up my conversation with Frank, but he'd be around in the morning.

May 21, 1992

By 4:00 A.M. I found myself outside reclining in a lawn chair with my notebook, writing close to my face, hoping the sun would rise a little faster. I looked over at our neighbor's little camper and noticed a light on. Frank and his brother were up, but did not come outside until a couple hours later, once the bugs awakened.

I heard a metal door opening, then vibrating as the groggy sun scattered light throughout the forest, improving my visibility. Frank cautiously stepped down from his camper, even more careful in assisting his brother down the two steps to the earth. He held onto his brother's brittle arm and compassionately lowered him down the steps. Time had no place. It only existed in Frank's mind as quality time because of the shortage. Sickness had stolen his brother's vitality. Old age had crept in and swiped most of Frank's vitality. It seemed unfair, yet I sat watching this display of affection and could only wish for such a relationship at such a time of need.

They sat side by side in lawn chairs, silently focusing on the forest when I arrived. A crumbled lean-to aged next to our camper, and Frank began his history lesson of the area a bit later.

"I've come out here since I was eighteen years old. We had that fireplace there right after they built it; once eight feet tall. We had big fires. People used to sleep in that lean-to and keep very warm in front of the fire."

My quick calculation determined the year to be 1928 when they first set foot on these parts. Calvin Coolidge was in charge of the United States as our thirtieth president. Frank looked at me as he spoke, and his brother looked down with his mouth ajar as if he was only half listening.

"How long did it take?" I asked.

"Two-three days," he responded, after a moment's thought.

"Yeah...two-three days," his brother agreed, nodding.

Logging trucks whizzed past the campground as we spoke, and Frank mentioned that "The Paper Company is big business here. They own all the land around here, but the public is welcome." Trucks raced through obscurity without a care for oncoming traffic around corners. Our main concern became escaping without getting cremated, and the brothers agreed that I'd notice dust kicking up in the road ahead. But there's nowhere for a vehicle to go on such narrow roads through the forest. We could see them, but they wouldn't see us, and we got the feeling that they didn't particularly care.

"Just stay on the 30,000 road," said Frank, "and you'll be fine. Those truckers are only on 30,000 for a short while before they turn off."

Frank sat up in his chair, not bothering to swat the three insects standing on his face, nor the swarm encircling his head. The swarm didn't appear to bother his brother either, so I felt silly swinging my arms around as if I was in a boxing match, shaking my head and moving in circles. Maybe they thought I was confused.

The bugs made us prisoners inside our own camper all day. We stepped out only for the sake of the dog. Another sweltering day made staying inside a difficult task for us, even with an oscillating fan blowing warm air. Dripping with sweat, we tried soothing each other with ice cubes, but even ice couldn't take the heat. Taking turns, we'd melt an ice cube on each other's face, arms, legs, and stomach. The ice could barely form in the freezer, so hot skin changed cubes to a lesser form in seconds.

Later in the day, we both felt large bumps forming on our heads. Tracy had two severe bites on her left upper cheek that began to swell. She also found two bleeding bites on top of her head where her hair parted and another bloody bite on her ear. The two bites we each had on our heads formed golf ball size bumps by the end of the night, and we worried because they kept growing. The night was full of bugs, but what kind?

We were concerned, disgusted, and ready to leave Maine. The bumps on Tracy's cheek swelled to where the bottom of her glasses rested. As hot as it was, nature forced us to close the windows because we detected gnat-sized insects inside the camper, and they were small enough to fit through the tiny openings in the screens.

Not only was our little relief from the open windows now gone, but we also feared having the little critters sleeping with us overnight. This distressed us, and as much as Tracy wanted to leave at that moment, I persuaded her that it would be wiser to get a 4:00 A.M. start. We already had a place to sleep and could avoid a confrontation with logging trucks.

May 22, 1992

Our 4:30 A.M. departure steered us from loggers and wildlife, bringing us out of the woods. During our long drive to Canada, we needed a bank, Laundromat, dump station, water, propane, and groceries: the usual, but all at once. It made sense for us to invest in a campground before leaving the country, even if it meant another night of Maine. Full hookups became imperative, and we found them about ten miles from the border in Jackman.

At the campground, we clapped bloody mosquitoes inside the camper, but at least we could use the air conditioner. Well, it wasn't allowed, but we did. Maine owed us that much as the sweltering heat wave continued. Our welts widened, and we finally learned more about them the following morning.

In the restroom, a girl advised Tracy that we had been bitten by Black Flies. Some people don't react; others do if they're allergic. We may have been poisoned, which would require medical attention, but since we had a five hundred dollar deductible, it would sadly take more than possible poisoning to get us to seek medical attention. It was certainly unusual, but an explanation seemed as comforting as treatment.

A French officer represented U.S. Customs. The uniformed man took my license, examining it long enough to make us uncomfortable. My hand was readied to take it back, but the moment was slow in arriving. The officer showed it to another officer, who directed us to park our vehicle off to the side.

The second officer informed us that he'd be conducting a search. Molly let him know that he was intruding, but I think she was more concerned for the welfare of her biscuits.

"Do you have any firearms or weapons of any kind?"

"No I don't." Molly must have thought he said "firearms or biscuits" because she barked twice.

"All right. I'm gonna take a look inside."

I wondered why he bothered to ask. He stepped into the RV after we extracted Molly. Standing outside, we could hear him opening and closing cabinets. Through the opened passenger door, we could see him reaching into our storage area above the cab.

"We have a step ladder if you'd like," I said, poking my head through the door, trying to be sarcastic. He politely declined and wrapped up the search. Strike one.

Bonjour. Arriving in Quebec put us in the mood to live their culture. We converted ninety kilometers into fifty-five miles per hour and listened to a French radio station as if we'd pick up the language. We became nauseated finding gas prices at $.65 per liter. Multiplying by four equaled $2.65 per gallon. Fifteen dollars missed the quarter-tank mark. Strike two.

We endured five hours battling the Canadian wind to reach Old Quebec City. My palms tingled from clamping the steering wheel. It wasn't just a steady gust. Secondary gusts slapped the high wall of our motorhome, jerking us to the side. Tractor-trailers aggravated our tense travel. Sand and dust sprayed across the road in our path, emanating from the fields as a forewarning. We were subjected to five hours of this constant brutality while I earnestly tried to stay on the road: Foul tip.

It was time for us to search for any campground. Stoplights tricked us. Poles stuck out from the side and the lights ran horizontally, blinking spastically red, yellow or green. Stop signs were the normal red octagons, but read "Arrêt," and directions included Nord, Sud, Est or Ouest.

Those signs we easily understood, but others were more complicated, and Tracy complained of feeling tense, closed in, and illiterate.

I pulled into a gas station with hopes of hearing an English-speaking resident.

"Do you speak English?" I asked, slow and loud.

"Li'l bit," the man replied.

"Camping. Do you know where there's camping?" I asked, enunciating each word.

"Gam-pang," he said, then stared.

I thought a moment. "Yes, camping."

"No," he replied.

Our second try brought us to a convenience store. "English?" I asked.

"Li'l bit."

"Gam-pang?" I tried.

She looked at me funny, so I repeated it. That made her look at me even funnier, then she walked away after motioning for me to wait.

"Can I help you?" came a hoarse voice from behind me.

The man startled me, and I started to ask him if he spoke English before Tracy's laughter brought me back to my senses. But he couldn't help either, so we referred to our camp books and tried to find our way around.

Finally, we located a campground as heavy clouds released some drizzle, a threat throughout the day. In the office, a lady greeted us in French.

"English?" I asked.

"Li'l bit," she answered, and by now we could've mouthed it in sync.

"How much is it to camp?" I asked, receiving only a funny look and a tilted head in return. "How much money?" I tried.

"Oh." She was onto something. "Thirteen or fifteen hookup."

We paid the lady, then started gam-pang.

May 24, 1992

Tracy began the day thinning my hair with shears; anything to save a buck. Then I strolled to the showers, but returned when I found that it worked better with a dime. We readied ourselves for Old Quebec, but it seemed every step in this foreign land required just a little extra work.

Old Quebec City came and went, and so did we. We fought our way into Canada and then deep into Quebec. This exertion exhausted us. After arriving, we confirmed our love for America. If ever in my life I felt invisible, this was the time. Canada was getting old fast, and the price of gas returned us quicker than we had planned. Even though the Canada we saw brought us through clean and beautiful farmland, the gas prices dictated what we could and could not do and we felt limited.

Aiming for America late in the evening, we discussed our unreasonable expectation of finding a twenty-four hour gas station. That was when we came upon Viagaz Avec Service and thought that it might be what we needed. I walked in to find the pleasing aroma of brewing coffee.

"Are you open twenty-four hours?" I asked, not caring whether he spoke English.

"No," said the man. "Eleven o'clock. Why? What d'ya need?"

44

"Just a place to park that camper," I said, pointing to the only vehicle that could be seen in his lot from where we were standing.

The hefty man with slicked back hair spoke so fast that some words almost passed others out. "You can park it here. Oh yah, truckers park here all the time. I don't mind, and it's safe here; haven't had any break-ins." He paused shortly and moved his eyes up in the air in thought. However, the little nook of a mini-mart did not allow his eyes to wander far. "Well, maybe a couple small break-ins. But they only took some cigarettes."

He was as helpful as a stranger could be, with a voice that sounded as if he was happy we had asked. His large eyes bespoke sincerity, and he really wanted to talk.

"I see you're just married," he said. "When was it? Last...Saturday?"

"No," explained Tracy. "it will be one month tomorrow. We're traveling the forty-eight states, Canada and Mexico for a year."

"Really?" he said. "How long's that gonna take you?"

"One year," I said.

The man explained that gas and most everything else is exorbitant because of free college education and health care in Canada, and cigarettes are a steal at $5.60 per pack at his station. The smokers are the ones who will pay for the health care. More than half the price reflects tax.

Having noticed that the RV battery cover on the side must have taken a ride in the wind, I asked Mr. Accommodating if he knew of any RV shops. He said he'd have an answer in the morning. He'd lived in Pompano Beach, Florida, for a while, but had moved back to his home in Quebec years ago. We were just happy that he spoke English.

May 25, 1992
Memorial Day

In the early morning, I walked into the station to fill up our two-gallon water jug. The same man stood behind the register. He owned the station and lived right upstairs.

"Drinking water?" he asked before I did. "Sure, right over there." He pointed to distilled water in an overturned five gallon dispenser with a tap. "It may take a while, but go ahead...you're welcome to it." His animated features lit right up as he spoke, highlighting his sincerity.

As I carried more water out than I left behind, Mr. Accommodating stopped me while he was waiting on another customer. "I found a service station to fix the door for your battery," he said. "I have all the information right here," he continued in excitement, pointing to a small piece of paper loaded with information.

Since the RV shop had to order the part, we decided to return to our homeland, but the gas gauge plummeted past empty and forced us to stop for gas with only about ten miles to the border.

When I asked for two dollars worth of gas, the attendant informed me of a five dollar minimum: state law.

"You mean to tell me that if I only have two dollars to go into an empty tank, then you won't give me the gas?"

"That's right."

We had twenty dollar bills, but didn't want Canadian change. Through all the commotion, I forgot about the ten to twenty percent U.S. exchange, and it wasn't the first time. Canadians must have a field day with Americans because they sure aren't going to offer up that information. It hadn't happened yet. Strike three. We were out.

Tracy grabbed a roll of dimes from our coffee can of change under her seat, which we used for payment before leaving skid marks up to the U.S. border. Hello America, and good to see you Vermont.

A state had never looked so inviting with the prevalence of green pastures, the Cold Hollow Mountains and the outlawing of billboards to preserve this scenery. We were out of a foreign land. Vermont smiled at us. Our moods were exceptional; a heavy weight lifted. Being thrown into such mesmerizing beauty and serenity after battles with wind, traffic, congestion, French language and conversions was precisely what we needed.

Winding roads twisted through the countryside, leading us up, down and around the mix of mountains and hills. Small country stores enhanced our peacefulness. Quaint towns dared us to count the number of houses while passing through. The folks who did inhabit these towns of northern Vermont even strolled about once in a while.

Tracy informed me that her pulse had dropped. I saw her slumped in the passenger seat with her feet resting on the dashboard, and I knew she spoke truthfully. She smiled and sang along with the radio. Sunshine beat a path through the camper. I had no doubt that her pulse had dropped. My pulse followed suit. Our vehicle had been much too large for Quebec, but snuggled up to Vermont. Everyone seemed to be getting along just fine.

When we needed a break from driving, I opted for the first pulloff I could find. We just needed to close our eyes for a bit and maybe have a bite. We were meeting Tracy's mother, Judi, in Burlington in a few days, but it wasn't exactly around the corner. When I shut down the engine, a sound persisted. It was a soothing one coming from the rushing stream just outside the bedroom window; a priceless song to mix into a swift dream.

Tracy and I melted into the cushions as the stream rushed us to sleep. Soon the stream took a turn and passed through my head, and I welcomed it. Resisting would have been impossible for me at the moment, but then again, I could have been carried away without a fight. The last thing I remembered was the breathing of the stream blending with my own.

May 27, 1992

Judy would be steering toward Burlington today, which fueled Tracy's excitement. Their closeness could only be measured by the fact that they once spoke on the phone on a daily basis. At this point, phoning her mother could only be done on Mondays, her father on Sundays, and my parents on Thursdays. If we had to be contacted for emergencies, they all knew who would be contacted next.

My sister, Karen, would also be joining us for my birthday. It would be standing room only, but we could manage for a few days. We landed at a campground on Lake Champlain. Out of the six New England states, Vermont is the only one without a seacoast. However, Lake Champlain displays a two hundred fifty mile shoreline containing the largest body of fresh water east of the Great Lakes, separating Vermont from New York.

Not even twenty minutes after pulling in, Judi arrived and settled into her new home. The excitement of reuniting with her daughter and the expanse of water from our windows enlivened her after the long drive from Connecticut. Now we had the opportunity to introduce Judi to camper life.

By nightfall, as rain pelted the camper on and off, bizarre animal noises haunted the woods just outside our camper. The sharp shrieks, chirps, and squeaks sounded off and on for about twenty minutes before the unidentified noise disappeared. The introduction for Judi had begun, but this was just the beginning.

May 29, 1992

Karen showed up by mid-afternoon, and the four of us visited the Burlington Mall for a stroll through this exceptionally clean plaza where musicians and artists abounded. As afternoon merged with evening, punk rockers made their presence known with black outfits to match their black shaved and teased hairdos.

An older and very short man, even shorter with bent knees, belted out tunes from the fifties on his flute. He played beside his opened flute case containing a crisp dollar bill that I suspected was donated by himself. He did a fine job with his instrument, but he wasn't eating steak for dinner on this night.

Burlington is a quaint little city with a big city trace, but in a Vermont sort of way. There was much to do in this relaxed city atmosphere, found only in the Green Mountain State. The hustle and bustle of a big city was toned down considerably in Burlington. Absent was the tightness in my chest from stress in the air whenever I'm in a big city.

This was an opportunity to prove to our guests that we could handle life on the road, and we returned to the campground for homemade meatball subs. I set the oven at three hundred degrees and attempted to light the pilot inside until we determined that all four stomachs were not ready to play.

A half-hour later, I returned to the oven. The knob already showed three hundred degrees when I went to reset it. I sat on the edge of the dinette bench with the long camping lighter and opened the door to light the pilot with my face down, eyeing the back of the oven. As the three others looked on, I inserted the lighter and flicked the switch.

My actions sent an explosive fireball directly into my face. The propane gas had been seeping into the oven for thirty minutes, creating this instant reaction. I ripped my arm back and slammed the door shut. Fog lingered over, and with my one opened eye, the events proceeded in slow motion. I could only see the three witnesses pained with shock, their mouths opened wide in disbelief and horror.

The bathroom mirror pointed out my singed mustache, beard, eyebrows, and bangs to go with the blurry vision in my left eye. That evening, after eating the meatball subs, we discussed what could have happened if more gas had collected. Propane is capable of turning our camper into scrap metal, reducing those inside to dental remains, and had certainly come close enough to that this night to receive the respect it deserved from me.

June 3, 1992

Tracy and I decided to spin by the Finger Lakes, and while thumbing through our free campground book, I extracted a wonderful campground in Gansevoort. The grounds came complete with water, sewer and electric hookups, and the place crossed our path. Our all-day drive out of Vermont and into New York would smear one hundred fifty miles of rubber to the road, and we planned on spending about four days catching up with our lives.

As we crossed into our sixth state, the air filled with the aroma of cow. The mountains of Vermont gave way to farmland in upper New York State, a side of New York neither of us knew existed. Tracy loves farms and craves to farm organically someday, so this was her bag. The farmland rolled with the terrain, following us much of the way. We drove through the searing heat from morning through late afternoon, and the farmland at least entertained us for much of the path.

Gansevoort eventually escorted us to the campground, where a short, shirtless, balding man walked up to our camper with his arms folded. My gut told me that the man did not trust us, and Tracy knew something felt wrong. He stared at us until I jumped down.

"Kin I elp ya?" he asked. His forehead and chest glittered in the sun.

"Yes. We have a book of free campgrounds, and this one is in it. I just wanted some information."

The man smiled after a pause, leaving me uncertain until he responded. "Ded you paus the restrant in town ind git yer free lunch?"

"No," I said.

"Oh, you din't?" Then he went on the attack. "How do you expict to git somethin' fer free? How do you expict tuh kemp fer free?"

His tone became irate, and in turn, my tone became irate. Tracy appeared by my side.

"This campground is listed as free," I enunciated. "Tracy, go get that book."

As Tracy went for the book, the man began to tell me that he didn't care to see it, but my rage interrupted him with reassurances to Tracy that we were going to show the guy the book. After one hundred fifty miles, the man was going to see the book.

"I know yer young," he started in, "and you belive thet there good thengs en life, and I don't blem you fer thet."

Tracy returned with the book, and I ruggedly opened it up to the New York section to find the ad. "Here it is," I said, pushing the book under his nose.

The man took the book from me with a tilted head and squinted eyes. "Yes, but thet's nut true. How kin you belive you kin get a kempground fer free? I pay eht thousin dollahs a year in texes."

He did what he could to belittle us, and I don't know if it was that or the tone of his voice that angered me more.

"Are you trying to tell me that this entire one-inch thick book is a scam?" I asked, fanning the book with my thumb. "We already camped at two free campgrounds, so I happen to know that they exist. There are lots of them in the Midwest. These small towns want to attract tourists. The tourists need gas and food, so it will be a boost to their economy."

Mr. Pessimist finally accepted our arguments, wishing us luck in our travels. That did nothing for either of us. Now we had to start from scratch, both of us exhausted once again. Since that campground was too good to be true, we had to pull into a mall parking lot to eat, nap, shower, and break out the map for an extended plan.

Pulling around the back of the mall, I aimed the camper for the lone remaining shaded spot, which would only satisfy half its length on this sticky day. Most important for us was a cool nap, so the back end of the camper became the beneficiary of the shade, which jutted away from the only tree in the lot. Our weary eyes sagged, but our stomachs raised the most hell. We were left no choice but to laugh it off.

We hoped a nap would sharpen us enough to persevere for an additional one hundred miles to Cooperstown, provided we didn't find anything else along the way. We even discussed asking farmers if we could sleep in their barn with the cows.

Another two hundred fifty miles brought us to Glimmerglass State Park, where a closed park office presented a sign indicating that campers cannot occupy a site until they register, so we occupied a site. After a day like the one we had, no sign was going to stop us.

June 8, 1992

A Frenchman eyeing the driver's side window needed $.75 from us so we could cross over the bridge to Canada. Once we gave it to him, he conducted a routine investigation from his booth.

"What nationality are you?"

"American."

"Any liquor, tobacco products, or firearms aboard?"

"None."

"Okay, how long do you plan to spend in Canada?"

"Just going to see the falls."

"You're all set...enjoy them."

The going rate was seven dollars to park in a lot, so we parked further away on the street, seeing the magical Horseshoe Falls from a distance. The intensity of the series of falls still created mist and steam from where we stood. The assaulting water surging over the edges offered no chance to the crumbling rocks below. This constant flow moved in slow motion like lava. Peeling our eyes from this outpouring felt challenging, but the time came for us to compare the Canadian side with the American side.

We drove back over the bridge, which changed its name to Bridge to USA, and paid three more quarters to the toll man. We had an easier time parking. Then we walked over a bridge spanning the Niagara River, making our way to the top of the falls within fifteen minutes.

It's been said that the American side is hardly worth the visit since the entire falls cannot be seen, so it turned out to be all the better. We had no great expectations. We stood over the top, observing the glass water disappearing over the edge as naturally soothing as the rebounding mist settling upon our faces, making us feel a part of Niagara Falls. The Canadian side, impressive in its own right, lacked this proximity to nature.

The downside of a trip like ours is that in an attempt to see everything, the duration of our stays must be shortened. However, with a variety of tastes we'll know where to return. Niagara Falls impressed us more than we imagined, but we had to make our way to Ohio.

Once we escaped the madness of Buffalo, we peacefully rolled toward our second Great Lake: Erie. Putting along the single lane, we became mesmerized by the miles behind and ahead. I drove along the roads as cars intermittently approached and passed. The haul silenced us. The mile-markers counted our miles.

Another green marker appeared far ahead. As it moved within eyeshot, I concentrated on making out the numbers, but an ambulance closing in behind us broke my trance. This was a highway. Not many cars traveled it on this day. I was fading when my side view mirror unfolded an unusual scene, which roused my eyes like eyedrops. The ambulance, speeding up behind us, looked like it planned to ram into our camper. My eyes bulged as this horrific scene unfolded in seconds. Suddenly, sirens blared, lights flashed and our hearts pounded. At the last second, the ambulance cut over a lane and passed on our left. This orange blur made me dizzy. Tracy sprung forward in her seat.

As I attempted to pull over, trembling from shock, the ambulance shut off the alarm and the lights. A medical technician popped his windblown head out of the passenger's side window, and waved to us with a big smile as the ambulance returned to the proper lane and settled into a normal drive. We returned the wave and the smile, accepting their congratulations, then tried to recover. Ten minutes later, our pulses slowed to normal.

Along Lake Erie we traveled, through the grape fields leading through the northwest edge of Pennsylvania and into the Buckeye

State. The reality of the trip emerged in the Midwest. For myself, Ohio marked the furthest west I'd ever been. Our shouts of contentment echoed through the camper as a sign welcomed us. Tracy shook the dog in her arms, her way of celebrating milestones. Poor Molly never knows what is happening, which is evident by the size of her eyes. For a mental exercise, I kept saying that we were in Ohio so that it would seem real, but to no avail. Repetition only made "Ohio" sound funny.

The free campgrounds start here, for the most part, because the states increase in size and open land sprawls endlessly. People are more relaxed, and the welcoming of travelers is basically unchanged in some areas from back when the pioneers flocked to these lands during westward expansion.

This was what we had in mind when trying to figure out if we could afford such a journey. The northeast had squeezed our budget with campground fees, and we began to panic. Now we hoped for long periods of time without that expense to worry about, especially since eight miles-per-gallon was skinning us alive.

The Corps of Engineers, a government-run program with free campgrounds all over the United States, had one residing on Berlin Lake near the town of Deerfield, twenty miles east of Akron. The all-day drive south of Lake Erie took us only to the Lake, not directly to the campground.

The closest we came to German Church campground was a church, so we pulled into the empty parking lot. After circling the church, I stopped the camper while we brainstormed for directions. Another car looped the church and stopped next to us, ready to pull out. Hesitation can prove disastrous, so I jumped out to the car.

A man relayed directions from the darkness of his car. He wasn't sure of the name of the campground, but described how to get to the campground he knew as being free on Berlin Lake.

"I believe it's called German Church. There's a lotta trouble up there."

"What kind of trouble?"

"Well...it's free. You won't get the best crowd hanging around at a free campground, but you shouldn't have any problems until the weekend."

It was only Tuesday. Tracy and I stayed in the parking lot, weighing our decision. We were spent, but should we still try to spend the night in an area that had just received a black mark? We had nowhere else to go, and darkness upon us.

Tracy started to shy away from the idea, but my answer was influenced by the fact that I sat behind the wheel, having driven enough for one day. She's usually right up there with the bravest, but it took me a while to talk her into at least looking into it, rather than losing the opportunity based solely on one stranger's word.

Each of us had Pepperguard spray in hand as we set off to the campground. If we so much as sensed trouble, I promised Tracy a quick exit. But I had a strong hunch that we should investigate. Following the directions down a residential back road, the pavement disappeared. Soon enough, the camper was rocking and rolling side to side down a dirt path called German Church Road.

Relief awaited us at the end of the dirt road, when the wooded path led to a clearing and a small yellow booth at the campground entrance indicated someone was in charge. Authority loomed large because of our image of Crocker Pond, where campers fend for themselves.

A trailer was next to the booth. Next to that was a campfire, where a large blonde lady, who appeared to be in her late forties, left her lawn chair for an interrogation.

"Can I help you?" she asked, as she made it to my window.

"This campground is listed as free in our book. We're from Connecticut, and we'd like to camp here for a few days."

"What I want you to do before you register is look for a spot. There aren't many left, and they're filling up fast."

She spoke firmly and boldly with not just words, but body language. She suggested we park in the first site around the corner from the office because it was level. Tracy and I looked at each other in agreement. We weren't about to disagree with her. After settling on the site, we completed the park loop to check out the clientele. The campground looked sketchy at best, as revealed by the light of fires and lanterns. It appeared the campers called this their home, but I knew of the fourteen-day stay limit, which even pay-campgrounds enforce to prevent permanent residency.

Her suggested site proved perfect. It certainly leveled the camper, which translated into a night's sleep without our heads sliding into the camper wall. It meant a refrigerator that would cool properly and a plate of food that wouldn't slide off the table if left unattended.

Since the site took up the corner near authority, we would have only one neighbor on our left to contend with even though we'd know about every vehicle coming and going. We convinced ourselves all would be safe, so I shut down the RV, and we rounded the corner to register.

The alert blonde stood ready for us when we entered the little booth she called her office to fill out some paperwork. When we had completed the forms, I asked Blondie if she'd experienced any trouble here.

"Not too much," she blurted. "Once in a while there will be some loud people, but if there's any trouble around here, I just call the sheriff to haul 'em away. I've only been here a few weeks, but I won't take no shit from nobody."

Blondie spoke with conviction, and she was really convincing. Her husband stayed in the trailer, but if trouble arose, I didn't think he'd be needed. She seemed a force to contend with, and no trouble would arise at site number one.

At site number two resided our neighbors, but Blondie warned us with bulging eyes that they'd be loud and obnoxious, and she was just waiting for a reason to oust them. We could definitely hear them, but still dozed shortly after returning to our camper.

June 10, 1992

Three families resided on the three sites to our left, but all convened on site number two. We arose to what sounded like third-grade recess, and our window provided the picture of grade school kids running wild through the three sites. They were screaming and beating up on each other. The grown-ups, and I use that term loosely here, sat out chatting by the continuously burning campfire.

As morning met afternoon, this scene continued with a rise in the volume. The smell of smoke and lighter fluid mixed into the air. The mothers had moved to the picnic table, which rested behind the lawn chairs encircling the fire. Their voices easily carried through the screens to our camper, and the subject moved from bars to drinking to smoking to fighting to sex.

One raspy voice spoke of how her first sexual encounter wasn't until the age of seventeen. A ten-year-old child with long blonde hair then took a seat next to her, breathless from running.

Raspy then continued with her thought, "And then when I finally did have sex, this is what happened," she said as she pointed to the girl with her thumb.

It didn't take long for our neighbors to prove themselves. The mothers sat around all day while the husbands worked, and we didn't have to bend our ears too hard to obtain that tip. The one small camper and several aged tents set up in the three sites indicated that they had been there for a while. A clothesline stretched from the camper to a tree in the woods, weighed down with a week's load of laundry, and every article in their possession appeared to be outside, from coolers to condiments. Most of what they brought camping littered the grounds on which they camped. The children loved being able to roam the campground day and night without supervision. The parents loved it too.

That night, the men returned from work with a replenished wood supply. Judging from the pyramid of logs, we would not outlast them. They decidedly looked like fourteen day limits, so we made the best of it. We spent our days reorganizing the camper, setting up our gazebo for an extra room, researching our next state, writing Thank You notes from the wedding and attempting to sprinkle rest and relaxation into this potent plan.

This campground seemed grubby, but we felt fairly safe, and even became the beneficiaries of wave greetings, sometimes from the hands of stone-faced bikers. We almost felt like we were a part of this little society in the woods by the lake, although we mostly kept busy amongst ourselves. Nobody bothered anyone else.

Molly walked us to the lake before darkness set in, then around the loop for a closer examination of our surroundings. We confirmed that most of the people in this thirty-six site park had settled into their shabby abodes as if the fourteen-day limit was not an issue.

Everybody sat outside catching the last of the sunshine, feeding his or her fires, when it occurred to me that we had the only motorhome in the park. Scanning the campground, I saw tents, tarps, and campers that looked like units built in the 1950s. Every automobile that passed through the park's stone loop contained a rattle from a loose part and a problem with the muffler. This was an all day and night occurrence.

They say that you get what you pay for. One morning, Tracy and I were reclining on lawn chairs beside the gazebo, soaking up the sun, refusing to let go of the moment. This enormous site challenged any site we had paid for up to this point. Our discussions wavered from our deep satisfaction of this moment to Mr. Pessimist in Gansevoort, who had told us that nobody can afford to offer camping for free. This was the man who told us that we were young, and that it was erroneous to believe that good still exists. What a negative attitude, but one that added laughter to our afternoon as we reflected on the chucklehead while the sun reflected on two reapers of this reward. Our laughter represented the last laugh, which we wanted to belatedly express to Mr. P. in Gansevoort.

In the afternoon, we strolled to the office, where we had a long chat with the manager. I told her that she was right on the money with our neighbors.

"Oh, aren't they terrible?" she asked in amazement. "They complain to me that things around here ain't like they were last year, so I told them that this ain't last year."

"The campground is free," I said. "How can they have anything to say?" She rolled her eyes.

"How long have they been here, and when are they scheduled to leave?" I asked.

She consulted her calendar for the answer, and I'm sure her curiosity piqued as well. After lifting up one page she said, "They've been here seven days and have seven more to go, and believe me ...when that fourteen day limit is up, they're gone."

June 12, 1992

On our fourth morning in Deerfield, we set off to the state capital of Columbus in search of Griggs Dam Campground. The holding tanks begged for mercy, forcing us to move on. If a certain place had no dump station, we couldn't stay long.

We rode through the Amish communities of Winesburg and Berlin, where rows of fresh and neatly plowed fields abounded, and the plain people roamed the area on horse-and-buggy, bicycles or on foot. We saw children weeding, cutting grass, or helping with other chores in the field, but never playing. This simple lifestyle was in plain view from the road, but we weren't convinced of its simplicity. The Amish kept their neighborhoods immaculate.

Tracy took the helm for a while. Through beautiful country miles she plowed. A small village intersection slowed the camper to thirty miles-per-hour, when we learned of drainage dips in the Midwest. Tracy, stricken with panic when the front of the camper dipped down and ground against the pavement, lost all control of her senses.

The sound of steel pressing and dragging thousands of pounds against the pavement made us sense permanent damage. Back up we came, like a boat negotiating a stormy sea. Tracy, perhaps instinctively, maintained control of the rig when the second round cremated the back of the unit and smeared the drainage system with the slowest of motions. The second scrape, even louder, dragged a bit longer than the first as Tracy guided the crippled unit to the side of the road. Shaken and scared, she lost her desire to continue on.

After pulling to the side, we remained in our seats in silence, hoping time would relieve our shock. Tracy, noticeably shaken, sat slumped with her arms hanging over the steering wheel as she snapped back into the reality of what happened.

"The road just disappeared," she tried to explain with a trembling voice.

Neither of us saw it coming. Checking for damage, we thought for sure the bikes were history, but they survived. However, a steady drip of green fluid came from a hose underneath the rear of the camper, appearing on the road. We thought it was antifreeze, but we weren't sure if it could be brake fluid.

I guided the wounded camper to a gas station, where an attendant believed the green fluid to be antifreeze leading to the rear-heating unit. Apparently a hose cracked, one that brings antifreeze from the front of the RV to the back.

This seemed to be a plausible explanation, considering no antifreeze remained in the overflow container, and I had just so happened to add to it earlier in the day. By the time we reached the Griggs Dam campground, I added antifreeze two more times.

The officer of the Columbia Police Department at the park entrance had no clue as to what the park was all about, and the park office had closed for the night. There were no pamphlets, no water hookups, and no orientation, so we entered the campground and picked a site at the beginning of the grounds because it seemed quiet.

We had to take care of business at the dump station, which had a foot-high cement block around it, preventing proper downhill drainage from the camper to the sewer. When I pulled the sewer tank lever underneath the camper, the hose clogged instantly. I had to lift the hose up and down, above the wall to drain and below to fill the hose again with camper waste. Ten lifts later, I was able to discard the rubber gloves and think about what I wanted for dinner.

June 13, 1992

Driving from RV center to RV center frustrated us, since no-body seemed to know or care to know the problem. One place had a repair center closed on Saturdays, while others couldn't get to it for a few days. Columbus proved useless to us, so north we limped toward Sandusky, adding antifreeze every couple of hours while keeping one eye on the temperature gauge.

We aimed for a rest area on the toll turnpike because it permit-ted one overnight. It turned out to be a truck stop and BP service station. Time was of the essence, so the BP boy in the garage fol-lowed me to the camper. His petite teenage girlfriend, with long brown hair hanging past her shoulders, followed him. She shad-owed him like a dog shadows its master.

BP boy stuck his capped head underneath the back tire where I pointed and said, "None of you two got AIDS, do ya?"

I assured him that we didn't.

"I gotta know, 'cause I don't wanna go touchin' toilet lines if ya do. Looks like ya mighta broke a brake line, and one of these tubes here is wore. You might wanna replace the wore tube."

"So that's brake fluid and not antifreeze?" I asked.

"Might be," he answered.

"Then why did I go through two gallons of antifreeze in two days?"

He hesitated before replying, "I'm not sure, but I'm gonna have to have my boss take a look. He knows a lot more about this stuff than I do."

That never happened because the station buzzed with business, so we agreed to have it checked in the morning. Pulling up to the garage after the overnight, another service attendant looked underneath then quickly refused the work.

"This deals with copper tubing, and we don't got nothin' to do with it."

A man at an RV center in Sandusky told me of his uncertainty about fixing our problem because they mainly dealt with the vehicle part of the camper, not the coach. However, he asked me to bring it down so he could take a look and either fix it or refer me to some place that could.

Upon arriving, a quick check by the mechanic confirmed that only a hose needed replacing. He not only referred us to a particular radiator shop, but called to set up our arrival.

The radiator shop, a large work area trying to resemble a garage, furrowed my brow. I searched long and hard for someone to talk to, but nobody was around. I felt like an uninvited guest. I finally found the bottom half of a man, who had his head submerged under the hood of a car.

"Excuse me," I interrupted. "I'm looking for something that resembles a front desk."

After a brief hood-rattling chuckle, the man popped his head out and referred me to the man in the Mack Truck. On the way, a mechanic, who had long red hair tied in a ponytail and was missing a couple of important teeth, stopped me.

"You the one with the motorhome?" he asked.

"That's me."

"Let's take a look."

Once on his back, he slid under the RV, then slid back with his findings. "The tube that feeds the heating unit antifreeze is wore. That must be replaced, but let me try to determine how." He slid back under.

About five minutes later, he reappeared. "Two things you can do. The first one will cost you forty dollars, and the second will cost sixty."

"What's the difference?"

"Well, one's forty...and the other's sixty."

"Besides price."

He explained the difference, which meant absolutely nothing to me. "Will they both perform the same task?" I asked.

"Yes."

"Then I'll take door number one for forty."

The mechanic fixed the problem within twenty-five minutes, and the bill only asked for twenty-four dollars, nearly one dollar per minute. What we thought would break our bank turned out to be nothing, and two much-relieved travelers sailed through Ohio.

June 19, 1992

Miles and miles of cornfields and grass fields followed Ohio into Michigan. Tracy's illness kept her up most of the night, so she slept in the back during my solo drive. The urgency to move onward forced me to get up and go, because daylight is most precious not just for the traveler, but for the driver.

The sign read: "Yes! Michigan Welcomes." No matter what kind of night it was, Tracy would kill me if I drove into the next state without her presence, even though Molly thought that a dog's presence would suffice. Once the eighth state of Michigan consumed us, we needed to figure out what the introduction meant. "Yes! Michigan Welcomes."

I can't say our combined effort could reveal what Michigan was all about. Michigan offered the Upper Peninsula, the Great Lakes and is even deemed a vacation haven; beyond that we knew nothing of this two-part state. This made us eager to learn about, see and experience Michigan. The plan sounded fine, but those Thank You notes were ridiculously late, so the free campground with water and electric coaxed our camper to the small town of Ithaca located north of the capital of Lansing.

Route 127 brought us into Michigan. The state received favorable reviews from us upon crossing that fine line. About ten cars acknowledged our sign by honking, waving, smiling or giving the thumbs up. Their genuine excitement shone through our windshield, planting a smile on me that carried on into Ithaca.

The age of our new-found friends followed no pattern. Young girls waved, sitting in the back seat of their parent's car. An elderly couple not only beeped and greeted us with a wave, but the lady turned her body almost completely around to get a good look. Guys and girls our age, as well as middle-aged drivers, welcomed us to their state.

By the time Tracy rejoined me, I was completely fired up and in love with the state of Michigan. First impressions are immensely important, and I spent the next twenty minutes filling Tracy in on what kind of people we seemed to be up against.

Being in the capital, the confusion and congestion chewed up Route 127 and spit it out as Route 27, and the long haul to Ithaca neared its end. However, that doubt associated with a free campground always existed, even after that final mile. Although our hopes were never high, it still incensed us to no end when we believed the long haul was over and it was not. Then uncertainty of where to drive next plagued us on top of all our other difficulties. We never knew our fate beyond the end of the road.

The upturned fields and plentiful trees resembled Connecticut, but the dark blue license plates may have influenced the comparison more than I'd care to admit. Farms were a frequent sight in this wilderness. Farms and barns and farmhouses of various sizes punctuated the state. We pondered the question of why barns are generally red. At that moment, Michigan presented us with a blue barn and a white barn. Michigan forced us to enjoy ourselves.

Curiosity scrambled our minds when the Woodland Park sign informed us that the park closed at 10:00 P.M. Passersby could have seen large question marks hovering atop our heads. Surely we could try parking at this lonesome place, but would we be driven out once we were settled?

As we circled the park, no bulletin board offered overnight camping. Although three sites with hookups were listed in our book we found only one, and quickly it became ours. Sandusky to Ithaca was no small task, so the opportunity to try camping in Ithaca proved to be our only option.

Just three bites into our chicken dinner, we noticed a police cruiser had invaded the park, circled slowly and then pulled up next to us. We knew he wasn't here to camp. As he prepared to interrupt our dinner, we discussed plans to eat and run. It seemed inevitable, but only time would tell.

Before allowing him to knock, I poked my head out the door. "How are you doing?" I asked.

"Good," he replied. "Do you plan on spending the night?" This pleasant officer with a British accent leaned on his right forearm, as if he were holding up the camper. He heard our intentions to stay, although we weren't strikingly convincing.

"Okay," he replied. "I closed the gate and put a chain around it, but the chain is just wrapped around to make it look closed. If you have an emergency, or have to leave for some other reason, you can get out by unwrapping the chain."

The officer bid us a good night and left us completely alone in the park, the amazingly tranquil park. Seldom did a car pass by on the town's main drag. The solitude was encompassing. The only noise I heard came from my head, which retained the sounds of the interstate. Long drives followed by utter serenity are like pouring water on a fire. The sizzling continued for a while.

June 20, 1992

Alone in the park the next morning, I pulled aside the curtain and surveyed the area through the bug-smeared windshield. Knowing that we were legal, the park looked considerably more attractive than the day before.

I spotted a water spigot and filled our plastic two-gallon jug, then lifted it into the refrigerator. However, this would not be the water we'd drink. There appeared a very light yellow-green hue, which was tinted enough for us to refuse it.

Not excited about unhooking the camper, I jumped on my bike and pedaled away through Ithaca to a small convenience store for water safe enough to pass down our throats. When I returned to the camper armed with two gallons of drinking water, we were able to sip fluid while pumping out notes. We now had the place and the time and had to take advantage.

For the second time in two nights, a police officer pulled alongside the camper when we were three bites into our meal. I opened the door when I saw him approaching, spanked by déjà vu with my greeting, "How are you doing?" It was at that moment that different ways of greeting people surged through my head.

After his response, "Good," I wondered about a stay limit at this little park tucked in the woods. More specifically, I wondered about a one night limit. That in mind, I allowed him to spiel about the unlocked chain around the gate.

"Have a good night," he ended with a smile. However, we didn't want to see him leave just yet. "And bundle up because it's supposed to be cold tonight."

Then he turned to walk away, but we both had questions for the officer. We had created these questions over dinner, but had a little trouble with the draw. Tracy and I simultaneously called out to him with incoherent sentences, but it did the job when the officer stopped to ask what exactly we were trying to blurt.

"How's the drinking water in Michigan?" I started.

The officer, who was about our age and had short blonde hair, returned to the camper door. He looked in and said, "All right...I guess."

That primed us to continue talking, but he became a little too comfortable with the questions.

"An officer told me that there were campers here last night...was that you guys?" he asked.

"Yes, it was." I agreed without hesitation, feeling like a toad for letting him go through that spiel about the unchained gate.

"Ithaca's a small town," he said, unaffected. "Not much happens around here. There's like...no trouble, really."

"I guess we must be pretty big news to Ithacans," I said. "Does everybody in town know about us?"

"Pretty much," he answered with a hearty chuckle.

"How's the crime rate?" asked Tracy half-kidding. "We don't have anything to worry about here, right?"

"Oh no," he assured us. "The crime is pretty low, really none except for drunk drivers."

"Have you been in Ithaca your whole life?" asked Tracy.

"Yes, I like it here. Small, quiet town," he replied.

The officer's return cost him his final twenty minutes until he went off duty. "You guys have a fun and safe trip," he ordered, "and thank you for stopping in Ithaca."

Over cold burgers, Tracy went on a tangent about the small town of Ithaca. "They give us free electricity," she began, "free water, a place to stay for a couple of nights, tuck us in, and thank us for coming."

Ithaca was a find. The small town in the Lower Peninsula provided us weary travelers a place to park with the luxuries of camping, and so we discussed a third overnight.

Later that evening, we both suffered flashes like this: "Oh my God! We're living on the road." It was a shocking revelation when the reality of our lives began to grab hold and shake us until we truly understood. The fact that it happened to both us on the same night was exceptional in itself because it was a seldom occurrence.

Here it flashed as we camped in Ithaca, Michigan, alone in the solitude of a small wooded park seven weeks into the trip. Although earlier flashes had occurred, they weren't as upsetting or terrifying.

Seven weeks into our journey found us sitting up in bed, each of us pillowed against a back corner of the camper. We then started working on finishing the Thank You notes. But as we began talking, the work slipped to our laps. We had become so absorbed in camper life that the honeymoon nearly escaped us. We had been working hard every day just to survive.

In order for the awareness of the honeymoon to survive, sometimes auto pilot had to operate. Many reasons for this journey rivaled for the forefront. Since our honeymoon had come as an afterthought and seven weeks had passed, our dream had taken over.

It's unlikely that newlyweds take off on a romantic honeymoon for a week or two and then forget about the honeymoon before it ends. We never had the luxury of sitting beside the pool sipping cocktails every afternoon.

In its place, we motored through the states. I was usually the one at the wheel, and Tracy was the one with the map and the dog. We drove through the night hoping for a parking spot. We bathed in the confines of a bathroom the size of a telephone booth every second or third day. That was our life. We respected our holding tanks too much to test them.

Delight for us came when we discovered a dump station after overflowing our holding tanks. Our brushes with death on the road ahead will stay with us forever. They weren't enjoyable, but they were unforgettable. We'd never stop during life-threatening situations to reflect on the honeymoon aspect of our journey. Whatever happened on our journey burrowed under our skin, staying there like the chill of a New England winter.

This became our trade-off, but we wouldn't trade it off for anything. The memories of a pool wouldn't be as binding. They wouldn't swim with our blood the way memories of this trip seemed to do. We were really living as opposed to living it up, the difference between long- and short-term memory.

Just shy of everlasting, the thank you notes sufficiently dwindled after the midnight hour. While moving through town to continue on the road the following morning, we spotted a mailbox and dropped off an enormous amount of mail. With our Thank You notes virtually completed, the Ithaca post office was probably on the verge of the most mail in their town's history. And with all of this mail out of the camper, we expected our gas mileage to improve as we headed north.

June 26, 1992

On this morning, we arose to a sunrise breaking away from land and early morning fog beyond Elk Lake, located at a rest area on Route 31 in Elk Rapids. After six nights of merely functioning in free campgrounds, we too were ready to detach from the land. We had had a mission to reach this rest area last night, and although the path led us to a four-hour stay limit, we pooled our resources so the three of us could stay twelve hours.

We rolled over the five-mile Mackinac Bridge. It is one of the world's largest suspension bridges and has linked the upper and lower peninsulas since 1957. Needing to experience Lake Huron for Great Lake number four, we exited the highway sooner than planned.

In St. Ignus, the camper stumbled into town for one of the country's largest car shows. Funky models, antique models, racecars, and convertibles surrounded us. We slowly pushed through town, feeling like we did not belong in this traffic.

People sat in lawn chairs on both sides of the road, witnessing a twenty-two foot motorhome pass between them. It was an open road at this time, but that did not make us feel less foolish about being sandwiched between model T's.

Eking along, amused and embarrassed, we reached the end of the commotion and began searching for our state memento. We collected a spoon from every state to represent each of the forty-eight states. We stepped into a little gift shop.

There we met Bo, a stocky man who looked to be in his fifties with slicked back hair. He began conversing with us from behind the counter, the spoon creating a curiosity in him that had us feeding him our story. His excitement showed as his eyes got big and his speech quick. "You have to see Mackinac Island," he said with exuberance.

"We'd love to go, but we can't afford to see it all," Tracy replied.

Bo urgently glided around the counter, asking us to hold on as he made a beeline to his desk near the store entrance. Sliding open the desk drawer, he grabbed something inside and returned to us.

"Here...now you can go. Since you're on the road for a year and can't afford it, now you can. Since you're in the area, you have to see this. Go and find out why. There's a lot of history and you can take a horse-and-buggy ride."

What Bo handed over to us were two VIP passes for a sixteen-minute, hydro-jet ferry cruise to Mackinac Island. He then whipped out a business card for a restaurant.

"Stop by here when you leave. They're nice people. Tell them that I sent you, and they'll give you a free drink."

As we bid our farewell, having chatted for about thirty minutes, Bo decided to follow us to the ferry. He brought us to where we needed to board, and before long, water shot high in the air as the ferry hauled us to our destination.

Once on the island, we just had to invest in a horse-drawn buggy ride, if not for our sake then for Bo's. No cars other than emergency vehicles are allowed on the island, and walking would not take us around this island fast enough. Besides, the horse piles decorating the streets made walking treacherous.

Our ride came when we stepped off the boat, and we spent most of our time either buggying around or investigating once the buggy stopped to rest. The island is three miles long by two miles wide with a high-cliffed shore, natural bridges, and caves. The odd rock formations complimented this intriguing visit, explaining Bo's enthusiasm.

But a few hours sapped our enthusiasm, and we saw dark clouds rolling in. It was the perfect time to return before rain entered the equation. The ferry rooster-tailed water again, rushing us back to St. Ignus to discover the Car Show had blocked us in a parking lot with closed roads all around it. However, once we ate and rested, the roads reopened and enabled us to drive toward Saulte Ste. Marie.

A rest area appeared on the map within fifty miles. A cup of coffee for me, tea for she, and gone were we. Interstate 75 would take us directly to Canada's sister city. Red lines on the map accurately portrayed the road. Deer signs provided continuous reminders. By the looks of things, though, these warnings were unheeded.

Four other campers were parked for the night with lights out when we arrived at the rest area, and this provided ample security for us. The uneasy feeling we got from being the only vehicle while attempting to pull off a free night's sleep can be a tad stressful, but not on this night.

Alone in the lot upon waking, we set off for the Soo Locks train tour, which would tote us over the bridge to Canada. It wasn't until mid-afternoon that we arrived to see a trolley, which we believed to be an authentic train upon reading an advertisement.

The seats we settled on were in the last row. They faced backwards, as if we were being punished. Two couples and a boy just shy of his teenage years sat behind us, which was actually in front of us. One of the guys, exceptionally tall, had the countenance of a lumberjack with a scar on his scratchy face and white bandages around his fingers.

In so many words, amongst jokes and laughter, Mr. Lumberjack told the big, sloppy man bent over in front of them to pull up his pants, which beltlessly sagged below the official construction worker's level. He knew that we were part of his audience, hearing our hysterical, yet smothered, laughter. His macho antics continued until the man in front of him took a seat.

Lumber Jack seemed to be obsessed with money, and every time an exchange or the possibility of an exchange of money occurred, the response was always, "More money. More money." When the trolley pulled up to the tollbooth on the bridge, he repeatedly said, "Gimme yer money. Gimme yer money." He was a character, but in this tourist trap, he was right on the money.

Two young kids, known as troublemakers to the trolley driver, trailed the train on dirt bikes. Lumber Jack, sitting back and struggling to relax on this seismic ride, began shouting to the boys to go home to their mothers. One of the kids, blonde hair falling to the middle of his back, prompted Lumber Jack to scream out in his roughest of voices, "Get a haircut."

The boy heard, but continued to pedal on, emotionless, until a retort became readily available, and did it ever. "Tell your mother to get a haircut," he replied, pedaling a few more revolutions before finishing his thought, "between her legs."

Everyone in the back of the trolley laughed to themselves, but Lumber Jack only smiled while his eyes searched for an answer. The rough-and-ready man who would never dream of allowing someone to get the best of him, sat slumped in his chair. He was speechless. The embarrassed smile painted on his face was equivalent to a white flag. The boys continued to follow, but within a few minutes the trolley driver's intercom chased them away.

If you've never experienced an earthquake and would rather experience a simulated tremor, this tour train would be your best bet. The tremendous vibrations forced us to perform that childish game of sounding a flat tone just to hear it bounce up and down. As for the ride over the locks into Canada and back, it was hardly worth our effort. However, the sideshow we witnessed was priceless.

June 28, 1992

Gloomy rain surrounded us as we crossed the Upper Peninsula of Michigan in search of a dump station. We needed to relieve our flooded bathroom floor, then we needed a Laundromat so we could again walk from one end of the camper to the other. We killed two birds with one stone at a campground.

"Can I help you?" asked a lady as she stepped out of her home with a coat over her head to block the rain.

"Yes. We need a Laundromat," Tracy answered.

"The door's open...help yourself," the lady replied.

"Thank you. We have another problem, also," I interjected.

"What's that?" she asked.

"Our bathroom floor is under water," I answered.

"Oh dear. You wanna use our bathroom?" the lady asked, concerned.

"No. I wanna use your dump station," I replied.

After meeting our needs, we traveled further west. Signs advertising pasties were spread throughout Michigan, so we finally succumbed and I asked a lady about pasties at a convenience store. She shot me a bewildered look before realizing that I probably meant the food.

Finally on the same wavelength, she informed us that a pastie is a delicious pocket sandwich stuffed with meat and potatoes; a favorite of miners in days past. Since pastie signs seemingly occupied every mile, we continued west with a future treat in mind.

In Munising, we picked up our mail, which Judi had gathered up at our PO Box in Connecticut and delivered about one week ahead of us. Our job was to sketch a route to a certain town and hope we didn't arrive too soon. The post office will hold mail for up to thirty days, but they won't track it down if it hasn't yet arrived.

Our time in Michigan long overdue, we cruised along Lake Superior, our fifth and final Great Lake, hoping to whittle away the distance to Wisconsin. Our one stop was to make Tracy's weekly call to her mother. Our calls home three times per week finally served their purpose. Judi had a message for me to call home, and although I didn't like the ring of it, I had a strong feeling that I knew what news was awaiting.

My suspicion proved correct. My ninety-two-year-old grandmother, Beatrice Maynard, known to our family as Mimmiere and the only grandparent I ever knew, had passed away. A prolonged illness claimed her life, and I had been certain that, when we left on this trip, we'd never see her again.

The previous Christmas, our family drove to see her in North Scituate, Rhode Island, because we believed then that she would not be seen alive again. That turned out to be the last time I would ever see her, and it served as our attendance at her funeral because now we could not return. My father understood; it was his mother, but that was just the way it had to be. By this time, her death was not a shock, but rather a deliverance from the pain she had suffered as she strived to join the centenarians.

My mind concentrated on my grandmother, born months before the turn of the century, as the setting sun set Lake Superior afire. The blinding reflection could have represented the light she was now seeing. Even our worries lightened as all tension lagged behind the beauty we beheld. I concentrated on the scene reflected before me, while the Eagles gently rocked the airwaves. Tracy and I observed a long moment of silence, perhaps intentionally. It was a time of sorrow, yet I wanted to jump out of my skin as a time of celebration shined before me. However, my body was sedated. My sadness and joy battled it out before dusk swiped it all away from me.

A rest area in Michigan provided our resting-place, about twenty-five miles shy of Michigan's Central Time and fifty miles from Wisconsin. We needed the rest, so Wisconsin had to wait until morning. Michigan was not a place where we would consider living, but we never imagined we would find the state so attractive, with so much to see and do. We had to push aside so many activities, but we did so many others that we exhausted ourselves and had to force ourselves out of the state long before we wanted to leave.

June 30, 1992

Another first occurred as we pierced our way into a new time zone. Central Time in the western portion of the Upper Peninsula represented another milestone, further and further from the place we called home. We agreed on a quick detour to a small restaurant advertising pasties. Most signs out here advertised pasties and pop. Soda for these East Coasters, thanks.

Sitting up in our dinette, Tracy and I each tried the infamous Michigan Pastie. It consisted of fried hamburger, fried chunks of potato, and some vegetables inside a crepe. It wasn't too bad...with ketchup. Although not the best food we'd ever tried, it certainly was not the worst. It smelled like fried hamburger and tasted like fried hamburger, plain and simple.

"Wisconsin Welcomes You!" read the sign. We'll take you through state number nine, but there's a large-scale problem with our first destination. Set your watch back an hour if you didn't already and buckle up as we make a detour away from the Apostle Islands, where a train that was carrying the chemical Benzene derailed in Superior, Wisconsin, creating a large, toxic cloud. Superior, Wisconsin and Duluth, Minnesota were evacuating in excess of seventy-five thousand people. The radio kept us updated.

Just thirty-five Wisconsin miles from the commotion, we back-tracked in Port Wing and headed south to a place to be named later. We had no concrete plans beyond the Apostles. We headed down the state, at one point witnessing a fox as it appeared out of the heavy trees lining the road, before illegally darting along the roadside and mixing back into the woods. Midnight struck by the time our altered plans took us to a free campground with electricity at Bruce Municipal Park, but we could not afford another delay after three hundred miles of tar.

July 2, 1992

Most of the roads we traversed in Wisconsin were county roads designated by a letter. County G Road whipped us along farmland and cows, passing well-kept fields at high speeds. Later, the reduced speed of twenty-five or thirty-five miles per hour escorted us through small country towns.

We drove through nothing but open fields, brown and green, perhaps scattered trees and bushes on occasion. We passed barns, farmhouses, silos, and one-foot high rows of corn, then slowly passed through meticulous little towns. Some towns lasted roughly twenty seconds before we resumed the fifty-five miles per hour speed limit, but this was the part of Wisconsin that we adored.

This defined paradise for Tracy, as she was able to observe more than enough farms in this dairy land. She sat peering out of the camper, able to see everywhere, far and wide. She just sat back in the passenger's seat with Molly sleeping on her lap. She admired the scenery, commenting occasionally on the solitude of these county roads and controlling Molly when the presence of the cows incensed her. One cow wandered into someone's front yard, but it seemed so natural there. A train approached in broad daylight, shining a bright headlight that appeared to be coming at us, but veered with the roadside.

Later in the afternoon, we turned the radio on to hear that the tornado watch had been lifted, and we felt comforted with our lack of awareness only because we now did not have to worry about it.

The free campground book led us astray once again as we landed in Horicon, the city on a marsh. The little old ranger amused himself with the thought of such a camping rate. However, he allowed us to park overnight, since we came self-contained and would be moving to Milwaukee in the morning.

July 5, 1992

After viewing a small fireworks display in Brown Deer, which is just outside of Milwaukee, we were ready for the Milwaukee Fest. This festival miraculously offered us its final day. Festivities usually took place the week before or after we arrived. Not desiring to get the camper caught up in the hubbub of this metropolis, we boarded a Park 'n Ride in Brown Deer, where a bus would shuttle us into Milwaukee and directly to the festival.

Upon our arrival, the lady at the ticket booth informed us that camcorders were not allowed. Leaving it with security was not secure enough for us, so we hopped back on the bus and made our way back to the camper to drop it off.

The bus driver recognized us and did not charge another fare, even though he wasn't the one who had driven us the first time. He was an obese black man from Little Rock with short black curly hair and a hint of sideburns. He put the shifter into drive after fruitlessly waiting five minutes for at least a third passenger

I asked the bus driver about all the "Adopt a Highway" signs as he maneuvered his large vehicle through the heavy interstate traffic. He kept glancing at us in his rearview mirror. I went out on a limb by suggesting that these signs perhaps refer to couples who are unable to have a highway of their own.

Glenn Maynard

The driver, with his stomach wedged into the steering wheel and not an inch to spare, began trembling. His entire body convulsively bounced up and down, silently, while Tracy and I examined him to make sure nothing was wrong. Up and down jumped his belly. Up and down in slow motion.

Then he turned to look at his passengers, and it wasn't until then that the smile enveloping his face indicated that he was enjoying a gut-wrenching chuckle. He kept repeating what I said, moving his head from side to side in disbelief, accompanied by after-chuckles. Even his eyes laughed whenever he bounced them off his rectangular rearview mirror at us. Then we arrived back at the camper.

Although he promised to give us a return ride and I continually repeated the request, he dropped us near our camper in the parking lot and drove away. We had only stepped off the bus to drop off the camcorder.

As we sat on the next bus, a girl in line behind us fisted seven dollar admission tickets for three dollars each. Six dollars later, I fisted two of them. Color Me Bad preceded Paula Abdul in concert. Although it was a sold out show, we arrived early enough for a hand stamp, which enabled us to sit on the lawn for free. Even the stamps were limited, but timeliness seemed to be on our side for a change.

A comedy show packed people under a large circus tent, and our heads peeped through the outskirts of the crowd to catch a half hour of laughs before catching the entertainment of the band who call themselves Plumb Loco. The music drew people up on picnic tables as they danced provocatively. The beer helped, I'm sure, but even without suds the band entertained this crowd.

An aisle separated our seats from paid admission. It didn't make much sense, but we didn't complain. Before the bands started, a teenage boy next to Tracy asked her for the time. Tracy glanced at her watch, mentioning that she was on Eastern Time.

"Where are you from?" asked the boy, as his mother looked on.

One seat separated our party from theirs, and when Tracy answered that she hailed from Connecticut, we chatted until the empty seat was filled with the boy's aunt. She had curly brown hair, dark sunglasses, and a face of stone, staring ahead emotionless as her sister explained our travels.

Although she did not say a lot at first, she ended up talking breathlessly for the next hour and a half until the show started. She had a mission to take what she called home, Milwaukee, and elevate it. It was nice to hear a native speak about their hometown in such a favorable way.

"How's the economy in Milwaukee?" asked Tracy.

"Pretty good. There are people out of work, but those are the people who don't really want to work because of Milwaukee's compensation package. It's a really good package, but for the most part, people here want to work, and want to work hard. There is work in Milwaukee if you're willing to look hard enough for it."

Her sunglasses stared straight ahead as if she was trying to hide her eyes from us, and her face remained blank. "People here are very religious," she continued. "They don't care what faith you have, just that you have a faith. Religion is a very big part of Milwaukee."

The beginning of the show interrupted the aunt's discussion. Color Me Bad and Paula Abdul rocked the amphitheater, but trying to beat the rush out forced us from our seats before the show ended. The poor dog had been pent up in the camper all day, and no concert could be good enough to allow a dog to suffer.

Walking out of the amphitheater brought us directly into an introduction of Bachman Turner Overdrive. After one song, "You Ain't Seen Nothing Yet," we had to pull ourselves away from the most entertaining festival we'd ever attended. We were wired from the excitement of the day. People buzzed around this festival in large numbers. The herds made it nearly impossible to turn around. We flowed toward the exit.

One of the most intriguing aspects on the road of life is that a different path will lead to a different experience, good or bad. Life on the road is much the same, and at the end of this path, a wonderful experience awaited us in Milwaukee. This one could have easily been passed over, and that goes for every other moment of the trip.

July 6, 1992

Our camcorder captured state line signs, not to mention our zany antics celebrating each state as a milestone done only in the privacy of our camper. Route 251 paved the way into Illinois, but no sign welcomed us to the state. It must have been a mistake; perhaps a small sign had escaped our vision.

The reasons for missing it weren't that important, though. What we wanted was the state sign, and we had none. Even after driving further into the first town in Illinois, hoping to catch a late welcome, we came up empty. We turned around, drove back to Wisconsin, and tried again.

Still seeing no sign to welcome us, we began to get desperate. Tracy grabbed the map, studying other routes to Illinois, but we felt it would be ridiculous to go out of our way. How badly did we want it? We wanted it badly enough, and at this point we prepared ourselves for anything. Lord knows we had the time.

We entered Illinois from three different routes, none of which helped us out. My impatience was amplified to anger. Though interstate ninety was a toll road, we thought it would certainly have a sign. Wisconsin welcomed us back three times, but Illinois wanted nothing to do with us. This frustrated us; an hour was wasted just chasing a damn welcome sign. How stupid, yet here I am printing the foolish act.

As we rolled to the tollbooth, we rolled our eyes. Illinois still did not welcome us. We lost an hour, paid a toll, and received nothing in return. I prepared to raise hell with the toll person, the lucky candidate being a short, heavy-set lady with glasses and a squeaky voice.

Slowly, I rolled up to the booth. After stopping and glaring at the lady, I calmly, though feeling silent rage, explained our dilemma. This upbeat woman somehow made me feel a little better about Illinois. Then I told her that since no sign would welcome us to Illinois, our last resort was for her to verbally welcome us to Illinois for our camcorder.

"Well, I welcome you to Illinois," her squeaky voice managed, flowing as smooth as honey, followed by a big smile. Illinois could do no better, so we thanked her and moved on, unable to believe her tale about our having missed a sign.

Rockford, our first major city in Illinois, offered Rock Cut State Park. We needed to flush out our sewer tank, for reasons I don't believe I need to elaborate on here. An older lady managed the park office. The structure resembled a shed, but the millions upon millions of insects dancing by its light prevented us from breaking through to the service window. The ranger slipped through the door with bug spray in hand, and after a series of heavy blasts, invited us into the office.

Two male rangers entered the scene, and the five of us began socializing. The old "Where are you all from?" question popped up, then they barraged us with what to do in Illinois. Two rangers rambled off potential visits not only in Illinois, but throughout the country, as well as the routes we'd need to take to get to all of these places. Tracy and I looked at each other briefly as they ranted; as if we'd remember every route.

To make matters more entertaining, the three rangers began arguing with one another as to which route was better and why. They further discussed possible construction on particular routes to particular sites in particular states.

One site that did spark our interest sat in the scenic northwest corner of the state in historic Galena. The people of Galena had presented General Ulysses S. Grant with a home on his return from the Civil War in 1865. Grant had eventually lived in Galena, known for the finest architecture in the Midwest.

After we left the office, our late sewer-cleaning mission was underway as Tracy filled the sewer and dirty water tanks with water. She then slowly inched the camper back and forth. I remained outside, making sure the hose from the camper to the dump station did not snap should Tracy drive an inch too far in either direction. We hoped her back and forth movement would cleanse the walls of the tanks, but if she drove too far, I'd be spending the rest of the evening in the shower.

Once the new day appeared, we accepted Route 20 from Rockford, where the majestic bluffs we meandered through made us wonder about Illinois being the most level of the prairie states. But Galena was really the only part of the state with hills. The distant views for the rest of Illinois offered miles and miles of flat plains.

Humidity sent rivers of sweat down our faces, and since it was too late in the day for a walking tour of Galena, we asked around for a Laundromat. Three loads of laundry overfilled the basket under our bed, lifting the mattress higher than normal.

The grocery store across the street provided us with a few items, air conditioning, and an idea of where to park for the night. We began by eyeing their parking lot and other areas in the vicinity, then hoped a native could provide insight.

Once the cashier freed herself of customers, I approached the thin, freckled lady who was wearing a red apron. The tall lady bagging her own groceries ahead of me stopped her shopping cart to eavesdrop. I stared straight into her eyes hoping she'd bundle and flee, but she barged into the conversation. She informed us that there were no all-night stores in town, only a campground down the road. The cashier couldn't help, and at that moment another man extended the line.

The cashier asked the lady standing next to her, but higher up in a booth in Customer Service. Now with the entire store involved in this one, we were pushed over to Customer Service in order to keep the line flowing.

She too started in with the campground bit, but unable to take anymore, I had to set her straight.

"We're on the road for a year, so we have to avoid camping fees whenever possible," I explained.

Once on the same wavelength, she put her chin in her hands and her eyes in the air, searching out serious ideas. When she saw one, her eyes returned to us.

"There's a parking lot to the side of this store, and I don't think the police will see you there...or the back street behind the store."

She was getting warm, but we needed more safety and didn't want hassles from the police. Then she followed with the clincher. "McDonald's is right on Route 20. They have a parking lot where truckers park for the night. That might be a good spot."

We parked next to another camper and between two tractor-trailers. The extra long parking spaces separated by white lines indicated a trucker's lot between McDonald's and Citgo, but we're always skeptical.

For reassurance, I knocked on the camper, but they told us they weren't staying for the night. Then I asked a trucker, and he shrugged his shoulders. Then I asked a boy in a McDonald's uniform as he stood outside conversing with a lady in a car. He told us that he sees truckers here when he closes up for the night and that we could try it. The lady interrupted to mention the campground down the road.

"We're on the road for a year, and trying to avoid that."

"Oh, but campgrounds are cheap around here."

Averaging over thirty-five dollars per day for the first ten weeks was not economically feasible, considering our bank account and holding plans for a year. It would not cut it, so we had to take desperate measures. Cutting out campground rates was a start. People seemed to look at it as only eight dollars, but we looked at it as eight dollars multiplied by three hundred sixty-five days. We couldn't do it.

A sheriff then pulled into the lot. As he drove by, the employee waved him down. Great. Now I had to ask the sheriff if we could park illegally.

"I don't think there's a problem with it," he said, much to my surprise.

After I parked for the night, Tracy phoned Connecticut and I began overhauling the camper. Our clean clothes needed folding, the bed needed making, and so forth. Darkness set in as the parking lot lights barely helped me see to clean the camper windows.

An older man pulled his clunking gas-guzzler up to the camper as I wiped the outside windows. When he rolled his window down, I walked over to his car and noticed his wife sitting beside him. A gruff voice mumbled from his large face.

"I just wanted to rib you about cleaning your windows at night," he said with a chuckle. "Where abouts ya from in Connecticut?"

"The Hartford area," I replied.

"Oh yeah. I think I know where that is," he said. "I used to be a trucker until I flipped my tractor-trailer over and rolled three times. Had my leg amputated."

This man's head looked as if it bulged with muscles, but his neck may have been on hiatus. His wife sat in the passenger's seat staring ahead, occasionally glancing over to see whom her husband was talking to this time. After all, he had admitted that he wanted to rib me about washing my windows at night just to strike up a conversation.

The former trucker rattled off places we had to see, although many were located in Wisconsin. On several occasions, I attempted to burst his bubble by speaking of Wisconsin as a thing of the past, but he insisted. This man told me a story about his hard life growing up on a potato farm prior to relocating to the Chicago area. He said that he had stopped because his wife needed to get some sleep before the last leg of the journey back to Chicago from Iowa.

Minutes after they pulled into a spot and parked, a tractor trailer pulled up beside them. The tractor trailer driver left the engine roaring for a couple of hours, making for a loud night even as we tried to shut our eyes.

July 8, 1992

Cornfields filled our view and bug juice filled our windshield as we meandered through the pig farms of Jo Davies County en route to Springfield. Slowing for a good look, we saw black and white pigs sliming atop each other, urgently moving toward something likely insignificant. The aroma they created disrupted our curiosity, and my foot returned to the gas pedal harder than before, but the smell traveled with us miles beyond the farms.

Our tour of Galena had us venturing through several antique shops for relief from the sweltering day. However, knowing Molly may be uncomfortable inside the stuffy camper forced us to cut the tour short. Each step of the tour tortured us. The weather changed our plans. This heat made no history charming. If we stayed in it, we would be history.

Since we could not conquer Galena in one day, we surrendered. Following Route 84 along the Mississippi River, thoughts of air conditioning in our heads, we settled ourselves into a free campground in Hampton. This was one of many sites offered by our friends in the Corps of Engineers.

This Lock and Dam on the Mississippi contained several roomy sites and a dump station. However, the little bugs negotiating our screens forced us to close the windows and use the inade-

95

quate oscillating fan. This fan was in no way a challenge for the heat of the evening. It benefited us only with its size; it was conveniently compact, though otherwise worthless metal.

Our venture out to feast our eyes on the Mighty Mississippi did not turn into the grand moment we had fancied. The infamous river, polluted beyond our wildest imagination, offered large sections of green algae and lily pads decorated with beer cans, garbage, and brown water. Riverboats charge good money for a cruise down this river. No thank you.

By eight o'clock the next morning we rejoined the roadway. We departed rather early because our refrigerator refused to cool properly, so we needed propane before all our food spoiled. The milk had curdled, and my coffee quickly pointed this out.

A wrong turn led us over the Mississippi River and into Davenport, Iowa. Turning around, feeling as though I had ruined our future arrival to that state, I returned to Illinois...without...you guessed it...a welcome sign.

Ripley appeared far enough away for us to stop for the night at their free campground, but the eight-dollar charge forced us onward, closer to Springfield. Dark clouds enveloped the sky, hanging in mysterious, mischievous ways, possibly carrying the rain in the forecast. Route 36 carried us into Springfield, but an emergency breakthrough on the radio altered our plans.

Those clouds were definitely up to no good. Radar had picked up tornadoes in the county we had been in and the county for which we were headed. Tracy clutched the map, revealing this highway with exits ten miles apart. We nervously eyed the clouds miles away over the plains while I created an image of a funnel, simultaneously trying to repress such an act. We had to move, but the only direction available forced us into the section under sky with the most menacing clouds. We hoped to be able to exit the highway and head back east in search of some type of shelter.

Driving through nothing but plains in a motorhome during this tornado warning was my worst fear realized. The exit offered a small cinderblock building, which would do us no good. I was living my own nightmare. We stepped out of the RV to scan the skies, which looked increasingly favorable for a tornado anywhere, at any time.

But I wouldn't have been surprised if one suddenly formed overhead. We saw an attractive faraway section of blue sky. The question was, could we make it there without being sucked into the sky? The possibility, being so real, belted me with fear.

Tracy's concern exacerbated my fear because this stuff usually didn't bother her. She seemed stir-crazy, as if she wanted to be out from under this particular dome of sky, which was falling. It unfolded all around us, but we had nowhere to go and no time to get there.

Having to act urgently, Tracy found a campground south of us in Pittsfield, where blue skies loomed. The tornado spun east toward Jacksonville at a rate of thirty-five miles per hour. With black clouds overhead on three sides, we opted for Pittsfield no matter what the cost. We needed solid structure, which campgrounds lack, but this seemed better than nothing.

I drove with my head sagging to the steering wheel and my eyes either peering into the side view mirror or through the windshield, awaiting the worst. Some vertical gray clouds urged me to look twice. My overly active imagination began hallucinating. The pedal touched the floor as I flew to safer skies, driving as fast as I could without being swept off the road by the wind.

"Forget the clouds," Tracy said. "Just drive."

"I can't forget the clouds," I screamed. "I can't just sit back in my seat and drive like there's nothing going on."

"But you're going off the road," she warned.

"I can't just ignore it," I screamed again.

The tension mounted. Our tempers flared. I did not have it in me to ignore the clouds. I feared for our lives and needed to see the clouds at all times. I kept looking at the small opening separating the clouds from the land all around, where tornadoes drop down in destructive ways.

Reports over the radio blared every fifteen minutes, but not nearly enough for me. Time stood still, and the camper seemed to do likewise in this everlasting dome. We followed signs to the campground in Pittsfield, driving down a road with gloomy clouds above. This was supposed to be our safe haven, but it still stirred uncertainty within us. The evil part of the sky seemed to be following us. The blue sky seemed to be in on this dirty trick.

Once at the campground, the old park ranger with a baseball cap atop his head slowly made his way to our camper.

"We're from Connecticut and have never been chased by a tornado," I said with a chuckle of utter nervousness, speaking faster than I'd ever spoken before. "We're not used to them and don't want to be. We were heading to Springfield, but this tornado forced us to head south, and here we are."

The ranger listened with half an ear as I rambled, undaunted by what I said, and soon a gradual smile emerged on his face as a result of my excitement. I began to feel I had overreacted, or maybe he was in on the whole thing, too.

"Oh," he finally managed. "I didn't know about the tornado warning. Haven't been listening to the radio."

I tried desperately to emulate the composure of the ranger. Tracy became calmer herself, having reached clearer skies, but it didn't look as though we had escaped danger. The ranger directed us to pick a site, and he'd be over to collect the six-dollar fee.

Once the ranger made it to our site, we sat at a picnic table writing up a registration form. He began telling us about Illinois and the tornado watches that he no longer paid attention to. He had plans to go into town later that evening, and it would never occur to him to change them.

The ranger lit a cigarette, smoked it to the filter as we were talking, then turned and flicked it to the edge of the woods surrounding the park. Tracy and I watched him flick, then our eyes met in wonderment of what it took to be a ranger.

Back in the camper, we turned the radio on to discover that we weren't in a good place after all. A radio station reported severe thunder and lightning storms, accompanying a tornado watch until midnight for the entire listening audience. Maybe we shouldn't have been listening.

The sky threatened to cry as darkness filled the campground. Light patches of fog intensified the scene. Now we had to worry for the entire evening. I wanted out of Illinois. Tracy suggested that we either go to a hotel or sit in the campground's bathroom for the evening, but neither would satisfy me. Nothing existed around these parts, and I wasn't sure that we should even be on the roads again with these threats.

Thunder rumbled loudly and furiously during dinner, raging from the heavens. It was accompanied by strobing, sporadic flashes of lightning. A tumultuous crack from the sky swiped any hope of our respite. The campground darkened, so we groped our way to the candles. Molly trembled and panted, crawling up and down Tracy in search of comfort from such a terrible monster. With most of the city in darkness, we could only stay tuned to radio updates from Springfield.

Rain soon pounded the camper, each individual raindrop empowered with a thud, and a constant drone of thunder kept Molly in a tizzy as she tried to bury her head under the blankets.

Outside the camper, we could see vertical streaks of lightning striking the ground. Stems branched off to attempt destruction of their own. A group of about ten people, some with coats covering their heads, began running for shelter under a pavilion.

Lightning strikes are amazingly less attractive from behind the window of a camper. Just a scrap of metal did nothing for my comfort level, but Tracy urged me to admire the way the streaks blended before hitting the ground. Even the nervous candles wavered from a bit of wind, which intruded from one of the corners of a window.

Good news finally entered the camper at eleven o'clock with the cancellation of the tornado watch and the easing of the downpour. Even better, I could finally start on the dishes, thus putting to rest a game of gin rummy in which I was getting trounced.

What a relief to be able to sleep without the threat of tornadoes, and Molly had an easier time of it too. She can't hear the weather reports, but she can sense them, and she certainly knows when a storm is assaulting us. If only we could feel as nonchalant as Tracy. This was the Midwest, but I could not take these threats anymore, nor could Molly.

One evening at this campground, Tracy wanted me to escort her to the showers. Since too many bugs flew in this forest, I didn't want to stand outside waiting for her to come out of the ladies room. Instead, since the campground was virtually deserted, I showered in the ladies room in the stall next to Tracy.

Before I could close my eyes for the shower, the June bugs had to go. Wearing nothing but flip-flops, I took one off to use as a weapon. While balancing on one foot, I went on a rampage, desperately trying to avoid stepping barefoot on the slimy floor. Tracy and I reported our June bug destruction process to each other throughout the extermination.

By the time the flip-flop rejoined my foot, thirteen brown June bugs lay cracked to death in three corners of the shower floor. Then I was able to shower as fast as I could. My imagination worked overtime, so it turned out to be one of my quickest showers ever.

As I began to towel-dry myself, I heard the bathroom door open and slam shut. In walked the old ranger's wife, who also needed a shower at ten o'clock at night. I heard Tracy talking to her loudly, mostly as a warning for me to stay put. I remained silent, calculating the odds. Seconds turned into minutes, but it seemed like a transition from minutes to hours. When Mrs. Ranger finally tucked herself into a shower stall, Tracy opened my door and ushered me out. I don't think I've ever felt younger.

July 11, 1992

We needed directions to a free campground on the third day in Pittsfield, which prompted the ranger to mention that he accepts traveler's checks. Ebaugh Park, located on old Route 36, was impossible to find on the new Route 36. The wonderfully updated book failed to point that out. The ranger set us straight, enabling us to pull away from the luxury of electricity to a more primitive lifestyle.

Dirt roads led us into this park, which looked like it had been deserted years ago as dictated by the overgrowth. Metal rusted and nature grew wild. The overgrowth gave this place a jungle-like appearance. Vines were strung from tree to tree, across from top to bottom. No designated sites existed, nor signs indicating overnight camping. Nevertheless, after the arduous task of leveling the camper, we called this place home.

This park sat in the middle of nowhere, according to the map. Waves of cornfields dominated this area, but nothing else could challenge them. Stretches of corn to all sides swallowed the road on both ends, but a slow, steady stream of cars still managed to flow. Most important to us was the fact that we could park here and get away with it.

Dark clouds gave way to rain, then thunder, then lightning. This prompted us to turn on the radio, which issued reports of severe thunder, deadly lightning, heavy rain, fifty-five mile per hour winds, and golf ball sized hail. I slumped in my chair, every ounce of nerve dehydrated.

This report frightened both of us. At one point, light winds began to shake up the camper a bit. We didn't know for sure if we should take the reports seriously, but if so, how seriously should we take them? Since the people of Illinois ignore weather reports due to lack of credibility, we decided to go with our only option: to weather the storm.

The storm didn't last long and Tracy tried to explain that to Molly, who again hid under the blankets, shaking like a leaf on a tree. The same dog that growls whenever I pick her up now sat below me at the kitchen table with her ears back when the storm began. She hates thunderstorms, and we'd been subjected to them every night in Illinois. It seemed safe to conclude that Molly wanted to move on to Indiana, and she wasn't alone.

July 12, 1992

We entered our eleventh state, Indiana: "The People of Indiana Welcome You." The offering of the state sign proved an automatic plus for Indiana. The contents of the message pleased us, and the opportunity to check its accuracy presented itself. We'd never been to Indiana or thought about what it was like, so now we tried to imagine what makes Indiana...Indiana.

Route 40, the most direct backroad toward Richmond, paralleled Interstate 70. A dynamic representation of Indiana began on a path called Old National Road for trade, culture and migration during the 1800s. Route 40 extends west from Cumberland, Maryland to St. Louis, Missouri. Indiana began defining itself: very flat and full of cornfields, history, and a slow pace; exactly what the doctor prescribed.

We eventually worked our way down the state to the town with the funny name of French Lick. It offered a free campground in the Wayne-Hoosier National Forest, a mineral water spring, and we thought its name really needed an explanation.

A lady rushing around the empty French Lick Laundromat found some time to talk. She informed me that French Lick originated from the nearby salt lick and from the French trading post set up in the early 1700s. This put to rest the runaway imaginations of Tracy and myself as we had pondered its origin.

The lady informed us that French Lick is the home of Larry Bird. She also claimed that she was friends with his sister.

"Larry's jus' one of us," she explained, holding onto the pride of the town, folding laundry as she spoke.

In search of relief from the heat, I asked her if she knew of a place to swim, and her southern accent surfaced.

"Go dowen to the ho-tel," Mrs. Laundry began, "and thy'll be able to tell ya."

"What hotel are you referring to?"

"Oh...there's a very old ho-tel dowen the road and it's being restowred. It used to be a Sharatan."

This hotel plan hardly thrilled Tracy, who pursed her lips after hearing the directions. We soon arrived at the French Lick Springs Resort, Villa & Country Club. This yellow hotel had a large white porch in the center with an overhanging red canopy; a massive structure in height and length. Tracy insisted on waiting in the camper.

I eventually persuaded her to come with me, mentioning that French Lick had evolved into a resort and health center in the late 1800s because of the artesian springs. We stepped up to the grand entrance surrounded by a golf course. Though we had not showered, we strolled up the steps leading to the porch and into this 1869 hotel as nobility met our side-to-side glances.

It seemed to be our appearance that had really held Tracy behind. We did not belong, but still we put one foot in front of the other with confidence, like we belonged and knew exactly where to go.

Hundreds of rooms filled this castle, including a mini-mall. It had a bowling alley, gift shops, restaurants and an ice cream parlor, and that's only what we discovered from a sign and a wooden arrow pointing downstairs. A girl sat in the middle of the lobby playing a harp, daintily plucking at the strings to accompany our footsteps. Tables swallowing one corner of the room offered hors d'oeuvres.

We returned to the camper to grab towels for a dip in their pool. Our agenda included cold showers, swimming, and the whirlpool, even though our blue and pink bath towels clashed with the small white hotel towels that everybody else brought. Tucked snugly under our armpits, we strutted about the hotel looking as though we belonged, even though our bright towels raised some eyebrows. When the Indiana heat burned us painfully with no relief in sight, we became members. Sometimes we had to resort to such tactics.

July 19, 1992

One town from Santa Claus and twenty miles from Kentucky, we decided that it would be in our best interest to have our squeaky brakes inspected. It took two attempts to find a garage set up to handle motorhomes. Many garages cannot fit motorhomes into their bays and give up the business because they're afraid to make money outside the shelter.

A young kid with black, curly hair and a sharp accent directed me into a bay by waving his two arms back and forth in the air while eyeing the top of the entranceway. Since we all heard the squeal of the passenger's front tire, he started there. The pads looked fine, according to him, which suggested the possibility that they had crystallized from sitting. I assured him that his presumption traveled six thousand miles off the mark.

Mr. Brakeman applied silicon to the rust on the outside of the pads to prevent scraping. He test-drove the camper, returning with his progress report. Although little noise remained, it would most likely only bother the dog. We owed him a mere twenty dollars, smiling through laughter as we rejoined the highway.

We reveled in our good fortune until we heard a dangerously loose part rattling underneath. It felt like the tire wobbled on its last bolt, about ready to pass us in the left-hand lane. This was serious enough to turn around and show it to Mr. Brakeman again after twenty minutes on the road.

He thought it might be a clip put on backwards. He pulled a tire off and made an adjustment to the pin. Since the pin had been correctly applied, he needed to hear the noise, which he now believed to be the shocks. After his quick adjustment, he bid us farewell.

We headed for the highway, but the problem recurred before reaching it. The garage, officially closed the first time we had returned, forced us on a frantic return mission or we'd be out of luck with our twenty dollar repair job.

Traffic jammed as the whistle of a train, once faint, now came howling through town between downed gates. This Soo Line persisted for fifteen minutes, and we had given up hope of ever seeing Mr. Brakeman again.

Two of the four bays remained open, so I drove into one of them, but nobody greeted us. We waited, knowing full well that garages aren't left open after a day's work, but it left us wondering just how different things were in these parts. The kid finally returned from across the street and figured out that he had checked the pin on the wrong tire.

"If it doesn't work," he said, "y'all come back. If it's all right, you go on."

This time it worked, and we did go on, even though we expected the noise to return all day.

Welcome to Kentucky: The Bluegrass State. A scenic beauty to this rugged terrain stretched out and pulled us in as we moseyed our way over the Ohio River and through the woods to Owensboro. Green predominated, and it seemed like every grass and plant reveled in overgrowth. These growths climbed hills with the camper, an attractive wildness in a jungle-like way. Vines connected elderly trees, more so than wires connected telephone poles. Hills brought us up and over, and we always wondered what would be over and around the next incline. Some states required driving and admiring, but our eyes widened as we tried to catch as much of Kentucky scenery as possible before that great ball of fire visited another part of the world.

Another fire reference sparked our interest in Kentucky as we crested a hill and hugged a curve to the left before sinking away from the tall, circular stack of stones that they called a fireplace.

Nobody cut their lawn, so the tall grass hill indicated that these folks fit in. Flames shot up, wickedly breaking off to the side at times, but still contained within the stones. The old couple sat around watching the fire in their front yard, and for a split second we watched them, unsure if the fire absorbed them more than the scene they portrayed absorbed us.

Leitchfield held another Corps of Engineers campground, the largest and best Dam campground we'd come across to this point. The sites, perched on a steep hill leading down to Rough River Lake, had the look of an expensive camping resort. When we pulled into the grounds and looked down the hill at all the sites, Tracy and I looked at each other, but said nothing. After ten weeks in a twenty-two footer, mere looks evoked messages, and this time they conveyed the fact that this area could not be free.

This place cost us nothing. Eighty-six sites had to incur serious digging to maintain level ground on this hill. Thanks to the Corps once again. But we had one problem. The reason we had come here in the first place was for the dump station we found out they lacked (partial credit to the book, which by this time had a success rate of ten free and five with fees).

We descended the hill and parked at a site close to the water and near the boat launch. It worked for us.

July 20, 1992

My nephew, Matthew, turned four years old today. I phoned to wish him a happy birthday. My sister said he was so excited when the phone rang for him that he sped into the kitchen to intercept the receiver. However, each time I wished him a happy birthday, he wished me the same. He said nothing more as I tried to get him to talk, yet he so badly wanted the phone. I wondered if he remembered his Uncle Glenn.

Standing at the payphone in a small private airport on a sticky evening, I saw flashes of lightning in the distance. An overgrown southern roach scurried around by my feet before joining a small population of beetles. Thunder cracked closer, and wind swept both the trees and my hair back.

We spent this stormy evening at the Dam campground for the second consecutive night, then set off for Mammoth Cave National Park. Having never been underground, we stayed at the park campground in order to get an early start in the Ticketron lines that extended hundreds of spelunkers deep.

Awakening in the early morning, we prepared to head for the visitor's center. I opened the back shade to discover a deer munching on the leaves below. It gracefully nibbled leaves, stopping to chew while cautiously eyeing its surroundings, then continuing the plentiful all-you-can-eat buffet. The fact that our camper sat a few feet away made no difference to the deer.

We tried to keep Molly from spotting the deer, but after we finished with our viewing pleasure, our guard eased, and Molly convulsively barked. This sent the deer further into the woods. Once Molly spotted the deer, she spotted the bed through to the mattress.

Two rangers led our group of forty through the thickness of ninety degree heat to the cave entrance to begin the Echo River tour. Twenty feet from the entrance, a blast of cold air smacked us in the face from the consistently fifty-four degree cave. If the tour ended then, we'd enjoyed our money's worth as we, in our deep-red sunburns, smiled.

The ranger led us on a three mile, three hour tour, which included a short boat ride on the underground river. Our tour encompassed part of the longest-mapped cave system in the world, exceeding three hundred thirty-five miles with additional passages still being discovered. Mammoth Cave is currently more than three times longer than any other cave.

After descending several steps, looking side to side for anything different, we saw a thin stream of water cascading down from the cliffs on the side of the entrance. We moved past the constant splatter, landed in the cave's largest room, then looked up to a cathedral ceiling in this three to four acre space. Tracy and I surveyed this massive underground hole with fascination. We had just stepped into planet Earth, but it felt like another world.

The cave, illuminated by electricity, had lights behind slanted slabs of rock jutting from the ground. This allowed us to see, but maintained the cave's mysterious aura as we passed through. During the War of 1812 between the U. S. and England, slaves mined nitrate, the essential ingredient in gunpowder, in this very room. When the war ended, the cave became famous, and guided tours began.

Over two hundred species of animals in the cave merited our attention. We scrutinized each wall for bats, crickets, eyeless fish and crayfish. The preservation of these species, the maze of passages, cavernous domes, pits, underground rivers and lakes, and the rugged topography, became the reasons for establishing Mammoth Cave as a national park in 1941.

Upon reaching a small, black rectangle the size of a matchbook, the ranger shined his flashlight onto it and called it a bat. We also saw crickets clinging to the walls. The group moved with the ranger's swift pace, but Tracy and I lagged behind the entire time. We eyed every wall on both sides, wanting to extract more than a mere tour allowed.

We walked underground, where some who came before us had never made it out alive. We took our time. The ranger admonished us for our reverence, but not even this could dampen our mood. Our steps quickened, though only temporarily.

Fat Man's Misery, the name of a passage fourteen to eighteen inches wide around the hip area, forced us to twist, turn and wind our way for two hundred feet through this slender, jagged series of rocks. Tall Man's Misery provided a backbreaking low clearance tunnel, which evolved into a twenty foot duckwalk. Stone steps descended, railings a must, and when the passage became even narrower, I felt ties to the crab family. A tourist not paying attention at all times would exit the adit with a sore head.

Further into the cave we strolled with the fast moving group. Our sneakers provided premium traction on the clammy, clay-like ground as we did all we could to keep up with the group and enjoy each awe-inspiring step. There were high walls with piles of rock slabs and chips at the base that had fallen thousands of years ago. We heard dripping sounds throughout this damp underground that kept our eyes and imaginations as active as the life forms surrounding us.

The highlight of the tour unfolded upon our reaching the Echo River, five cave-levels below the surface of the earth. Tall orange life-preservers straddled our necks before our group split in two. Extending above our heads, these objects clamped around our necks made any head-turn to the right or left impossible without entirely shifting our bodies.

Gumby came to mind as two boats and forty stiff-necked passengers paddled down the Echo River, which was just wide enough to turn the boat around. The ranger warned us against touching the cave walls; no arms or legs out of the boat because sometimes the boat met up with the cave wall.

While entering a low-clearance tunnel in this boat, I noticed the tunnel coming quickly, level with my eyes. Having no time to react, I ducked, but the preserver prevented me from doing so. Then the tunnel overcame us and my preserver caught up on the cave ceiling, forcing me to kneel on the floor of the boat.

As the tunnel clearance continued to diminish, I feared decapitation. My head vibrated as the preserver dragged and scraped on the ceiling. Incapable of dodging out of the way due to a life-preserver seemed horrifyingly ironic.

Once out of the boat, our group sped down a path with walls that resembled Swiss cheese. The cave tour ended with a reminder of the intense humidity, exacerbated by three hours of "air conditioning."

Nickel-sized hail pelted our camper as we prepared for take-off. Flash floods almost made the camper hydroplane off the road. Sheets of rain eventually forced us off the road, but we went voluntarily. We conveniently recognized a red and white restaurant, so we decided to wait out the storm at Kentucky Fried Chicken in Kentucky; had to do it in the home of Colonel Harlan Sanders.

Battling the drenching rain through the town of Horse Cave, we thought we had discovered a free campground and probably could have parked for the night. However, we refrained because nobody else occupied this overgrown horseshoe-drive that offered no designated sites. It appeared to be anything but camper-friendly.

Near the highway, we found another McDonald's truck stop where we settled for the night, wondering if we held the record for the most showers in McDonald's parking lots. Although these truck stops were loud, this particular one with a train encroaching on our peace and quiet, we still cherished them and rejoiced upon seeing them.

When Tracy and I collapsed in bed that evening, we reflected on the day, and something struck Tracy unusually hard. We had nearly shut our eyes for the night from sheer exhaustion when Tracy began regurgitating a disgusting story the ranger had told us about the impurity of the earth.

A true story about a cow and a refrigerator upset Tracy. These two items entered a sinkhole during the spring thaw and were found in the Echo River, several cave-levels below the earth. The water underground, once thought to be pure, had a dead cow in it.

As Tracy remembered the story, she lifted to her elbows with tired eyes no longer recognizable. I had never seen her react to anything so strongly.

"Think about it," she said, "we don't know a damn thing about our own environment. There's a cow and a refrigerator swallowed up by the earth and resting in water. What else? What could possibly be in the water we drink?"

Tracy transformed irritation into interest in this issue like I'd never seen her. I sat back and nodded in agreement as she continued her rampage, taking us back to Lake Erie State Park in New York.

"Remember the smell of dead fish on Lake Erie? Why were all the fish dead? Why are all the rivers polluted, and what is it doing to our drinking water?"

The ranger at that park had mentioned that according to biologists, the dead fish resulted from cold water late in the season. The fish come ashore for warm water, but it was too cold. Then silt happens upon the rivers, clogging their gills and suffocating them. The ranger offered his own explanation, saying that the lake was overpopulated, and that this was Mother Nature's way of dealing with it.

This instance also stayed with Tracy. The atrocious smell of the dead fish certainly would not make one soon forget, and it drove us away earlier then planned. More environmental issues crept up between the fish and the cow, but for the duration of the trip, Tracy remained alerted to these issues. Although we had been forced to conserve water in the camper, it changed the way we used it while away from the camper.

We became more aware of the abuse to the earth. America is hardly exempt. We'd cringe when passing discolored rivers, fields we thought of as the town dump, strips of smog lingering over cities, or dilapidated neighborhoods. What we didn't know was that we were gradually being introduced to problem areas, and we hardly saw it all.

Our environment worsened, and so did our attitude toward it. How could this be happening to our earth? What kind of person could have no regard for his own land? Now we could understand the tear running down from the Native American's eye in the

"Keep America Beautiful" campaign they used to run on television.

I hated witnessing the abuse this country has suffered, but Tracy went on a rampage. She bought books and wrote letters home and to the president of her former employer, explaining what they could do to help. She had never before believed that one person could make a difference in the world. Now she believed that she could make a world of difference.

If she spread the word about conserving water, for instance, then she alone would be responsible for thousands of gallons a year. Water covers over seventy percent of the surface of the earth, and yet we're faced with the problem of insufficient water to drink.

We recycled cans, bottles, paper and plastic. Anything we could do to help, we'd do. If nothing else, our satisfaction knowing we did our part drove us to continue our actions. It shaped the rest of the trip, and it will shape the rest of our lives, but the truth of the matter is that we had to travel close to America before opening our eyes to the planet. We had never meshed with the earth as we now did. The environment became our backyard, rather than a concept too large to deal with.

July 24, 1992

A disappointingly dull sign deciphered "Missouri State Line," but once we completed the bridge spanning the Mississippi River, a cement entranceway arched across the road. As we passed underneath, another sign welcomed us to the first town over the line. We found ourselves in Cape Girardeau, Missouri.

The intense heat made stopping at a red light a major chore, so we opted for a campground with the comforts of air conditioning. There's a point where money and oscillating fans mean nothing, and we had reached that point in Cape Girardeau.

We arrived at Trail of Tears State Park, an area dedicated to the long, anguishing route of the Cherokees in their forced march from Tennessee to Oklahoma. As we walked to the campground host's trailer, the retired couple had prepared to pay us a visit with money bag in hand. Eleven dollars for them, air conditioning for us and knowing that our money was well spent by the time we felt that first blast of cold air.

The air soothed us to contentment. We remained at the park through the next day, when we heard a 3:30 P.M. knock on our door. I threw my clothes on as quickly as possible, hopping around on one foot until the other foot made it through its pants leg. When I finally made it to the door, our hosts were sitting at our picnic table holding their hungry bag. The ranger mentioned that our elapsed checkout time now exceeded thirty minutes.

"Couldn't quite make it to St. Louis," I responded, popping my head out the door.

They only smiled, and then he extracted another camping contract. They waited for me to sign on the line and pay them the fee, then they walked back to their trailer to await tomorrow's outcome. The park was by no means full, but the host seemed to be right on top of our expired contract.

Later that evening, he walked by with a bowl in his hand as I lay next to the camper with my arms outstretched, flushing out the holding tanks.

"We're having a popcorn party, if you'd like to join us," he said, stopping for the invite, then slowly gaining speed again.

"Thanks," I responded, having no intention of going to his popcorn party. I began thinking back, wondering if I'd ever attended such an event. When I went to tell Tracy, she had overheard the offer and answered before I even formed the question.

"I think that would be neat."

Off to the popcorn party we went, joining the campground hosts and two other couples in a circle of lawn chairs. All of them had retired, so we sort of fit in. We spent the evening discussing everything from quilting to boating on the Mississippi to the Four Corners. They all welcomed us into their little circle, and our conversation lacked nothing.

By the time our short gathering scattered, we had swapped addresses with two of the three couples. It was nice to get out of the camper and hang, and the opportunity presented itself on this night until the bugs pushed us apart.

July 27, 1992

The inverted, glimmering, stainless steel curve designed by Eero Saarinen, known as Gateway Arch, commemorates the gateway to the west for thousands of nineteenth century pioneers. This St. Louis span across the sky also marked our journey west, crossing the state toward the two Kansas Cities.

What else would the most appropriate town to visit be other than Booneville, smack dab in the middle of the state, about twenty miles west of Columbia? With the summer heat laying it on thick, we became obsessed with reaching the free campground in the middle of Booneville, listed with electricity.

It was a long drive along the brown Missouri River. The heat forced us to continue on the roller coaster of Route 94, but brutal twists and turns through this cornfield countryside made me cautious.

After camping in a trashy mobile home park and then under the bright lights of a gas station, Harley Park in Booneville became our welcomed reprieve. Though it wasn't listed as Harley Park, the Booneville Fire Department assured us that they allowed overnight camping.

Perspiration drenched our bodies as we ran the extension cord over to the electric outlet inside one of eight shelters. We looked at each other and smiled while I turned the air conditioner knob, but our smiles diminished when the air shut off. Again, we turned the knob, and again the air went on and off. And so the cycle repeated itself…on and off.

The fan on the air conditioner and the oscillating fan proved insufficient, so we used ice cubes, face cloths, and ice cubes in face cloths. We tried anything to ease our fatigue. An ice cube dissolved in a couple of minutes when in direct contact with Tracy's skin, and relief disintegrated with the cube. When I returned to check the outlet for obvious problems, a breeze overcame me.

"Get out of that camper," I yelled to Tracy, and we spent the rest of the afternoon enjoying a breeze that never would have reached us otherwise.

Hours later, a light green car with an alarming exhaust problem struggled its way next to our camper. The big old car towed a small Scamp trailer, and a thin man topped with a brown cowboy hat got out. His old black boots carried him to where we reclined in our lawn chairs under the shelter.

He needed to know if overnight camping was allowed, and I assured him that I had verified it with the Fire Department and the grounds crew. This man in his forties toting his wife, son and daughter described a campground book that must have been the same as ours, then proudly revealed his Kansas residence. I told him that Kansas would be our next stop along our forty-eight state journey.

"Great," he said, and then shuffled on.

As dinnertime arrived and we cooked chicken on the Hibachi, our Kansas neighbors were returning from a little league baseball game that had taken place at a field within the park. The path back to their camper, which they parked across the field within the circular drive, had them passing by, so they stopped to chat.

I wanted to talk to these people. I needed to know what it was like to live in Kansas; a place known for tornadoes. I wondered… how could a family live in an area like that?

In the beginning, I almost considered making our trip through forty-seven states, but that would be ludicrous. It would defeat the purpose of why we were out here finding answers for ourselves through real life accounts and talking to natives. Tracy possessed no such phobia and comforted me whenever something severe mixed into the weather.

As the chicken charred, our Kansas friends felt as though they were interfering, and decided to run along after only a few minutes. I told them that we should get together after dinner, and they fell in love with the idea.

Mr. Kansas looked like a fifty-year-old boy with his cowboy gear all around him. His eyes seemed too close to each other, and Tracy noticed that he wore a large ring depicting an evil-looking skull. Were they your average church-going family of four, or could that ring suggest something more? The cowboy gear and skull ring clashed with his innocent face.

His wife seemed more reserved. She was a quiet woman of about equal age to her husband. She had short dark hair and spoke softly. The son and daughter were nearly teenagers, but intelligent and inquisitive beyond their years.

Mr. Kansas usually packs up and takes his family along with his job on a soil conservation committee, which moves him all over the country. They were headed east to Virginia, Washington D.C. and Baltimore, but the kids sounded more agog about this particular journey. After all, they didn't have a job to worry about, and we could certainly appreciate that.

After getting a feel for each other, the man began offering tips on Kansas, but I had to know something further. "How do you feel about living in Tornado Alley?"

Mr. Kansas responded with a thoughtful silence before his observations got underway. "We get them...and there have been some bad ones...but every state in the U. S. has gotten them at one time or another."

"But Kansas is known for them, and it seems like Kansas gets them all the time."

"Yeah," he agreed hesitantly, head tilted to one side, looking into the horizon where the sun had landed, causing the sky to turn reddish orange. "I guess we do get them often, but not as often as Oklahoma."

"We got one last year while we were at church," his daughter broke in, leaning forward on the picnic table and holding herself up with her elbows.

"Yeah," her father agreed. "The church spotter was able to warn us, though."

"Spotter?" I asked, raising my eyebrows.

"A spotter is someone who watches for tornadoes. This guy happened to be part of our parish, and we all went home early," he replied.

"You could see the white funnel," said his daughter, her eyes opening wide in remembrance.

Her father again broke in. "You could see it off in the distance all right, but we had time to drive home and get in our basement."

"What do you do if you're away from home and spot a tornado?" I asked.

"Get out of the car and jump in a ditch. Don't ever try to outrun a tornado. It won't work. They can be anywhere from fifty feet wide to a mile wide, and can turn at any moment."

Mr. Kansas began discussing how he grew up on a wheat farm and noted a misconception about Kansas as a state of mostly corn. He was adamant in getting across that Kansas is a state of wheat; the breadbasket of America. He was excited about the thrashing process, which separates the wheat from the straw, shaking his head from side to side while telling us that we had to see it.

"How's the economy in Kansas?" asked Tracy.

Another thoughtful stare produced another slow answer.

"It's...not...really that bad. We're not feeling it like the rest of the country."

It was such a relief to hear that. Everyone thought we were crazy for leaving in such a bad economy, but once we left New England, the economy didn't pose such a problem anymore. People went about their business with no stress from visions of pink slips dangling above their heads.

July 31, 1992

Escaping from Missouri became our mission, tackling Route 36 west through St. Joseph and into our fourteenth state of Kansas; sunflower and wheat state, and the Land of Oz. The land flattened as we crossed the state line into Elkwood, but the combination of recently-cut wheat fields, cornfields, and barrel-shaped rolls of hay forming these plains changed our irritable moods into sheer joy from what was unveiled before our eyes.

Blissfulness engulfed us, lifting us into orbit like the two other notable times while moving from Quebec into Vermont, and Michigan into Wisconsin. We rode our natural high as long as the light of the day held on, and the scenic route across these vast plains provided openness until the land met the sky. Concrete grain elevators were the only objects in all directions.

In Wisconsin, we noticed that farmland ceased while passing through the small towns. However, in this area of Kansas, towns did not let go of the farmland. Once in a while, we were treated to an old farmhouse in the middle of an open field. It had no neighbors or stores to interfere with its serenity, but looked out of place in a countrified way.

Further along, tall grass overcame a town. An old gas station with rusted gas pumps fueled grass inside and out, nearly blocking it from our view. Only a few other houses and buildings existed on this block, all engulfed in grass. This must have been a ghost town, or a grass town, but we only passed through.

Molly and I at the Geographical Center of the US in Kansas

Kansas is one of few states that allow overnight parking in rest areas, so we accepted the generous offer just outside of Marysville. This was both our destination and the place the Pony Express riders once delivered mail. When we pulled in for the night, a man at the rest area was walking his dog and muttering something to us, but from the camper we only saw his mouth moving around.

When I rolled down the window for audio, he explained that we could stay overnight. We knew, but welcomed his reassurance since that book of ours proved accurate only half the time.

Gentle hills carried us further west the following day to the town of Lebanon, where a nearby stone marker is erected on the geographical center of the continental United States. Most people saw rickety slabs of stone cemented together with a U.S. flag and a state flag, but we saw a landmark for our forty-eight state journey. As weary as we felt, Tracy wore a fixed smile, and I felt like I had reached the moon because of the gratifying feeling of accomplishment.

We stood in the center of America, the only ones who could say that at the time of our arrival. This lonely marker was ours for the time being. Molly, moving swiftly around the grassy area with her active nose in session, peed at the geographical center of the United States. Tracy and I cheered her on. To top off her moment in the sun, Molly did the next best thing, uncertain about why we cheered. She looked at us strangely, but we looked at her proudly.

In a dusty rest area with no shade next to a sign indicating six miles to Dodge City, our camper passed large farming equipment, then moved further into the arc before shutting down for the night. The heat intensified, and the freezer was unable to compete. We had no ice. We saw a gas station across the street and a train track behind us. Over a vast stretch of low cornfields sat Dodge City.

Our necessary showers came after skipping a couple of days, but we appreciated them more so as a coolant. We poured cups of water over our heads; nothing like it on a sweltering day. My hair still wet, I looked out to see a couple of cowboys playing Hackeysack, a game that had rivaled my college textbooks. My foot started twitching, and I knew then that the time had come for me to throw myself into their game.

Once outside of the camper, my moccasins took the necessary steps to bring me to the game in which Jason and Pete, both of whom looked no more than twenty years old, were engaged. Jason wore his brown hair short beneath his cowboy hat, and Pete had dirty-blonde hair and a baseball cap.

Before I reached them or even got a word out, they asked me if I wanted to join them. They both wore jeans and a T-shirt, which did not make the game easy for them on such a muggy day.

The soft leather ball hung in the thick air for the inside of my right shoe to kick it over to the backside before successfully returning it to sender. The action preceded introductions and questions, but I started the conversation when the ball landed in error for the first time.

"Where are you from?" I threw out for either to answer.

"Oklahoma," said Pete, as he concentrated on the hackeysack, which was thrown toward him by his partner.

"What are you doing here?" I asked, before firing the sack into Pete's chest, where he completed the play with good eye-foot co-ordination.

Jason couldn't handle the swift moving shot that was too awkward for his foot to play and almost pulled his groin. "Our truck broke down, and we've been here for two days," he explained. "We were fixin' to go to South Dakota."

As the game progressed, volley after volley, the two teamed up to tell their story. They had been with their boss, the three of them driving large trucks, when one of the trucks broke down. Two of the trucks carried wheat harvesters, and the third carried a trailer for their house on wheels. Six vehicles lined the rest area's semi-circle.

Their boss remained underneath one of the trucks with the harvester attached. They were en route to a farmer's wheat field in South Dakota, where they would pay the farmer for the wheat they harvested from his fields. In turn, the three would sell the wheat in South Dakota, and everyone would make out well.

"Dodge City sucks!" shouted Pete.

"Why's that?" I asked.

"Because we're broke-down here," Pete answered.

Aside from their frustration, the two were as amiable as we could hope to find. They sounded like Oklahoma, and they lived in Oklahoma, but I needed to know why. "You must get a lot of twisters in Oklahoma," I said.

"Get what?" asked Jason.

I tried "tornadoes," and they seemed familiar with that terminology.

"Oh, tornadoes," Jason replied. "Not like Kansas."

"That's what Kansas said about Oklahoma," I argued.

"Yah," he agreed. "We get some. I guess we do...but they're not that bad."

Pete broke in with a tornado story. "I saw a tornado once, and it lifted a roof right off a house. No windows got broke, and the roof landed right on the ground in one piece." His hands went out in front of his chest to reenact what he saw.

An hour of humid hacking diminished our effectiveness. We agreed that when volleys become impossible it's time to quit, because it's only going to get worse. I shook hands with them both, we wished each other luck with the road ahead, and I turned and walked away.

"Hey!" shouted one of the voices as I walked back to the camper. I turned around to see that it was Jason calling out from a distance, and he finished his shout. "We want you to have this." He fired the hackeysack across the rest area, and I moved a couple of steps forward to retrieve the toss that fell short.

Bending down to pick it up, I was honored by this token. I looked at the hackeysack in my hand and saw a one-hour friendship with two cowboys from Oklahoma whom we just happened upon. I held the hackeysack high in the air and looked back at them. "Thanks," I said, and brought the ball in to show Tracy, who had witnessed the kind act.

August 3, 1992

This morning marked the start of month four on the road and the end of the first quarter of our journey. So much had happened that it felt like the trip should have been starting the last quarter. It seemed incomprehensible that for the length of time that had transpired, the beginning was closer than the end. One year is a long time, but Tracy and I struggled with whether it was "already" one quarter through or "only" one quarter through.

We almost wished that the trip was finished after the life-threatening situation before us this morning. What began as a calm morning changed dramatically in the matter of a cup of coffee as the camper viciously jolted from side to side. To my complete horror, I peered through the side window at an undefined black mass of clouds sailing across the sky, heading right for us.

Tracy's eyes widened, wondering what was happening to us as the movement increased, knocking us around helplessly. I cracked open the camper door to look for the worst. The wind yanked me out as the savage suction ripped open the door.

No one hides in these plains, and I trembled while surveying the area. Tumbleweeds skipped across the road before me, papers whipped around, and dust kicked up, moving through the plains in a swirling motion.

Tracy didn't dare go outside, but I had to know what was happening around us. I felt so helpless. The black clouds surged overhead. I became numb, trembling with the thought of being in Kansas, overpowered by an assaulting storm, and nowhere to go but inside a swaying camper.

The convenience store across the street looked attractive, but I didn't think it was attainable as the wind could have easily toppled the camper in transit. What could we do? Should we go? Where? When? Would we make it? It worsened by the second. I imagined a tornado coming upon us too quickly for us to make any sort of move, and our lives would be something of the past. The storm had us.

Fighting my way back into the camper, I asked Tracy to turn the radio on for an explanation. She did, and all that blared through the airwaves was the dreadful tone of the Emergency Broadcast System, which was followed by a fervent warning: "There's a severe thunder and lightning storm going on for Dodge County. Wind gusts may get up to sixty miles-per-hour. Damaging hail and heavy rain is possible. This is a major storm, so take cover inside at the lowest level of a home or building."

We had to make a move right away. I jumped into the driver's seat and started the engine. After rolling off the leveling blocks, I reluctantly went out into the storm to retrieve them. I nearly got swept off my feet by the gusts, which were on the rise. The camper crept across the street. It creaked its old bones under obvious strain, but made it into the gravel parking lot beside the gas pumps.

The rectangular metal canopy over the gas pumps fiercely rocked back and forth. It looked as if it could land on us if we got out of the camper, but we had to get out. This equaled a nightmare in that we could see our shelter, but arriving there seemed impossible.

Tracy grabbed the dog, and we ran for cover against the direction of the wind. Kicking up dust along our dreadful path, we could smell the storm as it blew in. I yanked the door open, allowing Tracy and Molly to pass through to safety.

Terrified, shaken up, drenched from the heat and dramatics, we entered to see a calm storeowner sitting behind the counter. Once the door closed, he slowly lifted his head from the newspaper and greeted us as if it was business as usual.

He had short, black hair and a small frame, but lots of courage. We felt so foolish pleading our case to this native, who apparently thought nothing of the breezy morning.

"I thought our camper was going to blow over," I began. "We're from Connecticut, and we're not used to this."

The man arched his dark eyebrow, put down the newspaper, then put down the storm. "Ah," he began. "This is nothing. We get this all the time. Gotten some crazy weather this year."

His tone of voice was so low-key that it began to soothe us, though not entirely. His reaction amazed us. What was it with these people? The worst storm we'd ever found ourselves in, and this guy hardly noticed it through the glass wall he sat next to. He made no mention of Molly, who fidgeted in Tracy's arms, even though the dog grumbled a bit at the man who had the gall to appear in his own store.

We chatted with the guy for thirty minutes, buying only time, until the wind, though not entirely tame, was fit for travel. What amazed me most about this man was not just his calmness, but his nonchalant mention that it's probably too cold for a tornado, and that if he saw one he'd just jump into the ditch out front.

The categories of wind and clouds diminished enough for us to head into Dodge City, once known as "Hell on the Plains" and the "Wickedest Little City in America." This period, the 1870's when the boom began, was inhabited by wranglers, buffalo hunters, gunfighters, railroaders and prostitution, using Dodge City as a stopover along the Santa Fe Trail.

It was 1992, but Front Street replicated the late 1800s appearance with freshly painted signs: City Drugs, Beatty & Kelley Restaurant, and Long Branch Saloon. The main drag once had one saloon for every fifty citizens, but this cow town had changed. Legend has it that most people died with their boots on in drunken brawls or heated gunfights, but a storytelling competition is said to have possibly magnified the tales.

The Boot Hill Cemetery, named for a gunman killed and buried with his boots on, contained tombstones with harsh descriptions of how the deceased weren't quick enough on the draw.

We walked to the Fort Dodge jail, a small white shed-like structure large enough for ten standing inmates. I made the mistake of walking in first. Tracy took advantage, latching me in the cell until I agreed to her terms of release. First of all, I had to apologize for an earlier disagreement. She stood back with a mischievous grin on her face. I apologized and held onto the bars of the little window.

Another couple entered the scene, and just for a reaction, Tracy added to her demands. She received their laughter after demanding that I do laundry, dishes and make the bed for the rest of our lives together. I agreed to the terms of this harsh penalty just to get out of jail, and then she'd see about this prisoner's conformity.

While strolling through the museum after my release, we turned to see Hell's Angels members walking behind us, viewing the displays. They had a gruff appearance, all big and tall, sporting Harley Davidson leather jackets. Bat Masterson and Wyatt Earp were once called in to maintain order, but now they were long gone.

Tracy and I did not look at them for long, but rather stared into the display case. We pretended to read, unable to comprehend, merely waiting for time to pass. Ten of these bikers, all of equal or greater size, passed us while looking at the displays briefly. We felt relieved when they all moved on, and we were again able to entertain oxygen, then return to that notorious Front Street to watch a shootout.

Another unfavorable forecast pushed us out of Dodge City, then onward into the blackness. Bright flashes of light ahead of us only meant we were heading into it. The radio reinforced this with a severe thunderstorm watch for the Liberal area. Ten miles from Liberal was a rest area, and we had no choice but to land there. We could only face the music and hope for the best.

Lightning flashes intensified as we moved into them. However, the real storm raged once we pulled into the rest area. Tracy wouldn't let me park right away because of her fascination with the constant flashes of lightning. She adored the ingredients of her picturesque setting: total darkness, except for the flashes filling the sky and shedding light on the Rock Island Railroad Bridge spanning the Cimarron River.

Tracy kept shouting garbled expressions of awe as she set the camera on the tripod. The storm began to get too close for comfort, but she seemed to be unaware of the possible danger. After a short while, I returned to the camper. Tracy joined me there only when the drenching rain began. It was her moment, so I gave it to her, but not without contemplating her sanity.

Kansas never calmed down, nor did my nerves. Thunder, lightning and rain pounded us once again, while I vowed to be out of Kansas the following day. Winds picked up, and they sharply pushed and pulled at the camper like a tug-of-war. Here we go again. Lightning struck relentlessly, landing all around the rest area. Rain viciously pelted our windows.

When the storm increased to another level and the camper responded by whipping back and forth, Tracy and I sat Indian style on the floor of the camper until it passed. When she thinks it's bad...it's bad. When her courage is absent, I have nothing to hold onto. The weather report had merely called for thunder and lightning. There had been no mention of the Dorothy Gale-force winds ready to lift the camper off the ground.

Then we heard a radio ad aimed at newcomers to southwest Kansas, telling them of the severe weather they get and how to prepare for tornadoes. That comforted us, but shortly thereafter the weather settled. Mentally exhausted from the two storms of the day, we fell asleep fast. That night, I dreamed of a solid house with a basement as secure as a fallout shelter.

What a relief to wake up to blue skies, knowing we could make it out of Kansas alive, because I had really begun to wonder. I opened my eyes and sighed as I thought of the storms that had passed and hoped the threat would never again consume us. I glanced over to see Tracy peacefully sleeping. We had both survived Kansas, but my sanity depended on our escape from this state. We needed a gas station, believe it or not, at eight miles-per-gallon, and then we could flee.

An older couple running the small station took my gas money. I then gave them an earful about the weather in Kansas, which prompted conversation. Mr. Gas, a small, stocky, balding man, began lecturing me on how the Wizard of Oz portrayed the wrong image of Kansas. I had to disagree, but he wouldn't hear of it.

"I've lived here for sixty-two years," he began, "and I've never seen a tornado. I lived at Cape Cod for a couple years and barely lived through a hurricane. You guys get hurricanes in the East. I saw a lady on the roof of her house clutching her baby in her arms, and then a wave came up and swept them away, never to be seen again. I'd much rather live with tornadoes than with hurricanes. They're awful."

It's apparent that if you live with a particular natural disaster, you become callous to it. I can't imagine how people can live in areas with frequent tornadoes and think nothing of them. Then I saw myself downplaying hurricanes in the East, where I've lived all of my life. It's all the same, but no...not tornadoes. Kansas can keep them.

Pulling out and onto the road, I passed the station to see Mr. Gas standing in the doorway with an extra-large smile to go with his wave. He enjoyed our ribbing session, but I still thought he was out of his mind. His point was well taken, but Kansas still scared me.

Route 160 would take us north, then west into the most anticipated state of the trip. We had never expected to run to the mountains for shelter, but it sort of happened that way. Colorado could not have arrived too soon. If severe weather were to chase us away, then Colorado had to be the ideal place to end up.

Finally, we did arrive. The pedal touched the floor all day until reaching the state line, which also marked Mountain Time zone. Since we cheered every state line crossing, Colorado surely received the same treatment, but this time the cheers were louder and longer. We united with the Mountain State, even though it started out with the eastern grassy plains, and the drop-off in the horizon looked like the end of the earth.

Our mission upon reaching the southeast corner of Colorado was to look for the Two Buttes Reservoir near Springfield. The dirt road twisting to the reservoir offered us a slight roadblock. We saw nothing in the vicinity except small cows, which forced us to go slow.

Three of these cows stood in the road staring at our oncoming camper, looking as if we had some nerve to use their road. When I closed within fifty feet from the cows, they jerked away. This humorous scene had the cows darting clumsily back to their families and friends on the other side of the double barbed wire fence that wasn't performing its duties. All the cows took on distinct personalities with some of them gaping at us as if to antagonize us into chasing them.

The landscape transformed itself from flat plains as we neared the reservoir. Jagged dark brown and red rock formations did much to temper the plains, rising often as we rode into this canyon. Even though this area wasn't representative of Colorado in our minds, it still comprised high rock ledges and sharp, craggy, bulging rock formations near this reservoir, which enhanced the beauty in the face of the plains. It seemed that the plains had drastically attempted to shake their image, and this bizarre land resulted; a small-scale Colorado. This primed us for the real Colorado.

Tracy and I cautiously eyed the narrow and crusty dirt road that led to our destination. The steep drop-off to the right forced me to hug wheel ruts etched into dried mud at the base of the red rock wall to the left. This risky trail offered no extra room.

Me standing by the camper in Colorado.

Crawling through this tight spot, our camper sneaked along the lengthy wall and into an area where we parked for the night. We kept rolling around rocks and cliffs, having committed the camper to this path, but deciding to risk no more. Although we met no problems, the difficulties unnerved us until we landed in a turn-around.

We settled on this turnaround at the bottom of the canyon, which provided surroundings of layered red rock cliffs towering all around us. We had no reservations about this atmosphere. Its beauty could share three days with us after our rugged nights of stormy weather.

The heat made us crave a shower, after which our cleanliness put us on a pedestal as far as camping goes. In our bathrobes, we each snuggled into our own back corner of the camper, each with armchair cushions on the bed and material to read. We sunk down into our precious bed, and even our weariness felt like contentment.

Thirty minutes of reservoir silence injected into us an inner peace that had been lacking in Kansas, and we knew then that Colorado would be...was that thunder?

Minutes passed before verification came in the form of a louder rumble from the sky and flashes of lightning off in the distance. Molly had tuned into this activity first. Rain pinged on the roof, then thudded overhead, but Tracy's optimism convinced me of our safety here in the bottom of the canyon. We'd be protected by surrounding cliffs, which lightning would strike first.

Thud...thud-thud...thud. Accompanying lightning streaked viciously. Thunder roared and dragged, and each one crashed harder than the one before. Molly panted, and so did I. We were in Colorado all right, but still in the plains. We thought we'd be safe from violent weather just because we crossed the state line. Who were we kidding?

Our guardian angels appeared in a car that entered the canyon, zooming over to us with a message. Amazed at first that we would see another vehicle in this remote area, we then anxiously watched as the car sped within five feet of the side of our camper. One of the two young guys pushed his door open on the driver's side. He brought his warning to our window.

"If you guys plan on staying the night, you'll find yourselves under water in the morning. You won't be able to get outta here because the water level of the reservoir's gonna rise...so get your butts to higher ground!"

He jumped back into his car without waiting for a response. The driver sped in reverse, turned around, and trailed off around the rock walls and disappeared from our view. They left us wondering what our chances would have looked like in the morning. What a trek into this canyon, and somebody had persevered to the bottom just to warn us.

I started the engine and started out of this natural splendor. I drove toward the rock walls, then around the rock walls. It appeared that we escaped in time. Damn it. The wheel ruts that had been etched into dry mud were now reactivated, and the steep drop-off on the other side did not disappear. Tracy and I made eye contact briefly, but exchanged no words.

Forward...reverse...forward...stuck. We had no time for denial. Tracy grabbed the leveling blocks to stick them underneath the wheels. She thought she might be able to push us any which way. She stood in a bathrobe and sneakers, clutching two blocks of wood. She opened the door, saying nothing, just standing inside the camper and looking out.

Her delay made me uncomfortable. She finally jumped out and stuck the blocks under the tires on the right side. This proved to be ineffective, so she removed them.

Thunder shook the camper, momentarily making the three of us taller, caught off guard by the serious blast, which echoed through our bodies. There had been a reprieve in the rain, but I knew that if it restarted, we'd be stranded for the night with nowhere to go and nobody to help.

The engine revved as high as my adrenaline. My foot pushed the gas pedal to the floor after trying to go both forward and reverse several times. The camper rocked back and forth while I began to lose respect for the drop-off on the left.

I began grinding into the mud, feeling the camper digging deeper and deeper, and afraid to ease the intensity. I finally felt the camper beginning to crawl, inching forward, from edge to edge, before conquering the nasty ditch. The wheels pushed ahead, ignoring the seriousness of the left side drop-off. Tracy jumped back into the camper, sat in her seat, and sighed.

I trembled, frantic, sweating, and exhausted when I screamed in rage, "I wanted adventure...but not this much adventure!" Tracy laughed harder at the fact that I screamed the message in all seriousness. She brushed off our predicament. I couldn't brush it off simply because I could hear my heart thumping in my chest.

At the top of the reservoir, we parked for the night and took the presence of a nearby house to mean safety. Nothing was certain anymore, but when the excitement had ended, Tracy revealed what she had seen upon opening the door to put the blocks under the tires. The camper floor was level with the mud, and both tires on the right side had completely submerged. She then admitted that she didn't have the heart to tell me, never thinking that we'd free ourselves from the mud. Maybe it's good that she had said nothing, but I wasn't sure of anything anymore.

August 8, 1992

Having eased our way higher in elevation, the transition from plains to mountains inflated us with our realized expectations for Colorado. We drove through flatlands and shrubs. Massive rock formations appeared. On this cloudy day, shadows of distant mountains blended with the real mountains that bloomed in the horizon. Our bodies were dwarfed the further we drove.

Moving west along southern Colorado, we headed into the Great Sand Dunes National Monument. These are the tallest dunes in North America, hanging out at seven hundred feet, formed by winds across the San Luis Valley. Bordered by two fourteen thousand foot mountain ranges, the San Juans and Sangre De Cristos, the dunes had formed over thousands of years.

The sand piled at the base of the mountain seemed close, but driving fast did not seem to get us closer. Its immensity deceived us. A sign indicated several miles to reach them. Even standing before them deceived us. We noticed tiny dots. We soon discovered that the dots were people attempting to climb this dune. We agreed to give this pile a shot.

The bottom of the dunes resembled a large beach with high tide receding because of the wet sand and small streams rolling over our feet, burying them and making us smaller people. Before getting lost, we trudged to the base of this heap of sand, then considered our decision. Tracy started in, believing the top to be attainable for her. I believed I could do it too, but wondered if I was kidding myself. Up we plodded.

We were only capable of ten to twenty steps before having to catch our breath. This gave us time to view people at the top, the bottom, and in the middle, and then cherish the surrounding mountains, which became more of a treasure the higher we climbed.

Swells and creases in the dunes had us struggling to the top. We then had to slide back down before the ascent continued. Train cars filled with all of this sand are said to be enough to wrap around the globe twenty times. That's a lot of sand, but the pile remained mysterious and misleading.

At the halfway mark, Tracy dropped to the dune, becoming part of it. She then threw in the towel. We both lay horizontally on the sand, panting away, when I eyed the top and decided that I must get there. However, the dunes became increasingly steep, and no more than five steps separated my pauses.

The altitude was overbearing, together with the steamy summer day, but I pressed on. Heat stroke was the major concern and a frequent occurrence. I overlooked the concern, pressing on, toiling my way up when I should have called it quits.

The top looked so close that I felt I could reach out and touch it, but the mere steps up and down the swells negated all hope. This made me feel like I'd never reach it. But I saw people standing at the top of the dunes, so I knew it could be done. The question was whether I could do it.

Three-quarters of the way up, a man came striding down from the top, and in passing advised that I had a long way to go. I thanked him graciously and pressed on. Then a forty-one year old man from Ohio going my way caught up and slapped me in the face with reality. "It's all a matter of pride at this point," he huffed and puffed.

While crawling what we believed to be the last leg of the dunes after ninety minutes of pure hell, one last swell emerged, staring us in the face. Mr. Ohio and I were crushed, but moved on after collapsing for a stopover.

What a rewarding moment to arrive at the real top, no longer having to hear people running down saying that it was much easier to go their way. Our weary bodies, having been sapped of the last ounce of energy at the halfway mark, became one with the pile. Several minutes elapsed before we could energize ourselves enough to lift our faces off the dunes to appreciate the panoramic view of the San Luis Valley and Sangre De Cristo Mountains. We now viewed the very reason we had started to climb.

While scanning the earth all around us from this outer space and watching the ant-people barely moving on and before the dunes below, I detected a streak of lightning off in the distance. After hearing warnings about how often the high dunes get struck by lightning and how people on the dunes are even sooner targets, Mr. Ohio and I decided that we'd like to mix in with the ants below.

Clouds steam-rolled, and we did too, step-sliding to the bottom. The incline was so great that one step equaled three. With every step being a slide, seven minutes brought us to the bottom.

I met Tracy there, but she appeared much smaller than when I last saw her, having sunk down to her knees by the flowing water over the sand. After pulling up her roots, the black clouds and sudden gusts of wind pushed us into the camper, and away from the storm we drove.

Continuing west on Route 160 for about two hundred miles would bring us into the Indian ruins at Mesa Verde National Park, but we had to rush in order to get up and over the Wolf Creek Mountain Pass before dark.

The drive through the San Juan Mountains carried us through gorges, a drive sided by towering rock walls. Rocky cliffs, massive rocks and boulders encompassed this stunning region. However, dusk began setting in before we could hurdle the ten thousand eight hundred fifty foot elevation of Wolf Creek Pass. This was the first serious mountain we'd ever seen, never mind driving a motorhome through it. This had no place in our plans, but we had to move onward.

The only thing that we had going for us further into the pass was that our lane hugged the rock walls on the inside of the roadway. Darkness swallowed the scenery in increments as the narrow road became a dizzying drop-off with no guardrails. The exhilarating ride changed once I reached the top and headed down. Everything changed, and my shorts should not have been exempt.

Yellow signs began to take over the slope, warning about the seven percent grade, runaway truck ramps, road damage, construction, slippery when wet, and constant reminders to check the brakes. Having downshifted into low gear, the RV still raced uncontrollably, so I had to constantly jolt the brake pedal. Tracy kept reminding me that I could burn out the brakes, but what choice did I have since the lowest gear wasn't doing anything? My constant tapping of the brakes as the camper was whipping around corners suddenly filled the air with the aroma of burning brakes. Squeak...squeak, squeak...squeak.

Rain began to fall with my hopes, turning an already dangerous scene into a nightmare. Toothpicks could not have enlarged my eyes any more than when I went on this roller coaster ride down my first mountain pass under the worst conditions. Drivers behind us, unhappy with my speed, honked and flipped us the bird. Other cars passed us around narrow corners with no guardrails.

There were some crazy folks out on this night, and I don't know how all of the cars stayed on the road with their erratic driving. Here we were on this incredible mountain pass. Thoughts of death and burning, screeching brakes kept playing over in my mind, because of the steep incline. Somehow, I still had it in me to care about the cars behind me.

I was torn between our possible savage death and pleasing my fellow drivers. These anxious, agonizing moments offered little time for my mind to filter my thoughts through the proper channels. I had no time to determine sense. I could only risk a complete stop, and eventually I had to do so when my downhill speed started exceeding my control. I had no time to think, so I worked the brakes to what I believed to be their capacity, slamming them until the tons of metal scraped and fumed. I did not care about future brake use. If I could stop this once, no other time would matter.

After ten miles of this mountain pass, I let the camper idle while the brakes cooled off, not to mention the driver. My heart probably could have been heard echoing throughout the canyon. As Tracy descended the mountain, observing the awesome natural beauty before her, she commented on what a wonderful place it would be to die if a place had to be chosen.

I never saw a pebble on the way down, nor did I have time to think about funeral arrangements, but surely thought we'd need them. I trembled inside, waiting for the worst to happen, but I knew more danger would follow. It took me about fifteen minutes to muster enough courage to proceed down again.

Continuing down the mountain slowly seemed impossible, since our speed could hardly be contained in spots. Steep hairpin turns and uneven roads presented conditions I wish we'd never met. If the camper wasn't flying around switchbacks, it was having seizures weaving between orange and white-striped barrels.

Reaching Pagosa Springs felt mentally satisfying, but we weren't out of the woods, because the mountainous terrain persisted. In the Rio Grande National Forest, still avoiding campgrounds, we tried for rest areas along the way that never materialized. We also missed all of the county roads, which supposedly held free campgrounds, but our main concern was to get down the mountain safely.

Mentally strained and desperate, we searched for twenty-four hour places in town, though highly unlikely, and nothing popped up. Opting to pull into the next campground proved to be an act of desperation for us at ten o'clock at night. Five dollars later, we slept at a reasonable price.

August 10, 1992

Mancos offered a nice starting point because of its ideal location outside of Mesa Verde. The Mancos City Park provided a place to park the camper, and a pleasant old campground host received us and gave us an orientation of the grounds.

Driving to Mancos was no easy task through the mountains, and even with the carburetor adjusted, the camper refused to behave. The camper stalled during a long uphill battle, and whenever I pulled it aside there came a startling winding and grinding noise under the hood. Then there was a fierce boiling, so we waited thirty minutes before the engine cooled, then proceeded up and over the mountain.

Mancos City Park was full when we arrived, but the park host squeezed us in. This kind, elderly man sat with us at a picnic table and spoke at length. He instilled confidence in my mountain driving skills, telling me that I must be at a speed lower than twenty miles-per-hour in order to hit that lowest gear.

The park host crinkled his eyes when he smiled as he warned of what we had coming en route to Mesa Verde. I could test my new skills on this climb and descent. When we left Mancos for Mesa Verde, we asked the host to save us a spot because we'd be getting back late. He nodded his head in agreement, but said nothing.

The climb seemed devastating for the camper, but the important part was that I could tackle the mountains soon after Wolf Creek Pass. We could see the steep road leading up the mountain as we drove below.

That road took us several engine-rests during the twenty mile crawl to the top. The valley below on this cloudy day became our bird's-eye view, where shade spotted the earth. The greens turned lighter or darker depending on this shade, and the colors rode away from us and up into the mountain range behind. A tunnel carried us through the mountain, then back out to daylight.

In many instances in Colorado, my sense of perception failed. Sometimes I couldn't tell whether the camper ascended or descended the mountain, or whether the pavement leveled off. Molly also had trouble, barking at one side of the street while the herd of cows grazed on the other. She also lunged for the window for no apparent reason other than the altitude. At least that wasn't my reaction. Tracy had been to Colorado once before and had passed out from the altitude. So off to Mesa Verde went our motley crew, trying for a park blitz to capture as many ruins as possible in one day.

The Anasazi Indians occupied this high plateau rising above the Montezuma and Mancos Valleys between 550 A.D. and 1270 A.D., but much of their story is lost due to the fact that they kept no written records. Originally building their homes in the ground, the Anasazi, an ancient Navajo word meaning "the ancient ones," advanced to cliff dwellings. They built their homes out of sandstone rectangular blocks pasted with mud and water underneath the protective alcoves of the cliffs.

Hand and foot pegs scaled the Anasazi up to the cliff top, where they hunted game and farmed staple crops of corn, beans and squash in the fertile soil on the mesa top. They had to scrape holes in the rocks with their stone pegs. Many years of drought ended this community of farmers, forcing them to abandon these dwellings.

As the ranger led us down the stone park-service steps to the ruins, the faraway remains looked like a series of light brown models, or dollhouses. We could see tourists swarming all around them, but not inside. The many sections of ruins ranged from one-room houses to two hundred room villages. Whatever the size, walking before these ruins was like turning the calendar back about a thousand years, stepping on the very grounds of the Anasazi.

The fact that their buildings remain tells a story of these architects, survivors far ahead of their time, erecting structures resembling today's apartment complexes. They stood a couple stories high with windows on each level. They also constructed circular towers with windows and "Kivas," the Hopi word for "ceremonial room."

In some instances, we could see ruins by looking across the canyon to the upper wall on the other side. They built living quarters into the cliff, tucked away from perpetrators, but with access to the mesa top. I wondered if sleepwalking was ever a problem for them.

The Anasazi may have left because of a drought, but Tracy and I left because we had to get down the mountain before darkness hindered our drive, and there was no hypothesizing about that. Our descent in the lowest gear helped us to creep along, but I used pull-offs whenever vehicles trailed behind, earning hand waves instead of finger waves. This endless process overheated the camper only once, making it a success.

Once we met up with Route 160, the same route that took us into Colorado from Kansas, the southwest road beat sunset to the Four Corners. This is the only place where four states meet. It also introduced us to the desert, and this arid region felt like what we believed a desert should feel like. The dry heat made our thirst unquenchable; no amount or temperature of water helped.

The region was indicative of the alcoholism that plagues Indian reservations. Both sides of the road, strewn with empty bottles, showed mile after mile of litter. The drive included a most unusual landscape. It was fascinating yet unlivable, but this was home to Indians.

Mountains, mounds, rocks and spires looked thirsty and erose. A dull, light brown dominated the entire barren path. The long road unintentionally disguised speed bumps. The front and back of the camper took the brunt of them. We rattled up and down for miles as if driving on a road made up entirely of potholes. We felt confident that we'd be losing at least a muffler after this round trip.

Tracy, Molly and me by the camper.

We pulled the camper into a parking lot in New Mexico. The Indians had an L-shaped series of craft booths, where they displayed their wares. Jewelry far outnumbered other products. The nearby Four Corners monument, a flat concrete structure shared by Arizona, Utah, Colorado and New Mexico, had each quarter bearing a state seal. The Navajo and Ute Indian nations live there.

Tracy and I took turns walking to the center of the monument, where the Four Corners allowed us to occupy four states simultaneously. Bending backwards, we each had the opportunity to place one hand in Arizona, one in Utah, one foot in Colorado, and one in New Mexico to satisfy our quest. For some time afterwards, we gloated over this feat

August 19, 1992

We had two rigorous mountain passes to contend with before we could drop into Steamboat Springs, where Tracy's cousin, Dan, and his wife, Cat, resided. The Loveland Pass lofted us up to 11,992 feet, guided us through the Eisenhower Tunnel and dropped us into the town of Dillon. More problems awaited us at Rabbit Ears Pass at 9,426 feet. By this point in Colorado, the camper had endured severe beatings, causing it to overheat three times daily. This day was no less cruel, but the camper forgave us enough to get up and over both passes.

Along this one hundred seventy-five mile journey from Boulder to Steamboat Springs, we passed a couple of guys in a white moving truck towing a small camper. By the time we landed for the day, we had passed each other on the side of the road several times. One of us overheated at any given time, and it got to the point where we waved to each other upon passing.

Our whereabouts concerned Dan and Cat, but they figured we might be looking at some trouble on the hills. We finally arrived at their inspiring overview of the main drag, which was lit up and could be seen from their condo built into the mountain. We could also see the rodeo arena, but we weren't close enough to see the eye color of a bucking bronco.

On our third and final night in Steamboat, we became spectators in the stands at the Pro Rodeo and looked up on the condo. It was even better turned around, looking from the rodeo to the condo. The four of us enjoyed an evening watching western culture.

Just feeling the anticipation of the audience gave me a glimpse into life out west. Excitement was crammed into every nook and cranny of the arena. The cowboys rode the horses and the bulls, and they also sat among us. Their cheering made the atmosphere fulfilling before the show even began.

While the cowboys on both sides of the fence geared up for the rodeo, little boys with cowboy hats and boots tried to emulate their fathers, which seemed natural here. This little town appeared to be shut off from the rest of the world, tucked into a valley many miles from civilization.

The rugged rodeo began with cowboys, hardened from their lives in this sport, lassoing small cows with their accurately thrown ropes. They dismounted their horse, caught up with the cow, and lifted and flipped it over with both arms. They roped four legs together at record speed, hoping for the fastest time. The broncos and bulls just wanted them off their back.

Being at this rodeo was like being dropped into another civilization. Little girls took part in the rodeo by riding horses. A long line of little boys and girls ran after a goat with a flag on its tail. Tracy and I had hoped to experience a rodeo while out west, and found the cake and the icing in this little arena.

We also needed a pre-dawn departure to avoid the heat of the day and to get over the big humps. We owed it to the poor engine, and our plan worked without so much as a bucking, which had been characteristic of the camper on the way into town. At one point, we were tempted to enter it into the rodeo.

After a day of moving east, we hopped onto Interstate 25 in hopes of finding a truck stop. As we got close to Denver, an irritating scraping noise persisted from the right tire. We took an exit to a side street for a look.

Seven of eight lug nuts held the tire on, and with four loose, the tire had nearly come off. Tracy used a pay phone across the street to call a sales representative she knew, who had demanded that she call him when we got to Denver.

Vic was the man, and it just so happened that he lived on the other side of the interstate and promised to head right over. In the 1960's, Vic went cross-country on a motorcycle, and to this day claims that we haven't camped until we've "shit in the woods."

As Tracy conversed with Vic, I began speaking to a couple guys in their twenties from Iowa, waiting by the second phone. When I asked one of them what there was to do in Iowa, his answer truly fascinated me.

"Well," he said in deep thought, "there's them old people who live there. You know, they're really old...the things they do are old."

"The Amish?" I suggested.

"Yeah, that's it," he said, pointing to where the words may have been once they left my mouth.

Vic, a big man with short dark hair that he said had once flowed down past his shoulders, looked like a biker in some ways, but not in others. He was now a salesman and family man with a wife and two children. He bent down to take a look at the tire, whistling in disbelief. After tightening the lug nuts, he advised us to follow him to a place where truckers parked, until he could take us on a lug nut hunt in the morning.

Before he left, he strongly suggested that we allow him to treat us to dinner, so off we went, trying to forget what could have been a tragedy. With the lug nut in place, the camper stood fit for travel. We could finally leave Colorado after three weeks in the state we'd been waiting to reach since we had left home.

We heard reports of snow in the mountains of Montana, and every evening and some days chilled us here in Colorado. We had to think about the road ahead and formulate a plan to fly through the rest of the northern states and head south before we found snow. Money dwindled, and at this time we thought about picking up jobs in Arizona or New Mexico for some of the winter months, but it was premature at this point.

Route 14 from Fort Collins took us east into the Pawnee National Grassland. This area is preserved as the path the pioneers once used for westward movement. Although we used this path for eastward movement, the final road in Colorado moved us north on Route 71 toward Kimbal, Nebraska.

Cornfields had filled our minds whenever we imagined the Cornhusker State. Nebraska was flat and had corn, and that's what we expected, but we prepared to see that scenario only with appreciation. Maybe the state wasn't loaded with activities of interest to us, but we mostly enjoyed the serene countryside.

Welcome to Nebraska. A state line sign with a horse-drawn covered wagon greeted us. Our sixteenth state never flattened out like it should have. We motored through toward Scottsbluff, actually landing at the town of Mitchell, which offered overnight camping with electricity. A train track nearby never made it a secret when a train rolled through town.

After our night's rest, an early morning train became our alarm clock, ringing through town once again. A new problem with the camper begged for immediate attention. The heater's pilot would not kick in, so the nights had been cold even with extra blankets draped across the bed.

The normal frustrations squeezed in at an RV center in Scottsbluff as they asked us to wait, only to forget us. Then they sent us around the shop searching for the right person to talk to. When I finally met the right man, he told us that it was a busy time. They wouldn't be able to get to us for another week. The heater below the refrigerator had to be pulled, but the mechanic showed us a makeshift method of producing heat until the problem could be fixed.

From his knees, the mechanic reared back and swiftly kicked the heater with his workboot. This triggered the pilot light to fire, which in turn produced heat. He said it wasn't advisable to perform this method whenever the pilot did not trigger, but it would get us heat for a couple of nights. This was the best he could do.

Back into Scottsbluff, through bluffs and rolling prairie grassland, the Scottsbluff National Monument towered above. This eight hundred foot mound of sandstone, siltstone and volcanic ash became a signal for pioneers that the plains were ending and the Rocky Mountains fast approaching.

Between 1840 and 1866, wagon trains along the Oregon Trail carried Mormons in search of religious freedom and 49ers with golden minds in California: the hopeful and hopeless looking for that new start. It was 1862 when the groundbreaking of the Union Pacific Railroad and the Homestead Act sent forth a flock of settlers attracted by the free land offer, which resulted in the settlement of Nebraska.

In 1992, Tracy and I saw the mound only for its history. It now included us in its history. We'll remember it whenever we think of Nebraska.

From Scottsbluff, we moved north through the Agate Fossil Beds National Monument to a twenty-five mile dirt road en route to a free campground in Alliance. Nobody else wanted to travel this road, so Tracy and I enjoyed the solitude of the slow ride through additional rolling fields where cows grazed, farms prospered, and large birds soared.

We couldn't drive a mile without a large bird entering our vision. Two eagles entertained us. One perched itself on a wooden post as we pulled the camper alongside it. The eagle looked at us, then gracefully lifted itself off the post, flapping its wings until it rested on a large roll of hay. Many birds demonstrated their lengthy wingspans. Gracefulness accompanied us all along this road.

Rolls of hay spotted the area, sometimes in groups, looking like oversized, freshly baked loaves of bread. The last leg of this dirt road passed a turkey farm, where one of the turkeys walked across the road in front of the camper.

"Why did the turkey cross the road?" asked Tracy.

"Why did two...five turkeys cross the road?" I shot back after the birds poured in front of the rolling camper.

Although most of this road showed rangeland, every once in a while the treeless tracts of land gave way to a lonely group of trees earnestly trying to camouflage a white farmhouse. I pulled the camper aside several times so Tracy and I could soak up this beauty before us.

The road ran forever. Even so, we were afraid it would end. We provided our own competition. No car so much as passed us. Nothing disturbed us, so we plugged along this road at our leisure. If we wanted to stop in the middle of this road for lunch, I didn't foresee a problem. We didn't care if we ever saw another city. We didn't care if we ever saw another person.

Route 2 carried us out of the countryside and into Alliance, which is the location of Carhenge, a humorous replication of England's ancient Stonehenge, in its dimensions and orientation. Sixteen old cars were buried trunk down in a circle, and six other cars were placed atop them to form arches or capital T's. Every car was painted gray, including the tires. We laughed at the absurdity of this display, and left after touching the cars. We touched them just so we could say we did.

Further east on Route 2 we flew, crossing into the center of the state to the town of Broken Bow, where the state finally began to flatten out. Burn's Car and Truck Stop in Waco felt like a dream as I rumbled the camper to the back of their gravel parking lot, having put away over three hundred miles.

August 28, 1992

Along the ride north from Lincoln, we entered the town of Wahoo, which welcomed us twice with signs. Each time, Tracy and I yelled out, "Wahoooooo!" We needed the first grocery store we passed, and pulled into the Hinky Dinky. We wanted the world to know that we shopped at the Wahoo Hinky Dinky.

We camped overnight at Winslow Village Park even though the electricity no longer worked. A downed telephone pole next to the trash barrel with an outlet attached provided evidence of currents past. You bet we tried.

We landed twenty feet away from the railroad tracks that ran past the back of the camper. Trains again roared through the evening and into the morning hours between this park and the cornfields on the opposing side, but once again the clamor was nicely balanced with the serenity of this atmosphere.

As the west became populated, land clearing caused rain to wash sediment into the Missouri River. The pioneers referred to this Missouri River as "The Muddy," saying that the water was "too thick to drink and too thin to plow." Some things never change. We crossed the brown Missouri River into our seventeenth state of Iowa, which welcomed us with a sign that told us to explore the Heartland.

Our heater still blew strong, and sometimes the pilot didn't fire right away, so I gave it a swift kick until it changed its mind. The cool nights still forced us to wheel through these northern plains in search of relief, but to no avail. The camper and the hills rolled through the countryside, proving no shortage of corn in America. Smooth rows of corn, perfectly installed, waved as nicely as the hills that carried them. Here we saluted the kernel.

Dexter is a small town thirty miles west of the capital of Des Moines. It is host to a free campground with electric and water hookups at the City Park. Cornfields followed us the entire way. When entering the town, we needed a grocery store, and it surprised us that one existed.

"What's there to do in Dexter?" I asked the teenage girl with brown hair draped down her back as she handed me change from the register. She returned a look of surprise.

"Absolutely nothing," she shot back, forming a grin because I even asked such a question.

We knew she was telling us the truth when we could see the layout of the town from the grocery store. Located on the main drag, six connected buildings on each side of the street, the grocery store appeared to be one of only two stores currently in business. But this lonely little town in the plains satisfied our needs.

The campground doubled as a park with plenty of green grass, surrounded by fields of corn. Over a wire fence on one side bleated lambs, which did not fit well into Molly's plans. People used this park, though, unlike many other free ones throughout the country. However, we still roped up our ever-elusive peace and quiet.

A better description of Dexter came the next day when we pulled into Casey's, which included a gas station, grocery store, and pizza place. Tracy went in to use the only pay phone in town. She came out laughing and shaking her head from the note on the phone, which indicated a three-minute limit due to the fact that the pay phone also served as the store's business phone. After three peaceful days, Dexter became our history. The camper, the couple, and the dog pulled away, thus drastically reducing the population of the town.

September 1, 1992

With two museums on our agenda, we made our way to Waterloo, where the free museum decided that they'd charge three dollars, as revealed by an older lady with lipstick on her teeth. So we
moved a pinch north to the town of Waverly. This free museum
charged one dollar.

The Schield International Museum, designed by Vern Schield,
told a story that knocked the socks off Waterloo. Once through the
door, we received an exuberant greeting from a seventy-four year
old white-haired lady named Wanda, who found Jesus and had
never been happier in her life.

Her constant smile elevated her cheeks, and chuckles filled the
empty one-room museum building. We explained to her that we
wanted to see this travel exhibit because we were traveling ourselves. Wanda became so excited that she paid our admission. Although she only had one dollar in her purse, she insisted on writing
a check to cover the other dollar.

Wanda had traveled forty countries, married twice, lost one
husband, and turned to drinking Martinis every night.

"I had all the furs I could ever want," she explained, "I was
dripping with diamonds and rings and I'd traveled to all the places
I'd ever wanted to see, but there was still something missing; a

void in my life." She clenched her fist and placed it on her stomach as she discussed this void. "And then I found Jesus!" she continued with a smile that opened up like sunrise. "I've never been happier in my life."

Her bubbly personality was enhanced whenever she spoke about how she discovered the Lord. Wearing high heels and stylish clothes, the seventy-four-year-old woman drew attention to her white shirt patched evenly with red hearts throughout.

"See these hearts on my shirt?" she asked. She then looked down, while using two hands to pull it out straight. "This was my favorite blouse. Then I got stains all over it that even the cleaners couldn't get out. So I gave it to my friend, and she sewed these heart-patches over all of the stains, adding extra hearts to balance them out."

Wanda waited for the story to end before she joined us in laughter, at which point she let it out in a most hysterical way, nearly bent over as she remembered the time this happened. When our laughter dwindled, she decided to walk us through the tour before Tracy and I would walk around ourselves to catch the readings.

She showed us some of the items that Vern Schield accumulated through his travels to seventy countries. The items included a Russian Crawler Tractor, a two hundred thirty-six pound Giant Man Eating Clam from the Philippine Islands, elephant's feet, and a most impressive and unexplained one thousand year old smooth stone ball that stood about waist high. A man Vern met had wanted to throw the ball out, but had had no means of discarding it. Vern took it off his hands and shipped it home at a cost of four thousand dollars.

What actually attracted us to this museum in Waverly, Iowa was Vern Schield's 1970 canoe expedition from the Arctic Circle to the Gulf of Mexico. Accompanied in this excursion by one other, the five thousand two hundred miles began at Repulse Bay on May twenty-seventh and concluded at New Orleans on October seventh.

As Tracy and I began reading about this eighty year old man and his ninety year old wife, the couple slowly passed through the door. Wanda quickly gave them a rundown on the travelers fascinated with their museum, and Vern inched his way over to us.

For their ages, they looked to be in pretty good shape. Vern closed his eyes at intervals as he slowly told his stories, and after about fifteen minutes, promised to gather some material for us to take. Information on this man fascinated us, and it was an honor to meet someone of his caliber. Little did we know that another part of his story was about to unfold, making this chance meeting even more exciting.

Vern Schield is a self-made millionaire who started out with rags. He and his wife had found themselves down to their last dollar. The couple started out selling crushed limestone, but it was backbreaking work without proper equipment. A crane was too big for their needs; it lacked the desired mobility for his type of work. He needed a smaller version of that machine, so he invented the Bantam, a dragline built out of spare pieces of machinery. Ten years of modification by Vern, his brother, and two other farmers turned Schield Bantam into the largest maker of truck-mounted power cranes and excavators.

Vern Schield became a world traveler in order to manage his company's agencies in fifty-nine countries. Compelled to overhaul old, discarded machinery and equipment, he shipped and sold them at cost to missionaries and Peace Corps volunteers worldwide.

Vern became so involved with helping others that he sold his business, which had earned him eighteen million dollars a year, so he could devote his time to Self Help. He founded this organization to assist the Peace Corps' mission. His new interest was strong enough to sell what had been his life, so that he could have a hand in making life more bearable for those less fortunate.

Tracy wore a smile throughout the exhibits. She had already thought the world of Wanda, then the man responsible for the museum appeared. The building held such incredible people and stories that it was hard not to react in such a way.

They proved to be the most unselfish people that we'd ever come across. Take Wanda for instance. Here's a fascinating woman who had traveled forty countries and all fifty of the United States, and yet her reaction to our journey was more enthusiastic than any yet. Then there's Vern Schield, who had sold the business that made him a millionaire in order to get what would provide his inner peace.

The Schields exited their room of collections and memories, wishing us well as we headed to Minnesota. Wanda wouldn't let us leave without swapping business cards, promising to keep in touch and staying by the front door to get a glimpse of the camper and the dog. Then we left, but our correspondence with Wanda continued.

Nearly one year later, Wanda regretfully informed us of the death of Vern Schield. America had lost a friend. Tracy and I were saddened by the news of his passing as if we had lost a good friend, yet we had only known him for fifteen minutes. He had that kind of effect on people.

We headed north late at night on Route 71. Still trying to catch up with our week-per-state schedule after three weeks in Colorado, we had to take it out on the states that required us to backtrack. This sweeping dash west ushered us from Kentucky through Missouri, Kansas, and Colorado, which we figured to be the most strategic path for us to catch all forty-eight states. There had to be backtracking and zigzagging, so Nebraska and Iowa involved an eastward movement.

Getting to the center of Minnesota, a state that claims to have ten thousand lakes, even though the actual figure is closer to fifteen thousand, proved to be no small task. The promise of electricity and water lured us past the Minnesota border, where the Welcome sign glowed in the dark and was suspended in air. We took a wrong road and crossed the line before we had planned. I then backed up into Iowa, so we could at least look at the new state while Tracy balanced the crisp map, the flashlight, and the dog.

I turned the camper around, and we entered the new state from Route 71 to Jackson. The free campground charged, and so did we...away from the campground and into a nearby truck stop without even getting on the Interstate. The free campground book had done well for us on several occasions, but it was hard to think of those times after being scalped once again.

Since the free campground fizzled, so did our day off. It sounds funny to hear it put that way, but it's truly what we mean. My recently retired father fully understood what I meant when I told him that even without working, there's not enough time in the day. On the road, even for one year, we tried to catch everything we could, and ended up taking on too much. One week per state is not enough time to see everything, and states are bigger out west. Some states are even larger than Connecticut.

While inside the Laura Ingalls-Wilder Museum in Walnut Grove, I kept overhearing that a tornado watch had been issued for southwest Minnesota on the radio tucked behind the front counter. My ears bent back, hearing nothing else as I closed in on the radio. I then nervously asked the lady working if the tornado watch would threaten us. The old lady gave me a big smile and in a soft voice said, "I haven't been paying attention."

It was time for us to leave, and we walked outside to blue skies. We had planned on moving over to a town called Sleepy Eye, but we were much too tired. Instead, we visited the town of Tracy. Just a short drive west of Walnut Grove introduced us to the yellow and orange leaves of autumn. This was our first indication of the new season. At this point, the odometer told us about a twelve thousand mile journey thus far.

In Tracy, Tracy jumped out of the camper and ran under the sign that read "Welcome to Tracy." She giggled and smiled for the camera. I wondered if I should convince her that it wasn't really her town, but I didn't want to rain on her parade. After finding several other ways in which Tracy was of interest, driving through what quickly became a dark, cloudy sky, we headed for Franklin. Reports told of electricity and water there, but we did not hold our breath.

Distant and isolated thunderheads flashed electricity as we searched for this city park. This journey had become a night mission by the time we reached what appeared to be a park. We saw no indication of what the name or route number might be. It didn't take us long to discover that Minnesota is famous for losing travelers. We reached Franklin City Park, which was not marked with a sign, and set up camp.

While I was flipping through a palm-size notepad of phone numbers in front of a phone bubble in the small business section of town the following day, a young, pudgy blonde-haired boy slowly rode his bicycle in circles near me on the wide street. I had taken my bike off the back of the camper to pedal the short distance into town, unaware of just how small the town really was.

"What are ya doin' this afternoon?" asked the boy of maybe ten years as he slowed to a stop with his feet.

He took me by surprise. "What am I doing?" I repeated, giving me time to think of an answer, then wondering why I had to. "Ahh...making phone calls."

"Do you fish?"

"Not really," I said, sharing my focus with the conversation and the notepad.

"Well...ya wanna try? I have two poles at home, and you can use one."

"I think I'm going to have to pass," I answered. "My wife's back at our camper."

"Camper? Where are you camping?"

"At the park."

"The baseball park?"

"Yes."

"Oh," he said. "Franklin's a nice place. Let's go ask your wife if you can go fishing."

"I have things to do back at the camper." I replied.

Mr. Franklin came armed with one question after another. I couldn't believe that he would walk up to a total stranger, obviously an out-of-towner, and entrust him to go fishing. I don't really fish, anyway, but the lonely kid living in the trailer behind the phone bubble wasn't prepared to take "NO" for an answer.

Three kids rode their bikes past us on the street. "Nice haircut," he said to one of the bikers, a mischievous grin on his face, but received only a smirk in response. He rode his bike away once the kids passed, but returned while I spoke on the phone, eavesdropping on my conversation, though managing to falsely regurgitate my words.

"You're going to fifty-eight states?" he asked as I hung up.

"Forty-eight. Can't make it to Hawaii and Alaska."

"Why can't ya go to Hawaii?"

"Because we're driving a camper and there are no roads."

"Yes there are," he objected. "There are ya know."

Instead of more questions my way, I decided to turn the tables and try to get some information out of a Minnesota child.

"When does winter start around here?" I asked.

"Anytime now," he answered, after squinting his eyes in thought.

"When does it start to snow?" I asked. "Around Halloween?"

"On Halloween," he replied with confidence.

"On Halloween?" I asked for verification.

"Yes," he confirmed. "It starts to snow on Halloween."

He resumed riding his bike in circles once I convinced him that I wasn't going fishing. He disappeared, but returned a short time later. While I was on the phone, Mr. Franklin began tugging on my shirtsleeve. "Can you untangle my line?" he asked.

When I turned around, he had his fishing pole up to my face, but I motioned with my finger for him to wait; my index finger. Before I hung up, the inquisitive kid vanished, and I pedaled back to the camper uninterrupted.

September 6, 1992

The drive to a truck stop in North Dakota's capital of Bismarck became our record of three hundred forty-four miles for one day. The flat eastern portion of the state offered mile after mile of hayfields with barrel-shaped rolls of hay evenly dispersed among these fields.

Molly became infuriated with the large rolls of hay. She stood tense and shaking on Tracy's lap. She looked out the passenger's window, jolted her head left and right, and growled at what she must have thought to be a threat to our security. The landscape evolved from prairie into a rugged nature in the form of eroded Badlands. They were so bad that they were good, but we were glad that we didn't have to walk.

Free campgrounds are hidden in the most remote regions of the state, but since we had no problem checking out roads less traveled, we opted for the town of Zap. Perhaps the name of the town attracted us. Route 49 north of Glen Ullin toted us there.

Weather became a factor on this path. Rain and wind acted up. It didn't take us long to realize that wind in the plains is unforgiving, and a firm grip on the steering wheel is always advisable. We knew we had to eventually exit from Interstate 94, but signs only indicated exit numbers. Maybe travelers just have to know what exit they wanted, but we didn't, and ended up getting off and on several times. Some exits led only to a dirt road, while others led only back to the highway.

Glen Ullin took us to Beulah, six miles from Zap. Not wishing to take a chance, we filled up the gas tank at Subway. Luckily, we didn't have to eat their subs to get gas. Route 200 was a quick jaunt into the small town that we'd been looking for. A large sign to the left of the road greeted us: Welcome to Zap, the Little Town with the Big Heart.

We drove through a cool Sunday evening in this small town with all of the few businesses closed on the main strip, but we had to take a quick peek. On this Labor Day Eve, even the two bars were closed when we finally decided to splurge, so we went to the City Park for the evening. It wasn't free, naturally, but asked a minimal five dollars for full hookups, so we decided to take advantage for a couple of days.

On Labor Day, we took the bikes off the back of the camper, dusted them, and pedaled off into town. The sixty second bike ride wasn't too exhausting and was necessary in order for us to get some milk at the grocery store. It wasn't just milk we needed, though. We had questions regarding life in Zap, North Dakota. We wanted to talk to the natives and find out about the town's history. What do people do for a living, and how do they entertain themselves in such a secluded land?

Our first stop came at the grocery store, where we kicked our stands and kicked up dust while leaving footprints to the front door. The store was closed, and a van had parked in front of the little post office next door. A lady, looking down as she shuffled her mail, closed in on the mailbox in front.

"Excuse me," I interrupted. "Is there another grocery store in town?"

"No," she said with a chuckle. "There's not enough people in town to keep a grocery store here. This one just closed their doors because there's not enough people. You'll have to go to Beulah."

Across the street, Tracy used the pay phone. I decided to stroll into one of the two bars to check it out. Maybe there'd be a dartboard. Even better, maybe I could haul a drop of milk away from them. Standing before the bar next to the few sitting patrons, a middle-aged lady with brown curly hair smiled, then asked if she could get me something.

"Would you have a small glass of milk that I could get to go?"

She stopped in her tracks, donning a blank look on her face. "Milk?"

"Yes, just a small cup to go."

"Well, I dunno," she began. "I never got a request for milk before. By the way, could I ask why you need milk?"

"For coffee," I answered.

The bartender averted her eyes, focusing on some spot in the air that did not exist, then shook her head. Obviously bewildered, she walked around the bar and breezed past me, then out the front door.

So there I stood in the middle of this Zap bar, wondering where she had gone, since she offered me no clue. After a few minutes, I slowly strolled out the front door, where I met her on the sidewalk. She held a gallon jug of two-percent milk a quarter of the way filled.

"Here...how's that?" she asked, handing the jug over to me.

"What do I owe you?" I asked.

"I dunno....," she said with her head tilted, holding the jug up in the air and wearing a puzzled look as if this was The Price Is Right. "How about fifty cents?"

I flipped her two quarters, expressed my gratitude, and warned her that we'd probably be seeing her later in the day. She had a bar to tend, and we thirsted for nightlife in Zap.

Since this bar had apparently closed early the night before, Tracy wanted to make an afternoon of it, sitting down to our first beer by four o'clock. We ordered from the same lady behind the bar, who now referred to me as The Milkman.

A group of four girls several stools down and to our right joked with the bartender they called Carol, and one girl to Tracy's left nursed a beer bottle. As Carol placed two beers in front of us, she turned to the girl to our left and told her that we were traveling through forty-nine states.

Of course we had to set the count straight, then engaged in conversation with this small brunette who hunched her shoulders as she leaned against the bar with her elbows. Through the hour that this girl remained, she provided insight into what it's like to be a Zap native.

People really lived here, and they were friendly, but people are friendly in the entire state of North Dakota. Any given day on the road, passing motorists will always wave. It was no longer simply one motorhome waving to another because of common interest, but rather genuine people wishing a good day to everyone. It amazed us that people took the time to greet strangers.

The thirty-seven year old girl at the bar sipped at her bottle of beer as she told us that her sisters from Bismarck give her hell for living in a town that doesn't even have a grocery store.

"They ask me how I can live in Zap," she said with a higher pitch to indicate resentment of her sisters' opinions. "I like it here...it's quiet, and so what if we don't have a grocery store. It's only seven miles to Beulah."

She told of how Zap had received national media attention. This had taken place in the spring of 1969, during a spur of the moment Zip to Zap. One thousand people zipped to Zap just to party. This tripled its population and created havoc, eventually requiring the National Guard.

Meanwhile, the four giggly girls to our right began to laugh harder and get louder as the afternoon aged. Tracy and I continued to order beer, and Carol continued to bring them over with a smile. The six of us occupied this bar for the longest time, and it was an enjoyable evening.

These girls sat on stools, but huddled together as they began to get crude. Shots and mixed drinks poured into them at a steady rate. "Let's toast to prostitution!" shouted one girl, and four wobbly glasses clinked together.

Carol shook her head with an embarrassed smile as she leaned against the bar with her right hand. She walked away saying that she'd seen it all.

The girls seemed to have more fun once they began spilling their drinks. Then they spilled their guts, talking about sex for most of the night. Their husbands were coal miners in town, obviously not home enough.

When the drunken female population had had enough spirit, the bar quieted down. Tracy and I then converged on the electronic dartboard, infamous for shooting a dart back faster than it was thrown. We played several games as the evening wore thin. At that point, Tracy decided to call home from the pay phone outside while I snuggled up to the bar.

A young coal miner with short black hair and a mustache attached himself to a stool, separating us by one seat. He had no trouble starting up a conversation.

"I'm William," he said, sticking his hand out for a shake.

I shook his hand and introduced myself.

"I'm a coal miner in town," he continued. "I love the job, and I love the location."

"People are certainly friendly around here," I said.

"This is one of the friendliest places I know," he said. "Everyone waves whether they know ya or not. I wave to everyone I pass on the road. It's just the way it is here, and that's what I like about it."

When a gray-haired patron entered the bar and challenged Carol to a game of darts, Carol decided that he should be her partner in a game against William and me. We accepted the challenge, but I wondered how this bartender had no qualms about serving a miner.

A few games passed, and Tracy returned from the phone to be my partner. Carol went back to her job, and William was traded to the gray man's team. The beer continued to pour into us as we played, but somehow the shots got better. Tracy and I continued sweeping sets.

As the evening progressed, the bar cleared of all other patrons. Tracy and I sat at the bar talking to Carol and her husband, Gilbert, a stocky man with a cowboy hat, who stood beside his wife behind the bar. Carol mentioned that she had seen us pull into town the night before, which is a sign of a very small town.

Gilbert told us that Zap had only one policeman, but no crime existed there. We mentioned that we were staying at the Zap City Park, and the monthly rate was seventy-five dollars if we chose to return to town for a while after the trip.

"You can park the camper on my lot," Gilbert offered. "All it would cost you is electricity, which runs about sixteen dollars per month, and you can stay as long as you want. I have electric, water, and sewer from the time I had a camper."

This town of Zap had settled as a railroad town with a mining industry in 1913, but wasn't incorporated as a village until 1917. A Northern Pacific railroad official, Mr. Pettibone, named the new village Zap because of the coal mine at the edge of town. He based the name on a coal-mining town in Scotland called Zapp. He Americanized the name of this one-square mile region.

When we left the bar, Tracy and I pedaled down the middle of the wide, silent street a bit under the weather. As exciting as the night turned out to be, I had indulged a tad too much. Tracy can verify that one.

Before leaving Zap the following morning, we had a couple Zapian things to take care of. We owed the Zap City Park box ten dollars, but had only five singles to slide into the wooden dollar slot. Our change for a twenty would come from the post office. The lady we spoke to was also on the City Park Committee, so we paid her directly without having to return to the park.

Passing the bank during our farewell drive through the rest of town, we roared with laughter after discovering that it was in the inside of a mobile home. A short dirt driveway led to a drive-through window. All this was for a town of three hundred, and this was in the midst of a boom.

Our final Zap memory came after a quick stop into the bar to say goodbye to Carol. Tracy asked me to go behind the bar for a photograph. When I did so, Carol grabbed me and gave me a big hug, offering Tracy the chance for a cheek-to-cheek photograph. All this from a lady we hadn't even known a few days ago. That's North Dakota, and it's also Zap.

September 10, 1992

What a thrill we felt, being close to Mount Rushmore. Never would we have visited South Dakota just for this attraction, but now it almost smiled upon our doorstep. There are so many attractions in this southwest corner of the state, but when the day began, we wondered if we'd be doing anything due to the clinking and whistling in the engine. We could not put off finding an RV center even though we found ourselves in the middle of tourism.

When a mechanic asked me to start the engine, we heard no noise even remotely foreign. The engine actually sounded pretty good. The mechanic jumped in and took a ride with us up and down the Black Hills, a fairly decent challenge, but the engine still behaved well.

Finally, a slight rattle took some concentration to hear, but the mechanic could only offer a suggestion that the U-joint might be the cause, eventually spelling trouble for the driveshaft. His seventy dollar estimate entailed one day to chase the part down in Rapid City, so we agreed to return if the problem worsened.

The mountains leading to Mount Rushmore steepened, and the camper choked, spit, and sneezed to the top. The earlier problem recurred and intensified as we wound our way up. We resigned ourselves to the fact that the work had to be performed on the engine, but we wanted to view the faces carved into the mountain first.

As we ascended the mountain, roadside trees gave way to a clearing, allowing a distant view of what we had come to see. There it was...Mount Rushmore, but additional trees blocked the monument out again until we could stand before it.

Gutzon Borglum's sculpture required ninety percent dynamite blasting and ten percent hand carving by a crew of over three hundred sixty men. Mount Rushmore, named in 1885 after New York City lawyer Charles Rushmore, became the dedicated site in 1927 by President Calvin Coolidge. The Memorial site had smooth grain and a fine texture of stone that appealed to carving. Unfortunately, lack of funds and bad weather prolonged the project, which lasted fourteen years and cost $990,000.

It was time for us to see this work, so our quick steps moved us to the visitor's center before feasting our eyes. Standing before Mount Rushmore felt better than I imagined. A genuinely patriotic feeling delivered shock waves through me as I focused in on the individual presidents who paved the way for the creation of the United States as we know it.

George, Thomas, Theodore, and Abraham stared blankly over our heads, admiring the country that had become as much a part of their lives as their lives had become a part of the country.

I had no idea that this popular attraction would be more than faces in the mountain. Tracy could not break away either. Enraptured, she did not want to lose the moment any more than I did, and that was the reason for our moment of silence.

Not wanting it to end, we agreed to return to the camper for dinner, then watch the lighting of Mount Rushmore at night. Turning and walking away, people silently walked into the spot in which we had stood. They stood in awe. No words, no motion, just reverie.

Later in the evening, we took a seat in the amphitheater for the park ranger's lecture and a thirty minute movie on the achievements of these four presidents. Here we gathered amidst an amphitheater of a couple hundred people, and the spirit of America waited overhead in darkness. What a sweet moment to be cherished forever. As we enjoyed it, we overheard other inspired people in the crowd stating facts about what they were about to see.

Me as the fifth head on Mt. Rushmore

This patriotism and excitement dissipated during the most miserable display of behavior imaginable for such a time. As the park ranger cleared his throat to begin his lecture, we saw two adorable blonde-haired girls climb over the bench to our row. They landed just to our right, while their parents smiled at kids being kids. The girls giggled softly and wore precious grins. Looking at one another caused them to laugh harder.

A large, middle-aged lady with frizzy brown hair, sitting a few benches ahead of us, ruined the moment for everyone sitting there on this night. She rose from her seat, turned her whole body around, and screamed, "You kids shut up!"

Her husband's head remained forward and his arms remained folded as he pretended that he didn't hear a thing, or pretended that they weren't together. Everybody who heard this outburst, which included just about everyone with ears, stared at this lady with gaping mouths. A silence swept over the amphitheater. It was no longer a sacred silence. The two girls looked sadly at their parents for protection against this evil force.

The children looked confused, as though tears would soon flow, not knowing what to do next. People looked at their neighbors, and the mother of the girls made eye contact with Tracy.

The father of the girls sat tall with long brown hair. He leaned back in his chair with his arms folded, trying to manage coherent words after such a shocking display. "Get used to it lady," he finally retorted in a deep, but calm voice. "It's gonna happen for the rest of the night."

The fat lady didn't sing, but rather belted out another rude comment as though the Americans there tonight didn't already hate her. "Then why don't you take those kids home?" she screamed in an even more psychotic way. This time she remained in her seat, but turned her body, offering her profile.

Again, everybody looked around, and the screamer's husband fixed his eyes on the ranger. No other words were exchanged, and the two girls went back over the bench to sit and be comforted by their parents. There was no excuse for this outburst, and to think it came before four of the most influential men in America. We made the most of the night, salvaging what remained of the spirit.

The National Anthem soon filled South Dakota, restoring the emotion that I thought would be lost. The crowd either sung along or hummed, but it was hard not to do either.

When the Anthem concluded and the American flag waved high up front, the illumination slowly began. We first noticed clouded outlines of the heads, then facial features, and finally the faces could be recognized. The monument continued to brighten, and the patriotic feeling was restored. With the screamer silent, we could finally enjoy the moment. By the time everyone began to exit, the faces aglow were not just those on the mountain.

Everyone rose from their seats, whispering about this wicked lady who seemed to have disappeared unnoticed. A bunch of proud Americans united on this evening to celebrate founders of their country, only to be momentarily put off by a lady who had no business being there with that attitude. A noble moment swallowed up a terrible one. Although the noble moment may have prevailed in the end, Tracy and I will always associate one with the other. We joined the whisperers as we moseyed back to our home.

The camper acted up even more while descending the mountain. It sounded as if a loosened part could drop to the pavement at any moment. Instead of sticking around the Keystone area, we thought it wise to return to the truck stop in Rapid City, saving us the one-day delay of chasing the part down in that city.

Reaching the truck stop caused us to breathe a little easier, and the lady behind the counter told us that the mechanics began work at the crack of dawn. We tucked our camper away in the back of the lot, away from the area populated by trucks.

By 6:30 A.M. our camper sat in the large trucker garage being examined by a tall, thin man with dark hair and a mustache. A young short kid with a Metallica T-shirt assisted him. They were unable to identify the problem, and I did not want to mention the first opinion we had gotten. Then the younger kid told me that he needed to take it for a test drive. He then jumped into the driver's seat.

Before I knew it, he had started the engine and pulled out of the garage with Tracy and Molly sleeping in the back. I wondered what raced through Tracy's mind. I wondered if she thought it was me driving. I could only watch and wonder.

Onto the road he drove, traveling away with Tracy and her dog. I envisioned Molly running up to the cab, which was separated from the camper by a thin orange curtain, and freaking out on the mechanic. As fast as he pulled away, he returned looking as though nothing strange had occurred, explaining what he thought the problem was. I felt confident about having the U-joint replaced, but I had to hear Tracy's version.

The young mechanic ordered the part over the phone and came back out to the garage to await delivery. I figured that it would be fun to put him to a test.

"So," I began, "did the dog give you any trouble?"

"No," he hesitantly replied, somewhat taken aback. "I didn't even know there was a dog in the back."

"Yes, my wife was probably holding her back."

"Your wife!" he said, as his eyes nearly bulged out of his head. "Nah...oh no...I don't believe it!"

"What's wrong?" I asked.

"I was swearing at the traffic," he said, embarrassed, shaking his head back and forth in disbelief.

Tracy's version was a tad more descriptive as this kid screamed obscenities to every other car on the road. She figured out what was happening and stayed in bed, trying not to make noise, while holding Molly and her laughter under the blankets.

When the bathroom door began swinging open and closed, Tracy quietly crawled down the hall, gently clicked it shut, and crawled back to bed. The irony of it all is that we had been warned many times that my lack of mechanical ability meant that we would be taken for a ride by mechanics nationwide. We certainly were taken for a ride (Tracy was anyway), but the bill did not even topple forty dollars, which meant that we nearly sliced the cost in half by driving to the city that had the part.

The tall mechanic began his final touches under the camper. Tracy sat on the toilet wondering if she should wait since the guys' head was directly underneath. A tough call, but he returned to his feet before our final decision came through. We had to wonder if he had overheard our debate.

Four hours after entering the garage, we pulled out and started for the Badlands with morning still very much intact. The magnificent drive into the park provided bluffs, buttes, and gorges of red hues. Sixty-five million years were present in the layered formations of sharp ridges, spires, and knobs; erosion at its finest. It was like driving through gigantic sandcastles and dunes that lined the road.

A sign on the way in advertised helicopter rides starting at ten dollars, so we decided to fly since neither of us had ridden in a helicopter. Within thirty minutes of our decision, Tracy and I sat behind a bubble about to rise over land that the pioneers had found to be bad for travel.

Up and away we went, shooting off the launch pad, then over the Badlands for a two-minute loop. The bird's-eye view was a unique way to see this erosion; a sea of wrinkles where flat land gives way to Badlands. Tracy and I spent the entire ride leaning forward into the bubble to examine the scene below. The formations continued beyond our sight, but for ten dollars the pilot refused to whirl us to Hawaii.

This region was so arid that nothing quenched our thirst, which eventually returned us to our camper after a jaunt in and around a footpath. Tracy had brought along a bottle of what seemed like dry, but wet water. These were Bad Lands.

Out of the brittleness we drove, our sights on Wyoming to the west. Erosion continued on the way out, and the pieces easily crumbled upon touching them. South Dakota became history. Not

Glenn Maynard

far from Rapid City was Box Elder, so instead of shacking up at that truck stop in Rapid City for a third consecutive night, I chose to treat Tracy to a McDonald's parking lot next to a Conoco station.

September 12, 1992

Having over one hundred miles to pass from the Black Hills to Lusk, Wyoming, we set out after a late start and a stint encircling Wind Cave National Park. Here the buffalo loitered in the streets, some leaving piles of scat larger than Molly. We could only briefly visit with the bison though, because a long drive awaited us.

A couple of days with full hookups at the park in Lusk would enable us to relax in the sun and clean up the camper. No matter how clean the camper was in the morning, there was no way that it will be clean by sundown.

Before we left on this trip, we envisioned tidiness every time we motored along. In reality, however, dishes piled in a sink too small to accept them. We always needed the road in good time.

Not everything flowed ideally, so we had to make adjustments to make life manageable. But at this point, we hardly thought about the reality of our life. For us, traveling became a day to day routine just like going off to work. We always had something to take care of before setting off for the day.

We would do our chores, then work at getting to a certain destination. By evening, if we parked before midnight, we researched the next state. We highlighted interesting places in pink highlighter on the state maps, then highlighted free campgrounds within the same area as the attractions in yellow.

As we tried to conquer these highlights, we'd research the next state, so it wasn't tough to lose sight of our different life on the road. This is why the sudden rushes of reality seldom occurred. It felt like an eternity from our departure, and Tracy and I would reminisce about the early days of our journey. The memories were so deeply ingrained. A catastrophe became our only enemy. Nothing else could stop us.

Through the Black Hills we meandered, twisting and turning, rising and falling. We passed through small, dusty towns and large cities before being released to the prairie once again. Bluffs appeared and gave way to small mountains before meeting up with our twenty-first state of Wyoming: A Great Land Outdoors. This welcome sign included a cowboy maintaining a Bronco, one hand on his harness and the other waving his hat in the air.

Here was the cowboy and Rodeo State we'd been waiting for. We saw the old west before us as we accepted the continuation of Route 18, which headed south soon after entering Wyoming. Our new state flattened after a turn southward, but soft, distant mountains emerged from the earth like clouds spattering the horizon.

Bluffs entered our windshield picture, and so did a couple of trains to the right side of the road heading toward us, veering with the road. The park in Lusk could not help us. An open shower stood lonely in the middle of the grass. The supposed facilities failed us, including a sign dictating no overnight camping. We had put too much faith in Lusk, so their offering frustrated the hell out of us.

I grabbed our maps and camp books to research Plan B, and we found a free campground fifty-five miles west in Douglas. Darkness began to set in, and a fierce wind began to blow as we continued the drive.

We were exhausted, sick of driving, could barely see through the bug-splattered windshield, and had to continue on for at least another hour in the dark. We continued on our journey that would perhaps land us at a campground that might exist. If not, then we could remember Wyoming as merely a dark drive.

Our westward movement continually delayed darkness. It truly fascinated us to follow the sun, even though it had retired for the day. The sun hid, but we knew where it had tucked itself away because of the one spot lighting the horizon below the earth, our exact destination. Complete darkness pushed us along from behind. Sunset was my favorite time to travel, and it seemed to camouflage any turbulence that may have occurred when the sun shined.

We no longer had a problem with our earlier misfortune in Lusk. Now it stood as a small inconvenience. If it had worked out, then we would not have traveled this far ahead, and would have missed an inspiring sunset. If we'd stayed in Lusk overnight, the entire rest of the trip would have had a different outcome. A restaurant along the way to Douglas had a large gravel lot for trucks and campers, and although we stuck out, it worked just fine for us.

The western states provided an east to west landscape beginning in the plains then gradually rising into mountainous regions where the sights began. The drives could not have been more pleasant. Wyoming was no different as herds of antelope roamed the vast rangeland until we made our way into the mountains.

The town of Hiland at an elevation of 5,998 feet had a population of ten people. The smallest population we saw had five people, with the only signs of a town being a bar. Apparently a town out west cannot exist without one.

What amazed us most about Wyoming was its small population of just over five hundred thousand people, spread across the nation's ninth largest state. Connecticut squeezes over six times as many people into its boundaries. So much land out west, and so few people, which makes it amusing to see the conglomeration of a city. Spread out!

September 16, 1992

Route 26 helped move our camper west from Casper to Jackson Hole, where mountains sprouted all around, but our strategic stops prevented the camper from overheating. When the console covering the engine became too hot for my right leg to lean against and the ice melted instantly in our cups, we knew to give it a rest.

The Grand Teton mountain range rose high above the valley floor, towering seven thousand feet above the Hole. Since it was getting dark, and we had no place to sleep, we descended into Jackson, where houses sprinkled the base of the mountain. Searching for a truck stop seemed futile, even after we decided to follow a truck route.

We entered the city, driving around tourist sites such as gift shops, restaurants, and saloons. What we couldn't find was a place to park. Tired, hungry, and sick of the road, we only wished to turn off the engine, even in the middle of the main drag. I simply cannot push beyond a certain point, and I was there. Tracy admitted being as spent, so I couldn't turn to her for driving.

Continuing south of Jackson in search of parking was a shot in the dark, but desperation maddened us. About ten miles past the tourism, we entered a pulloff for regrouping. The gravel parking area was a small semi-circle for those interested in reading a historical marker. We pretended to be interested in reading, although we were more interested in sleeping.

We really didn't think we'd last at this roadside pulloff, even though it was ten miles from Jackson in a remote region, but when our eyes reopened, a new day shone upon us. Our alibi had us falling asleep while reading the historical marker, but we saved that one for another time.

Having no choice, we pushed our luck and kept returning to this historical marker night after night, until the fourth night we laughed it off. Out of principal, we couldn't succumb to this convenience. The lot was ideally located in the middle of a mountain, which rose and ran along one side of the road and descended to the Snake Valley, located a dizzying distance below. The view from the shelf we parked on made us high, which became the second reason for our return.

September 18, 1992

When the Teton Range started to rise nine million years ago, the Jackson Hole formed. After the sea that covered this region retreated, earthquakes created the fault line and subsequent smaller earthquakes continued to push the range higher.

While standing before the majestic Tetons, we were dwarfed, to say the least. Sun reflected off the snowcap, but finer details ensued with the trail that took us closer to the range.

After spending the day at the Jackson Hole Art Festival, we were advised to drive through the park at dawn or dusk in order to see the abundant wildlife, and hopefully our first moose. That's exactly what we did, driving through the park looking for a campground. Barbed wire fences separated the road from the distant marsh.

While following this marsh long after the setting of the sun, we came upon an animal that looked like what we'd been seeking since Maine. It lifted its head from the marsh, and water dripped off palm-shaped antlers. This was evidence enough that our first moose stood before us. Although darkness began to steal most of the description, I yanked the camper to the roadside, and we got out for viewing and photographs from a great distance.

This moment had taken months to arrive, but standing and watching this bull's head go down, then back up, and seeing the antlers swing about with each graceful head turn made it all worth our while. The moose decided to lie down, ending any hope that Tracy had of additional pictures. Dusk blocked her, and the tall grass hid the moose effectively.

A park ranger told us that we could park anywhere in the National Forest, so we took advantage of the Bridger-Teton National Forest for shuteye. A pull-off, although quite small, looked more than sufficient for us weary-eyed travelers. The pull-off had a very steep drop-off down the mountain. The blackness of the forest helped transform it into a dark abyss.

The area was Black bear territory, so after pulling into the spot, we decided that we were level rather than getting out to confirm that fact. Earlier in the day, we made the mistake of strolling into the Million Dollar Cowboy Bar, where we hopped up on the saddled bar stools and sipped Ginger Ale. There we viewed a stuffed grizzly, viciously smiling, standing high above us with its paws and claws out in front. That picture stayed with me through the entire night, and I tried to sleep with my eyes wide open.

The wind picked up, jerking the camper toward the drop-off. A whistle emanated from puckered lips in the corner of one of the windows, so I gave up on trying to fall asleep. I wasn't sure which picture was worse: the camper skidding down the mountainside and crashing on the perilous rocks below playing in theater number one, or being gored to death by a large predatory bear in theater number two.

I had set my watch for 5:15 A.M. for a wildlife mission, and all that I wanted was to fall asleep and be rudely awakened by the beeping of my watch alarm. Tracy fell asleep shortly after her head hit the pillow, and I despised her for it. Every once in a while, I watched her soundly sleeping, and I wanted to rouse her from her sleep for a quick lesson. I only managed a couple of hours of sleep before my watch beeped, but the aggressive wind stirred me moments before the alarm.

It was as dark as when we had given up on the moose the previous evening, but we continued the search. We closed in on the Tetons, watching the sun rise up from behind. It was such a fulfilling moment in this early morning with birds chirping, sunrise before us, and knowing that we never went over the cliff or to the maul.

As weary as I was, I could only think about the wonderful light of this new day. Tracy kept asking me to stop the camper so she could jump out with the camera and tripod. If it wasn't the golden leaves of autumn on the trees which caught her eye, then the positioning of the sun every inch it moved above the Tetons turned her on.

I watched the excitement on her face while she screened her photographs. She possessed the intensity necessary for a telling photograph, and that's exactly what she got.

The three Tetons rise over twelve thousand feet. As we closed in on them, we discovered that this fact increases their grandeur. Coming to a stop sign, I slowed and glanced to the right for cars, but spotted something else. An animal stood in the middle of the road, too far away to identify. Wasting no time, I moved the camper down this road faster than I should have been going. I didn't want to lose the animal.

Closing in on this thing, we discovered it was actually one towering animal and one much smaller animal at its side. We witnessed our second and third moose. Our elation peaked as we flew down this narrow road, but twice I had to slam the brakes because of deer crossing the road ahead. Normally we'd be excited to see deer, but we had moose to catch, and they appeared to be waiting for us to close in on them.

We ended up getting close enough to the moose for me to wonder whether the big one was going to charge the camper. At the moment, it seemed as tall as a giraffe. The mother and child ran for the forest on the roadside once they saw the camper within one hundred yards of them.

We stopped the camper where we thought the moose to be, and looking into the forest, we saw two moose hiding behind thin trees, watching us. After a couple of minutes, the moose turned and ran deeper into the forest, so we turned as well, and continued back the way we were headed before this detour.

Moose four and five stood still in a tall grass field, but once cars began to pile up on the roadside, they were scared away, easing their way through the grass until the threat was diminished. Then came the elk. There were herds of them, either huddled together or moving in and out of the forest set behind the field. High-pitched mating calls echoed through the air in bugle-like fashion, sounding like Rudolph, steam billowing out of their mouths and noses. They didn't seem too concerned with stopped cars, only with finding a partner.

The buffalo outside Yellowstone National Park

For us, this was the Greatest Show on Earth. Wyoming had by far provided the largest showing of wildlife, and the land did not do too badly in our ratings, either. Climbing up the state brought us to Yellowstone National Park, the first national park in the world, designated by President Grant in 1872. It's also the largest and most popular, but our autumn arrival toned down the usual crowds.

Upon entering Yellowstone, our jaws dropped and our eyes widened from shock. It was a tragedy to see the devastating effects of the big fire four years earlier in 1988, which had charred almost half the park. Bare and burnt trees, standing and fallen, enabled tourists to look far into the forest while driving through. This devastation traveled with us for too many miles.

Our search began for the infamous Old Faithful Geyser, which faithfully shoots 3,700 to 8,400 gallons of boiling water 100 to 180 feet into the air every 77 minutes on average. While we were sitting on benches with a group of tourists who had the same idea as we did, a buffalo sniffed its way onto the field containing the geyser. It seemed far enough away from the geyser while it grazed and looked up as it chewed. I still wondered if it had distanced itself enough from the spectators. It was very mellow, but very large, and people aren't their favorite company.

The geyser looked like a large pitcher's mound. It consisted of light, dusty ash, slightly raised above the playing field. The hole in the middle constantly shot out steam, as much as an idling automobile on a cold winter's day. Once in a while the geyser would tease the crowd with a spurt, a hush would fall over the crowd, and the mound would return to idling. Forty-five minutes after we arrived, Old Faithful exploded, gushing white, thick steam and water into the air like a house on fire.

The buffalo paid no mind to the massive eruption taking place to its right, but the geyser settled down within ten minutes. The crowd dispersed when the geyser stalled, and we weren't prepared to stay behind with the buffalo, so we left too.

On the way out of the park, more cars braked and pulled to the right side of the road, this time because of a coyote rummaging in the sagebrush for food.

In the Hebgen National Forest, a sign greeted us at the entrance to the campground: WARNING! CAMPGROUND CLOSED TO TENTS, TENT-TRAILERS, POP-UP VANS, AND SLEEPING ON THE GROUND. HIGH BEAR FREQUENCY.

That was unsettling, so we let Molly outside before it got too dark, hoping she'd do all that she needed to do. We searched the campground while out with the dog, and I felt certain that we would see a bear. I was prepared to detect anything that moved. However, we saw nothing even resembling a bear.

Returning to Yellowstone in the early morning, hoping to see the large animals now that we were out of danger, the scene inside the park looked as if we were driving into an inferno, or meandering into clouds. Steam was suspended over these active fields on both sides of the road. Other areas contained yellow grass fields with steaming bald spots shaped as oddly as puzzle pieces. This mysterious aura lingered everywhere in the park as we chased down the hot spots.

This morning introduced to us hundreds of elk, more than we'd seen in our combined lives, but I guess that wasn't hard to beat. A couple more coyotes roamed in the same setting as we'd seen the day before and hundreds of buffalo were spread out all over this park, proving that this once-endangered species had made a valiant comeback since the late 1800s.

Steam was visible from anywhere in the park as we prepared for a day of hiking to see more geysers, fumeroles, and mud pots. As we pulled into Mammoth Hot Springs, the tire on the front driver's side scraped with each revolution, and the sound intensified as I slowly drove into the parking area. I asked Tracy to drive while I jumped out and got down on one knee to see if anything jumped out at me. Nothing jumped, but it wasn't as if I knew what to look for.

The screeching noise became so loud that we didn't feel good about driving. Rolling down the mountain slowly, listening to the tire sound as if it was going to leave us, I eased the patient into the Conoco station for medical attention.

The attendant wasted no time coming out for a listen as I rolled the camper to and fro, but Mr. Conoco admitted right off the bat that he couldn't diagnose the problem. He suggested that we move into Gardiner, Montana, five miles up the road. We had no choice but to do just that.

Nobody could help us on this night, so we crossed into Montana and followed our free campground book to a fishing access area. Telephone poles offered no lighting, and the moon didn't help much. Although it was impossible to see, I managed to direct the camper across the opposing lane toward an entrance sign. High beams confirmed Yankee Jim's River access in the Gallatin National Forest.

The sign existed, but we could not see the entrance. I squeezed the camper between two trees. What we expected to be a long trek through the forest turned out to be a search for the ideal place to park on the gravel circular driveway right next to the road. Once through the trees, we found home.

We were encapsulated in Big Sky country. I didn't think it possible, but it seemed like the sky had dropped down some. The sky seemed to close in all around us. The stars seemed within reach, and the horizon looked closer than usual. Tracy and I decided this was the only place we wanted to be right now.

Pulling into this dome called Montana was special because it's all land and few people, just the way we like it. Our halfway point fast approached as this twenty-second state smiled upon us with its offering of this beautiful place to rest our weary heads. Some spectacular feeling came over me as we entered Montana, and I attributed it to the lack of the hubbub of tourism we'd experienced the past couple of days.

After the pressure of trying to see it all in Grand Teton and Yellowstone, we now noticed a great weight lifted. Rolling into Gardiner equated rolling into a soothing, relaxed, and gentle atmosphere. It saved us from that affliction called tourism. This was a dramatic change, like when you come into a house on a cold and snowy winter's day, then slam the door, and sound of the howling wind is transformed into silence. We savored the moment then melted with the swift river nearby, which became our music as we slept.

What I discovered when I awoke put me in awe, and it was what we had set off to find last May. Being the first one up just as the light of this new day began to enter the valley, I pulled the back shade to find our camper in a low valley surrounded by towering mountains of rock. Crumbled pieces were piled at every level, and a half moon still maintained its presence in the sky. The Yellowstone River still rushed past as it had while we had drifted off to sleep the night before. Infrequent echoes from passing motorists came and went. I could hear the sound of their motors trail off then dissolve into the horizon.

My mood was instantly transcended into an inner peace that crept into my body, taking it hostage. I enjoyed this peacefulness, this lonesomeness. I inhaled deeply and exhaled gently, feeling more alive than ever.

Needing to take in the entire picture, I strolled to the Yellowstone River about ten seconds away. The soothing water, swirling and twisting its way along the narrow river of protruding rocks and past the banks containing it, constantly provided the tune we so cherished. Standing small, admiring the scenery before me, I searched for wildlife, but saw none. That didn't matter, though, because life prospered all around, and to me it was wild.

Sometimes we simply could not pick up and leave a place, and Gardiner qualified as such a place. We needed another night to fully appreciate its offering, and we had only seen a couple miles of Montana. We wanted stability for a full twenty-four hours, and what better place than where we were? A plane or an automobile would be our only infrequent disturbance, so we agreed to use this area as a stopover.

The next day, we drove parallel to the winding Yellowstone, hoping to move further north to a free campground listed in Butte. We believed a gravel road to be the route to a campground, but no signs verified this. We gave it a try, but the camper began to suffer greatly from seizures. By this time, Tracy had crawled to the back for a nap. However, she could only sleep through this rumbling for a short while, because it only intensified.

After working her way to the front, Tracy related to me the effects these earthquake-like rumblings had on the camper. While lying on the bed, she glanced over to see the stove and counter jumping out of place. We wondered about gas leaks. She saw every cabinet shifting about. I tried to navigate seven miles of this wide, bumpy, gravel road, traversing land that apparently led to nowhere.

Five miles became a thirty minute drive over what seemed like limestone. Thick dust seeped in, saturating the camper. It smelled so putrid that it prevented us from breathing. We took short breaths to prevent ourselves from turning blue, but the fierce odor forced us to entertain that possibility. We both lifted our shirts over our noses so we didn't have to inhale fully. The world behind us was hidden in dust, and we wondered what it would be like to follow a car.

When a vehicle approached, we had to quickly roll up the windows. Even that wasn't enough to prevent the thick coat of dust from enveloping the camper's tables, counters, bed, and everything else inside, including the occupants.

When I waved down a truck coming toward us, the man stopped, got out, and walked over to my door. We needed to know about the end of the road, and he advised us that it wasn't what we wanted. We had persevered down most of the road for naught, and had to backtrack.

It was much easier for us to skip the free campground idea and find a truck stop near Helena. I'd surely have fewer gray hairs, and we'd be able to breathe. Sure enough, a truck stop appeared in town, and right now it looked like the finest truck stop America had to offer.

While attempting to take a siesta, it wasn't long before I awoke to the sound of a tractor-trailer completing the job of backing into the parking spot next to our camper in a dirt lot. The truck nearly extracted our passenger's side mirror in the process. It wasn't merely the engine's rumbling going through the camper. The trailer contained livestock, and these all-too-familiar cattle danced around, hooves against metal, echoing throughout the mountains of Helena. Molly must have been exhausted not to notice, but she did eventually, and protested as never before.

September 24, 1992

A little north and a little west of Helena is the quiet ghost town of Marysville, which brought us six miles down another dirt road. This time our shirts did not cover our faces. The inconspicuous town sat well protected; the beginning of the road indicated only the Marysville House, but not the town.

I stuck my left arm out the window and pulled over a school bus with just one young girl playing passenger. The bus driver answered all my questions and said that I'd find the ghost town at the end of the road. So we continued on, rumbling into town.

Marysville began as a boomtown in the 1880's and 1890's at the time of the Gold Rush, but was abandoned shortly thereafter. Two railroads tracked through town. Sixty businesses had been established, including two newspapers, and the town was once Montana's leading gold producer and richest gold mine area in the world.

Although the Marysville House Restaurant was opened for tourism and some people called Marysville their hometown, the place certainly had the look of a ghost town. The few roads in town contained strings of abandoned houses and buildings. They were broken down, some to the foundation, and others boarded up.

Marysville epitomized a ghost town. Houses had either been abandoned for one hundred years or burned to the ground. The last ghost town we visited in Michigan exhibited only an old railroad depot; this was what we imagined a ghost town would look like.

More problems troubled our motorhome, and we prepared to shell out money to get them fixed because this had gone on far too long. On top of the recurring noise from the front tire, something had to be done to stop the camper from overheating in the mountains before we moved up to Glacier National Park.

A tire center in Missoula pulled the tire off and found no reason for the scraping. We left the garage without shelling out any money, and the noise diminished. As for the overheating, we knew it wouldn't be so easy, and only wanted the problem fixed. There had to be a logical reason for this overheating, but different mechanics offered differing opinions.

One mechanic decided that we needed a new thermostat. Another mechanic said we should rip out the old thermostat and go without one. A third mechanic blamed our overheating on the timing set at sea level. A fourth insisted that the radiator needed to be flushed, and a fifth mechanic held that we needed a new radiator cap. Each mechanic spoke with conviction.

The next tire center down the road narrowed the solution down to either replacing the thermostat or cleaning out the radiator. The cheaper of the two was the thermostat, so we took our chances without a guarantee because it seemed like the only logical solution.

Tracy and I knew next to nothing about radiators and thermostats, and maybe the price tag indeed spoke to us, but from our experiences with instant overheating in the mountains, we agreed that the hissing might be the thermostat crying out for help. The twenty-five dollar job turned into a sixty-five dollar job because a bolt broke while the mechanic attempted to get the thermostat out of the housing. He had warned us about the possibility, and sure enough it happened. With the thermostat replaced, at least we'd know if that was the solution once the mountains presented us with a challenge.

September 25, 1992

Our destination was Hungry Horse to pick up mail at the post office. We gave the thermostat a run for its money, and it passed with flying colors. The console, which previously could not have been touched by my right leg within five minutes of driving, now felt cold after a full day of climbing mountains. We prayed our good fortune would continue.

Inside the post office, I asked for the general delivery mail for Glenn and Tracy Maynard, and a big smile lit up the face of the little old lady on the other side of the counter.

"Oh...I'm so glad you kids decided to show up," she began. "I kept getting mail for you, and I wondered when you'd arrive."

Before leaving, we told her about our travels. We also told her how we chose funny named towns for mail delivery, and her town of Hungry Horse qualified hands down. She enjoyed the little anecdote, then gave us directions to the Hungry Horse Dam. This would be our starting point for Glacier National Park the following day.

Trees with golden and reddish leaves lined the dirt road leading to the reservoir as we peered down into gorge-like valleys. Once over the dam, a sign indicated that we were approaching Grizzly Bear Country.

189

With nowhere else for us to go, we let Molly use the bathroom. Then we plowed through the thick forest along paved roads no better than some of the gravel roads we had mixed ourselves up in. After pushing our way miles into the forest, we risked a dirt road, hoping it would lead us to the campground. It had more bumps than the first, and signs were virtually nonexistent.

A quarter-mile down this slow road, our front tire became agitated more than before. The scraping noise intensified rapidly to the point where we thought the tire would leave us. At least it wasn't dark yet. The light enabled me to stand before the camper and inspect it as Tracy rolled it along.

I saw no indication of the origin of the problem, but we surely had had enough of this tire saga. To my amazement, I discovered that the noise wasn't on the driver's side as it had been. Now it had moved over to the passenger's side, scraping louder than before.

Tracy suggested that we back up to where the dirt road met the paved road, where we started. There was a pulloff at that junction, and we could further examine the problem without blocking the road entirely, should another vehicle come around.

Moving ever so slightly in reverse, I thought for sure we were risking permanent damage. I cringed at the intensity of the scraping, knocking, and screeching, but we had no other recourse. Upon reaching our destination, a large dusty pulloff surrounded by forest, I shut down the engine for the night. We agreed that we should deal with it in the morning, since we already had a place to stay overnight.

Then the rain began with this sudden outburst from the sky, and we realized there were no forest trees to prevent the downpour from reaching our roof. Each drop reached us with full impact. As further luck would have it, the only food that we had for dinner was a roasted chicken, which is not advisable in Grizzly Bear Country.

Our only real dilemma after the aroma permeated the forest was when Molly began to dance in front of the door. Tracy and I stared at each other, but could say nothing. We went so far as getting down on our hands and knees and trying to bribe the dog to go on the plastic rug runner, dangling three biscuits in front of her nose.

When that failed, I started the engine to create noise. As Tracy held the flashlight, I stood in the doorway holding the leash. Molly jumped out to the ground. Tracy pressed against my back, her chin resting on my shoulder. The flashlight followed my every move. I looked out into the darkness of the surrounding forest to see florescent eyes staring at us. Startled, I yanked the leash, ricocheting Molly back inside the camper. It looked as if she were having her debut in aviation.

"What was there?" Tracy asked. She didn't see it.

"I don't know," I said. "I saw glowing eyes."

My second look, after a few seconds for my eyes to adjust to the darkness, presented a raccoon standing on its hind legs with its paws jutting out in front. The animal stared me down, but soon scrambled away far enough for me to let Molly perform without incident. That was the last time she had to go out that night; we ended up going to bed extra early so the dog would too.

The next morning, we made it out of the forest and back to the dam, where I proceeded to pull the tire off the camper. I found nothing. I thought that maybe a piece of brake would drop to the ground, but when I returned the tire to the camper, the problem again disappeared. We moved up into Glacier without more repair bills.

Unsure if our twenty-two foot motorhome could drive on Going-to-the-Sun Road, I popped into the visitor's center for verification. I ended up listening to the park ranger lecture two backcountry campers on the dangers involved in hiking. The two guys with shoulder-length hair and winter coats only wanted a backcountry camping permit. They got much more than they had bargained for.

The old ranger had white hair in a crew cut and a scratchy voice that filled the small room. He sat erect, not looking at either of the two, who appeared to be in their mid- twenties, but rather fixing his eyes straight ahead. He spoke in a monotone voice. Inadvertently, he spoke to everyone in the room, and his warnings carried weight.

"Make noise on the path," he began, never taking his eyes away from the far wall. "Bears are scared of noise, but never startle a bear up close. Don't cook anything that smells good. If you do, cook it away from where you're sleeping. Hang all cooking utensils, food or clothes that you cooked in ten feet high in a tree. That way, the bears won't get them. Only take a water bottle and a flashlight with you in the tent when you go to sleep."

The ranger never showed an ounce of emotion, speaking as if he wanted to get a rise out of the newcomers entering the room. That's what he did, as the visitors wondered exactly who the ranger was talking to, but still seemed sort of interested in the content.

"Mountain lions have attempted to kill people over the past couple of years...and Grizzly bears have been successful. If a mountain lion comes within one hundred feet of you...just play it cool. If it comes within fifty feet of you...pick up a rock. If it comes within twenty-five feet...try to hit 'em right between the eyes."

At this point, as the situation he hypothesized became dire, he looked up at the guys, then finished his message. This indicated the seriousness of their last chance: "If you miss, and he comes at you...pick up another rock and try to KILL 'em with it."

His eyes widened as he related the last ditch effort. Although few people occupied the visitor's center and most were scattered, all were standing facing the ranger with one ear trained on him. The two hikers didn't seem to be fazed. They signed their lives away, making the risk all theirs.

I was next in line after this long lecture, and when the guys moved away from the counter with their papers in hand, I asked about the twenty-two foot length on Going-to-the-Sun Road. The ranger looked at me sternly and said, "Legally...you may go on the road. But be very careful."

Going-to-the-Sun Road elevated us into snow-capped mountains. The forecast called for sleet and snow. We couldn't avoid harsh weather this late in the season. It began to get very cold and windy, and the drop-off went straight down. Early on in the drive, we had to decide if we should risk slick roads ahead, but the prospect of reaching the clouds thrilled us.

The altitude we were in was high and rising, and views into and across the valley made our heads spin. Traveling through what appeared to be Paradise put us in the clouds with snow eye-level on a surrounding mountain. We soon looked down on these mountains and across the valley of pines and autumn-golden trees.

Far up in the mountains to our left, we noticed several white Mountain goats clinging to the rocks like spots of snow. A black bear tangled with cliff edges the best it could, stepping cautiously.

Crawling our way to the top, we noticed slush on the unprotected right side of the road. A couple of inches of snow covered the left side at the base of the rock wall. A light fog overcame us, and when the road curved, we found ourselves heading for a white wall. I carefully hugged the middle of the road before reaching Logan Pass, our destination and temporary resting-place for the camper.

The console was cool, and so were we. A snowplow rested in the middle of the parking lot with snow remnants on the ground ahead of its shovel. The sky looked like snow. We could only afford to keep moving through the park to St. Mary and onward and westward via Route 2. This path would take us across the panhandle of Idaho and into Washington.

Outside the park, a sign indicated that Canada was just fifteen miles north. This new side of the mountain placed us in temporarily sunny skies. A complete rainbow arched across the sky. However, as we climbed higher and twisted our way around the eastern edge of the park, severe weather knocked us around. It never did snow or sleet, but rain assaulted the camper, and wind tried sweeping us off the road. Hairpin turns and steep drop-offs greeted us while we tried to weather the storm. Even after the park, the rain and fog continued.

An earlier billboard had told us of a truck stop in Kalispell, so we ended up there. A couple medium-sized trucks, back to back, occupied a dirt parking lot near the street. The parking lot was next to a twenty-four hour restaurant. A sign indicated no parking. I saw a dump station in back. It was late, and we were too tired to move on and find better. We used the trucks to block us from the street, then shut down and called it a night.

After the morning dump station, we had other needs to fulfill along the day's two hundred mile journey. We needed drinking water, potable water, a Laundromat, and grocery store, and we weren't going to worry about that clang in the engine.

We embarked on a tiring drive on what turned into a sunny, brisk afternoon. The time and money factor began eating away at us again, forcing us to eat up the miles. I gazed at the endless road, and Tracy gazed at the scenery on the side of it. The only words came from the radio. On and on we sailed.

Tracy suddenly pointed out at the road, but no words could come out, and it was too late. My response did not kick in quickly enough. My swerve proved useless to the small deer that crossed the road for what would be the final time.

Stunned, and with both feet on the floor, I could only direct the RV to the roadside before stopping. We both were numb. Another car stopped next to the deer in the middle of the road, and then next to our camper about one hundred feet ahead. The driver leaned over his female passenger in order to see me higher up in the camper.

"You gonna pull it off the road?" he asked.

I had no immediate response, staring at them, paralyzed by the impact. I replayed the scene over and over in my head. "I guess so," I finally managed. I struggled to respond, but my mind raced, tripping my tongue. "I never..."

"Yeah," he interrupted. "Just pull it off the road so nobody else will hit it."

I agreed, but could not rise from my seat. I could only gaze into the side view mirror, hoping it would disappear. I did not want to do this, but I had to.

Tracy sat slumped in shock and tears, feeling guilty that she could say nothing to save that little deer. The man's passenger looked past me to Tracy, asking if she was all right. Tracy avoided turning her red eyes to the lady, slowly nodding up and down. Her hands covered her face, and rubber gloves covered my hands. I hopped down from the camper after ten minutes of deliberation.

Standing motionless, eyeing my destination, I still couldn't take the necessary steps. It felt as though my feet had been sewn to the earth. Then an older man walked to the scene and beat me to it, grabbing the deer's legs and routinely pulling it aside. I hopped back into the RV and began to drive away. This time, I used the side view mirror to thank the Good Samaritan with my left hand as I carefully edged back onto the road. I knew he couldn't see my appreciation, but I could do nothing more as I hit the gas pedal. I needed to leave the scene now that everything had been finalized, and I knew Tracy didn't want to linger longer.

Tracy's sorrow resulted from having seen the deer on the roadside fluttering its tail in the sunshine. She became mute while seeing it nearing the road, never imagining it would become our challenge. It had happened in a split second. She had had no time to react. My last-second reaction had me cutting the wheel across the line into the oncoming lane, plastering the deer between the headlights.

As we continued driving, the cab became more silent than before. Neither of us could speak, especially about the incident that just took place. It had to be repressed. Now awake, I could drive a little easier, but it wasn't going to be an enjoyable day. Maybe the focus should have been on the fact that this was the first deer we'd hit along our fifteen thousand mile trek.

There was usually a lot of noise in the camper as we celebrated each thousand miles with hoots and cheers. The fifteenth was quiet, passing unnoticed. Big Sky Country was behind us after eight days. Although I might not want to live in Montana, I'd surely return. What we liked most about Montana was the feeling it gave us.

Late at night, pushing our way west through the panhandle of Idaho, a sign fast approached, glaring from our headlights: Welcome to Washington. Our twenty-third welcome came from the Evergreen State. It was also the state which would bring us to the Pacific Coast. It was the furthest state from home. No further west could we travel. More so, the next state of Oregon would be the twenty-fourth of forty-eight, marking the halfway point of the trip.

As usual, everything of interest to us resided in the western part of the state, so we only admired the points in between as we drove across Washington. From Spokane, we traveled up to Chewelah, where we spent a few days at the free City Park with electricity. Once our break from travel persuaded us to continue on, we moved through North Cascades National Park and onward toward Seattle.

October 3, 1992

Wishing for an early start to Olympic National Park, I tried to rouse Tracy from bed, but a problem kept her there. She was exhausted from a sleepless night. A major battle immediately erupted between us. I separated myself from her rage, sitting up at the table with coffee, but that didn't last long. I wasn't pleased with being held back. This wasn't the first time we had had this issue. This had happened more than I would have liked.

I sat at the table until she exploded. She'd had enough and wanted to go home, calling me a slave driver and saying that I pushed her past her limit much too often. I sat at her side, searching my mind for an appropriate response.

As bad as this moment seemed, I knew that she would rather see more of this country than return home. I couldn't see her throwing fifteen months of planning and five months of action into the fire. I knew it wasn't true, but being in the heat of battle, I asked her what it would take to make her happy.

"I need a rest," she pleaded, screaming. "You push and push, and I can't take it anymore." Her tone calmed a bit, and her wishes unraveled. "I need a solid week off to do nothing…catch up on sleep and watch television…vegetate. I need a week with full hookups."

When I thought about it, I felt that it would be money well spent if it would make her happy and excited again about traveling. Our rush through the northern states because of winter's approach was nearing its end, so we could afford to take the time now. More importantly, we had to take the time now.

We ended in agreement, and Tracy decided that we could do Olympia National Park while being so close. Then we would park for a while.

Route 101 continued to circle around to Port Angeles, which is the gateway to the park, but we found that no roads pass through the interior. Time was of the essence because of the deceptive loop around to the Hoh Rain Forest, which had swiped most of our daylight by the time we arrived.

It was especially dark where trees canopied over the road, and although we could see in some sections, the darkness disallowed our appreciation of the splendor before us. A campground sat within the temperate rain forest, so we headed deep within the park, but not very far in proportion to the size of the park.

The campground had a bulletin board indicating that fees would not be collected until April, so we happily parked for the evening. That first sign we appreciated much more than the second, which warned us to beware of cougars.

What a display that greeted me when I awoke, stepping out of the camper and into the rain forest. All that I could see was verdant green in the trees, on the trees, hanging from the trees, and on the ground. Just to check, I looked to the sky. It wasn't green, but it wasn't raining either; a small miracle in itself since there's more than twelve feet of rainfall in the coastal rain forest annually.

Epiphytes, plants living on other plants without coming in contact with the earth, give the rain forest its jungle-like appearance. Mosses, lichens, and ferns create the rest of this atmosphere. Nurselogs, which are fallen trees, help to nurse seeds into new trees. As the logs break down, new trees sprout. The trees grow out of other trees in enormous sizes every which way. Some fallen trees reached eye-level even though they had been decomposing for years.

A trail that Tracy and I took, the Hall of Mosses, put us well into this magnificent forest, where lichens and hanging mosses predominate. The hanging mosses resembled overdoses of tinsel on a Christmas tree. The streams running through the forest offered water so clear that it sparkled.

The trees were grandiose, whether they towered above us or fell to the ground. The earthy smells accompanying our journey along this path were so fresh, natural, and pure. We inhaled deeply and often, breathing in what every human being on earth should breathe. Yet nobody gets this opportunity, with all the pollution pumped into our oxygen, so we remained here for as long as we could.

Once we had seen and smelled sufficient green, we moved on to find a place to recuperate. Tracy and I became ecstatic when we caught a glimpse of the Pacific Ocean, which became quite a milestone for us.

"Stop," she said. "Let's get out and see it."

There were still many miles ahead of us to reach civilization. We had a long drive south through Humptulips to Aberdeen before returning east to Olympia. Our options remained to be seen. We had an extra minute, but not much more, so I pulled over and we stood on a cliff overlooking the Pacific.

Ruggedness met us with our first Pacific view. Driftwood was piled on the beach, and signs warned of the danger and swiftness of the tides. We stood content on top of the cliff, holding each other in the stiff, cool breeze. We hoped for the moment when we could safely dip our toes into this large body of water, one continent away from the body we grew up with.

October 6, 1992

Tracy remained in the camper playing with the roof antennae, in search of her soap channel, in the early morning at our campground in Puyallup. I walked into the office for the camping rates and discovered that the sites included cable television. Before I had gone in, Tracy had mentioned that she only needed a couple days of vegetation. I reserved two nights before returning to the camper and telling Tracy not to bother with the antennae. She more than welcomed our arrival at this campground.

Whatever Tracy wanted would be granted, so our break in Puyallup stretched into four days. She did just what she said she needed to do: she vegetated in front of a mindless television. I enjoyed the layover too, but I could have continued on. She teased me about being the king of the five-minute nap.

A long trip over the Columbia River on Route 82 ended in Oregon. Our exuberance pushed us through to this twenty-fourth of forty-eight states. A westward journey had us chasing sundown once again. The blinding reflections soon hid below the earth, leaving only our reflections on what the first half of our trip had given. We decided we wanted to do it all over again, but we had new territory to conquer.

Along the Columbia River Gorge, past the Dalles, and through massive bluffs we traversed, trying to find a place to settle. The ruggedness of the rangeland and bluffs resembled western Nebraska. The landscape above the Columbia also showed up below in the reflection on the river and against the golden backdrop of the sun that had now set.

Rest areas in Oregon told us of a twelve hour stay limit in a twenty-four hour period with no overnight camping. We took this as a multiple choice and satisfied one of those rules.

This rest area, with loud tractor-trailers, sat beside the Columbia River. We settled down for the evening. This turned into our loudest night yet, and Tracy was unable to sleep all night. However, we found ourselves there when the light of the next day came shining through our windows. The noise persisted in the morning, prompting Tracy to request an early departure. I'd never seen her so serious.

As time passed, so did exhaust through our muffler. The camper had never sounded worse, as if it could qualify for the Indy 500. It also sounded like I had stuck playing cards in the spokes of the wheels. Something had to be done, so we stopped in Hood River where an all-day muffler job meant forking out two hundred thirty dollars, our largest repair bill by far.

The mechanic suggested that we tour the town while he put the camper on a lift inside the garage. This meant we had to barricade Molly from the front with several seat cushions. We didn't want her to attack the mechanic should he need to get under the console inside the cab.

Backfiring in the muffler resulted in a muffler-explosion, blowing it apart. This turned out to be the reason for the noise and smell. But the mechanic had further difficulties with installation. A previous owner had installed a 1980 engine into this 1978 unit, jimmying the muffler to fit. This didn't jive, so our problem would not be gone altogether.

We left for Portland poor, driving over and around the massive city via extensive bridges. Oregon provided another striking example of desolation for many miles then a bombardment of population in one small area. Portland was minuscule in relation to the desolate land preceding it.

Once through the intricate web of bridges, we pushed our way to the Pacific Ocean in search of a rest area for the evening. The rest areas indicated on our map never appeared, so our haul continued.

We eventually saw a state park from Route 101, the road forging a path down the coast, which provided our shuteye. It appeared that the map referred to rest areas as state parks, so we did what we had to do. Tracy was tired, and I fought desperately to keep my eyes open, but they came dangerously close to shutting, so I entered the next State Park.

A large sign clearly stated: Day Use Only. No Overnight Camping. So we did just that. We, and anyone else on the road on this evening, were safer with the camper here. The park sat beside the road, so we could see and hear the few passing motorists. We could also hear the savage surf pounding against the rocks below.

The Pacific Ocean crashed just below us, making us feel as though the waves were about to topple us, but we could not see a thing. The picture would have to wait for morning. That is, if we were lucky enough to remain that long.

Our luck prevailed, but not even the light of dawn could have roused us into leaving. We didn't leave by choice. The drain on the bathroom floor pumped out a noxious, sulfur-like aroma. We had used too much water for the dishes, so the holding tank had overflowed. Thank God the dirty dishwater is separate from the sewer.

Once a dump station swallowed the rancid water beneath the bathroom drain, we followed the rocky shoreline south. As bold as it may have been, we pulled into another state park for the evening, amongst crashing waves, and were never disturbed. These ranked as our favorite campsites this far into the trip. Parking our camper right next to the Pacific Ocean, it felt as cool as the ocean breeze.

I remembered seeing a picture of a camper parked on a beach with people circled around a cookout. I had kept that image in my mind since before the trip, and now these state parks in Oregon came awfully close to my realization of that picture.

When we sailed further down the coast the following day through Lincoln City and Gleneden Beach, we saw gray smoke billowing into the sky. With our recent stop at Mount St. Helens in Washington, a volcano was the only thing to which we could compare this distant disaster. In the clear, frigid day, smoke stretched far and wide across the blue sky. We had to learn the cause.

People in stores told us that they weren't aware of smoke outside, but that it might be "slashing." Further south we drove, unable to get an answer, finally pulling into another State Park in Newport for a break. An older couple in their truck pulled in, parking beside us, while Tracy and I admired the coast. I greeted the lady passenger, and she made a comment about our being far from home.

"The other side," I said. We strolled over to them with our arms folded in an attempt to keep warm.

Although this older couple was dressed smartly for this weather, they showed no discomfort from the cold even with their windows down. They both had stocky frames and appeared pleasant and plain. These farmers from Oregon just wanted to chat, but the crisp ocean breeze did not make it easy.

They informed us that the smoke, which now served as a cloud cover in a strip across the entire sky, indeed was "slashing." This is when the timber industry burns fields of stumps and thick undergrowth necessary to regenerate the soil. The replanting of trees to start the cycle all over again follows this process.

We asked them about a place to park the camper for the night while eliminating fees, delicately put. They both pointed across the nearby bridge out of Newport to a parking area across the bay. They said that a state park was in the works, but people park there for free all the time, and some folks live there. This couple had even camped there themselves, and nobody bothered the campers.

After our discussion, they started their truck and told us to follow them over. Although we could see it, the site was not easy to drive to. We hopped into the camper and spanned the bay behind our newfound friends.

Once we arrived, they turned around, tooted the horn, and went about their business. We found ourselves back on the Pacific Coast atop rocks leading to crashing waves. People were scattered around this long, narrow park. Some campers looked pretty settled, but we didn't foresee any problems with the natives.

Darkness turned Newport and the bridge into a spectacular display of lights, glowing and brilliantly reflecting against the bay. The sharp, cold gusts felt strong enough to carry us over the rocks and into the water. However, the beauty of looking across the bay at the side of the bridge and to the city of lights beyond far compensated for the cold.

We felt uneasy rocking around to the mysterious sounds of seagulls honking their horns overhead. The crashing of waves could have been hitting the side of our camper for all we knew. Still, we somehow managed to get some shuteye. This may have been a lot of trouble to go through for a night's sleep, but we had to park outside, and it seemed a small price to pay for coastline beauty.

October 17, 1992

Having finally broken away from the coast at Coos Bay, we spent a night under evergreens in the Umpqua National Forest, parking in a pulloff in cougar country within the Cascades. Again, Tracy and I decided the camper seemed level enough and we felt sure that Molly would not have to go to the restroom until the light of day.

This location enabled an early start for a quick circle around Crater Lake. This water is far bluer than the sky and deeper than any lake in the country at 1,932 feet. It is the second deepest lake in the Western Hemisphere and seventh deepest in the world. A crater at the top of Wizard Island rises seven hundred sixty feet above the water, a striking mark off to the side of the lake.

Mount Mazama occupied the site of Crater Lake almost seven thousand years ago. Then this twelve thousand foot volcano underwent a series of eruptions, creating the caldera, which now contains the lake, filled by years of snow and rain.

A long road encircled the lake. Each overlook provided a new angle of the same evergreens riding the crater to the top. One long look at this unusual body of water satisfied our craving, so we moved on. We wanted to see a little of a lot, rather than a lot of a little. Crater Lake seemed to fit into our plan. This unusual attraction only required a little time, and our Oregon chapter neared the end.

We invested in matching traveling hats during our final Oregon stop at the Pendalton Woolen Mills. With our new acquisition, we had less than two weeks to see Idaho and Utah before picking up my mother-in-law in Phoenix for her ten-day vacation with us.

The passing of a few days put us near Idaho, but we had many problems to take care of when we awoke at a truck stop in eastern Washington. After I took a sponge bath with the remaining water in the tank, we needed more water for Tracy. Furthermore, the camper began backfiring, losing power, and still had an exhaust leak. The leak seeped into the cab and was the possible cause of Tracy's headaches.

When I started the engine, which needed about five minutes of warming, Molly did her usual thing. She jumped into the passenger seat, as if we could possibly leave without her. Scanning the parking lot, she focused her eyes on a heavy man with thick glasses, standing by his car in front of us. She became so upset that her little head began to shake back and forth. Then her barking began, which got the man's attention. I believe it could get a deaf man's attention.

The man stared at Molly, a grin on his face, and began to slowly take steps toward her. Then he changed his route when Molly started biting the window during her fury, and he walked to my window instead. He came over with that same simple smile he wore on the other side, and I rolled down my window. "She's not as tough as she sounds," I confided.

After our brief discussion about the dog, I asked him if he would have a guess as to why the RV was backfiring. The guy went on a tangent, emphasizing that we should have the spark plugs checked. We needed only a spark plug wrench and extension, both Greek to me. He continued to talk theory, and I interrupted to ask if he could see if his wrench fit our plugs, just to see.

He removed the console from inside the cab and began playing around, talking more than tinkering. I never noticed a second guy walking through the parking lot to our camper because my head had been tucked below the windshield.

He entered the scene and pretty much shoved the first guy aside, taking on the task of solving our problem single-handedly.

This guy appeared to be on the ball. He stood tall and muscular, and began hands-on work.

Every time the heavy man began to speak, or might I say tried to advise Mr. Do-it, he would be shot down. The first man and Mr. Do-it surrounded the engine and exchanged ideas. Mr. Do-it haphazardly answered while checking the plugs, removing the distributor cap to check the points, and taking a screwdriver to scrape the inside edges before reinstalling the cap. He sounded surprised after noticing a thin rubber tube that had somehow come loose.

"That could be your problem," he said. "Right there. It's your vacuum hose, and it could be what's causing your engine to backfire."

He started the engine without the hose attached and revved it, and we heard the pop of backfire. Then he reattached the hose, revved it again, and the engine sounded quiet and strong. The first man kept trying to butt in over his shoulders, but Mr. Do-it seemed too busy concentrating on the task at hand.

This man claimed that he wasn't a mechanic, but liked to tinker with engines. After he finished the job, we thanked him kindly. Then we watched him walk away through the parking lot, kicking up dust on the way to a tractor-trailer idling across the parking lot. He opened the door, then climbed up and in. When I thought about this team, I asked the first man how he knew the second. He surprised us when he insisted that he had no idea who the man was.

Mr. Do-it had just crossed the lot to fix a troubled camper, a problem that most mechanics couldn't even figure out. It truly impressed us and comforted us to know that good really does exist in this world.

Now he lined up as part of a ten-truck convoy, and our opinion of truckers changed instantly. Before, they had just been those damn tanks that rolled over small guys on the highways, but now we knew that they were a community of real people. We had slowly become familiar with them from the many truck stops, but it took something like this to realize that they aren't just robots flying around the country.

The first man continued talking long after Mr. Do-it left. He had a hand in assisting me with filling the water tank. Without his presence, we would still have been in need of a mechanic. He got the ball rolling, and then helped to get the camper rolling, although he hated to see us leave. But we had to roll over one hundred miles from Washington to Idaho, and we did it without any further trouble from the camper.

Tracy tried to convince me that Molly deserved credit for the camper being fixed, but no. As far as I was concerned the barking was more of a nuisance, but she was a great rascal to have protecting the camper.

I attribute my interest more to my curiosity than to my belief. Either way, a Washington newspaper printed a story about Sasquatch sightings on an Indian reservation in Idaho, so that's where I wanted to go. Certainly, I did not expect to see Bigfoot, but who knew? I really, if nothing else, wanted to talk to people who did claim to have seen it. Tracy decided to go along for the ride.

We arrived, having moved from Clarkston to Lewiston. Could there be a correlation between these neighboring cities of different states and those early guys? We were as sure about this as we were of the state line marking the end of the first half of the trip. The beginning of the second half was about to unfold.

We passed the state line from Washington to Idaho, cheering our accomplishment. The second half of this trip did not seem attainable. We cheered and hooted some more, then continued on to look for a place to stay overnight. Our day's goal had been reached.

This was a monumental moment, but so truly inconceivable. After all we'd seen, there was still more, and just as much. The money we had started with may have been far greater than half-spent, but we had done all the necessary backtracking.

Having made it this far, we knew we had it in us to conquer it all. If we had to fight tooth and nail, then we considered it done. Corporate America may have lagged behind us, but we had no problem picking up some work in order to finish the trip. Then again, we wouldn't have a choice. In the meantime, we'd just live this life until it became essential to stop.

Our next adventure took place after dawn hovered over Flying J's truck stop. An historical park on the Nez Perce Indian Reservation in Spalding became our destiny, and mountain-sized hills on both sides of the road ushered us in.

An employee of this park claimed to have seen Sasquatch. We entered the center, walking toward the female ranger who waited for the next question. She made me feel like I should throw my numbered ticket in the little round basket and order one pound of thinly sliced American cheese.

Anyone in his right mind would feel apprehensive about asking another human being about Bigfoot, and I've been told that I'm in my right mind. So I felt silly, wondering how to ask questions about such a creature during the entire drive here. Tracy wasn't about to touch this one. She made it clear to me that I'd be on my own.

Before ordering, I reached into my right shirt pocket and with two fingers clenched the Sasquatch article. I placed it on the counter. With a false sense of confidence, I questioned her about its accuracy. She looked at me with a grin, her long brown hair hanging down far past her shoulders, then looked at the clipping placed on the counter before her.

"Oh...that thing," she said. "Yeah, someone said they saw Bigfoot over in the hills of this visitor's center." She then turned and pointed through the wall of windows to the terrain that climbed higher and higher. Her thin hair followed the turn as it swung past her shoulders.

"It stood like a human, but it was all hairy. Then they had a man stand up in the same area, and he was microscopic...so this had to be big," She informed me.

"And that's why they call it Bigfoot?" I asked.

"I guess so," she continued. "They went up to the site and measured the footprints. They measured thirteen inches...smaller footprints, indicating a female Bigfoot."

"Oh!" I queried. "They distinguish between a male and female now?"

She smiled, agreeing with the crazy sound of the statement.

"Do you believe in Bigfoot?" I asked.

"No, I don't think so," she continued. "They haven't found any dead bodies."

"You're right. Who here saw it?" I asked.

A girl working downstairs was the one who had seen it. Although I asked to speak to her, the meeting never happened, so we moved on to another hot spot.

Lapwai is the home of Donald's Café, where the Bigfoot Burger is served. We pulled into the parking lot and hesitated for about twenty minutes. I simply didn't have the guts to walk into the lunch crowd and ask about the Bigfoot sightings.

A Community Center on the reservation, a place where four monsters had been spotted in the hills beyond, would be our last chance for sightings or conversation. An Indian with a yellow hard hat on his thin black hair, who looked to be in his mid-twenties, stood at the entrance of the center with a stop/slow sign, assisting traffic through the construction. As I turned in, he confirmed that we were headed into the Community Center. We pulled in, parking with the dining room window facing the hills, and had lunch.

A half hour passed, consisting of cereal, relaxing at the dinette, and oh...glancing into the hills. I started the engine and rolled the camper to the exit, where the Indian showed us the STOP side of the sign. Standing about ten feet from my window, he asked if we had found what we had been looking for, and I responded with a "yes and no." My answer prompted him to turn the sign into a walking stick as he took steps toward the camper. "What was that?" he asked.

"Bigfoot was seen in these hills. Have you seen him?"

"No," he answered matter-of-factly, looking up at the portion of hills in question. "I guess some people said that they'd seen four of them. One other time, four more were seen in a field, and a helicopter shining a light down began to close in on them. All of the sudden...they disappeared—they were gone."

"Do you believe...in Bigfoot?" I asked hesitantly.

He looked back at the hills, offering his profile, and the squint to the side of his eye indicated deep thought. "I believe it's a spirit. My ancestors have always said that it existed as a spirit, so it's been going on for a while."

"What about the footprints? How do you explain them?" I asked.

"Spirits can be physical," he replied.

"What's your nationality?"

"American Indian."

"What tribe?"

"Shoshoni. My family background goes back to when our tribe was driven away to the reservation. My family escaped...hid...and were able to remain here."

Thus, we continued through Idaho, resigned to the fact that we would not see Sasquatch. We didn't even try a Bigfoot burger, but I had received verbal responses, which was second best, realizing that I'd see nothing of the real thing. I was just hopeful and curious...dreadfully curious.

We felt like ants weaving the camper through the massive hills, which grew as we moved on. Occasionally, we had to peel our faces off the windshield while attempting to peek at the peaks.

Sometimes travels through a particular place can be influenced by mood, whether good or bad. Route 95 to Route 55 to Boise became so inspirational that we had to use a pulloff so that we'd be able to arise again to such a setting.

Some mornings can easily start off on the wrong foot, and for me this always occurred when cold nights required much heat, which reduced the battery power. On this morning, I arose before dawn, shaking from the cold. I had to start the engine to build battery power, which in turn would generate hot air.

I also require coffee in the morning, which I usually sipped while reviewing the plans for the day or writing in my notebook before Tracy awoke. My options: freeze while I brew coffee, get heat and then brew coffee, or try for both and receive little. Either option took at least thirty minutes, then it was time to face the day. This wasn't exactly a microwave lifestyle, but, overall, a preferred lifestyle.

We found there were no bad routes through Idaho, so we decided to go to the moon. Craters of the Moon contained black lava beds as choppy as freshly plowed fields. Tracy and I walked up to a spatter cone and hung our heads overtop, getting a view from the inside.

The cone was filled with what looked like broken and charred stones. These cones had been formed during a volcanic eruption when clots of pasty lava stuck together as they fell back to earth. Our pace quickened once we learned more about this unsettled ground.

Volcanic activity began about fifteen thousand years ago. The last activity occurred about two thousand years ago. The activity generally occurs about every two thousand years. Even though the seismograph in the visitor's center had no activity forecasted, we still continued swiftly through these fields of lava. Our conclusion of Idaho sent us wheeling through Pocatello and racing to the Beehive State, which is king of the national attractions with five parks and six monuments.

October 25, 1992

A tall sign with a picture of a natural arch of stone welcomed us to Utah as we were moving right along at State number 26. A footnote on the sign advised that Utah is still the right place.

From top to bottom we were in for a treat, descending into Salt Lake City at the foot of the Wasach Mountains. The Great Salt Lake also calls this place home. Because this lake receives water from streams and inlets, but has no outlet, the salt content is eight times saltier than the ocean. It is second only to the Dead Sea, making it almost impossible for the human body to sink because of the buoyancy.

Tracy was ailing and had been for several days. We seriously considered a doctor. She hadn't been to the doctor on the entire trip, and I had been twice, which was not the norm. We rode our ailments to the limit in most cases, usually victorious at the end.

I had never imagined that Tracy could tough it out for the entire year, but that she did. We came close to seeking a doctor for her, but she fought off the fiercest virus to come along. I had never imagined that she'd be as tough as this trip required. I had also never imagined that this trip would be as arduous as it turned out.

By no means had this been the stress-free pleasure trip we thought it would be, sipping cocktails by the pool like a vacation would dictate. We had no time for that. We were traveling, not vacationing, so the acoustic guitars and art supplies in our storage area were rarely used.

We had great intentions behind every item in storage, but instead mainly involved ourselves in daily routines. We had constant concerns for simple things once taken for granted. A certain place may have water, but was it drinkable? Can we fill up our water jug, then pull it out of the refrigerator and consume it without snarling our lip and leaving an aftertaste until the next day? Wildlife? Weather? Neighborhoods?

The battle of camper maintenance was as ever-present as the possibility of breaking down in the middle of the lonely desert with the mechanical know-how of that "box of Cheerios." Bill wasn't kidding when he had said that. Sure, we had a box of tools under the bench of the dinette, but what the hell would we do with them? We had them in case someone stopped to help us.

After several more useless attempts by mechanics to solve the exhaust leak, we headed down the state through Park City, Provo, Price, and Green River. The phenomenal desert trail unfolded like a scene out of the Flintstones in Bedrock. Erosion of uplifted layers of red sandstone and limestone, once mud and silt holding up ancient seas, spread across the southern part of the state. It was a definitive picture of aridness.

We tackled Canyonlands National Park, Arches National Park, and Natural Bridges National Monument. The drives to get to them impressed us as much as the parks themselves. We felt the entire state of Utah should be designated a National Park.

It seemed impossible for Utah to be part of Earth, not to mention our own country. We feasted our eyes upon a region of mazes sculpted by the Green and Colorado Rivers. The most unusual rock formations included red, brown, and pink buttes, fins, arches, windows, and spires, all in the most remote region of the United States.

Each of the parks made us wonder about material possessions, but the most wondrous indulgence came on a hike through the Needles section of Canyonlands. Tracy and I went our separate ways around the towering mushroom-shaped rocks.

Over and around these massive rocks we hiked, and at one point I spent ten minutes crawling to the top of a mushroom for bragging rights. This strenuous risk required leaping, crawling, and pulling, but I had to do it and couldn't wait to show Tracy where I ended up.

When I made it to the top, gasping from the struggle, enabling a view of the surrounding canyon, I yelled out to Tracy below. She did not appear, nor did she answer. I kept yelling her name, which echoed throughout the canyon, until finally she appeared...on top of another mushroom across the way, which stood far higher than mine. She asked me what I wanted, and I told her that it was nothing; just wanted to know where she was.

Our final effort ushered us through Natural Bridges and to the visitor's center because of a sign indicating that our vehicle stretched one foot longer than the road through the park permitted. After a long delay, the young ranger with short blond hair came from the back room and apologized. I asked if he collected fees, and he gave an affirmative reply to which I whipped out our trusty Blue Eagle Pass, just to bust his stones about the delay.

When I asked if he could bend the rules since we only missed the length by one foot, or twelve little inches, he glanced into the parking lot to take a look. "Oh, that's nice. That'll be fine."

"Great. It's getting late, and we still have a drive ahead of us, so we're just going to whip around the loop real quick...at the posted speed, of course."

"Of course," said the stunned ranger, an uncertain grin on his face. "You must have been reading my mind. The speed limit would be best."

Winding our way out of Natural Bridges, we came upon what appeared to be a German Shepherd standing in the middle of the road with its tongue out. Slowing down, Tracy and I finally decided that it wasn't a dog after all, but a wolf. It gazed at us for a while, maybe unimpressed with the color of the camper, though that was hard to tell. But it trotted to the left of the road, up the steep incline of the hill, mixed in with the trees, and we never saw the wolf again.

October 29, 1992

When our constant movement became commonplace, and we became accustomed to traveling and the passage of time, we pinpointed our necessary progression a month prior to our reunion with Tracy's mother, Judi. We allotted a certain number of days per state in order to end up at the airport in Phoenix on Halloween.

Tracy sure was excited. Five months had passed since their reunion in Vermont, a time that had scurried into the past as a distant memory. Just two days remained as we rolled out of Utah and into our twenty-seventh state of Arizona. Tracy shook the dog back and forth in her arms, and I howled and hooted as we crossed into this new state.

We'd surely be back to Utah, though, as we had plans to bring Judi to Bryce and Zion National Parks in the southwestern part of the state. Night driving became essential for Tracy, who wanted to get close to Phoenix. After a long day of canyons and bridges and driving, she requested an additional two hundred miles in the dark. She not only wanted to get to Arizona, but through the entire Navajo Indian Reservation to Flagstaff.

Molly wasn't terribly excited about this, though, because we had been going strong all day and had already treaded one hundred miles of roadway. We landed in Mexican Hat for a break, recouping with coffee and hot chocolate. Having stretched our limbs and filled our cups, we began walking to the cab to continue on as the eleventh hour played a tune on my watch.

Molly wasn't sold. Usually she was the first one to the front, but this time she dragged her feet. Positioning her body toward the bed in back, her head faced the front as if to say, "All right, come on guys! I think we've done enough driving for today."

Tracy grabbed the weary dog and explained to her that we had to do a little more driving because we'd be picking up Grandma in Phoenix. Molly eventually passed out on her lap as we pushed on.

Through the reservation we cruised, greeted by warning signs we'd never seen before. One of the signs read: Watch for Animals Next 20 Miles. Every twenty miles stood a new sign. Then came a sign for the next one hundred twenty miles, and we wondered why there wasn't just one sign warning of animals in the entire state of Arizona. This very cold night at a truck stop in Flagstaff flabbergasted us because we had thought it wasn't supposed to be cold in Arizona.

We performed last minute camper maintenance the next day in Flagstaff in forty degree weather. Together, we scrubbed the unit inside and out. We needed winter jackets because of the cold and cherished the heat shooting from the dashboard during errands.

It wasn't until evening when we set out down Interstate 17 for Phoenix, about one hundred miles south. Phoenix ignited the horizon from afar. The glow seemed more than city lights. By now, we not only shed our jackets, but also had the windows down and our opposite elbows pointed out toward the cacti on the sides.

Phoenix welcomed us with seventy-five degree temperatures at ten o'clock at night. It was like night and day, and we kicked ourselves for not doing our chores on the bottom of the mountain. It didn't matter because this was the warmest we'd been in a while, and we instantly fell in love with Phoenix.

We pulled into a twenty-four hour restaurant in Apache Junction with our sign on the back of the camper facing the back of the building. By the time I put the shifter into park, my eyes were nearly closed. This restaurant parking lot seemed risky, but driving was riskier.

One further detail describes our desperate parking spot. It was a bar, and while drifting off to sleep, boisterous drunks awakened us. They made our very selves the subject of ridicule. Tracy was more awake than myself, and kept trying to bring me back to life. They scared Tracy with comments about our sign. They claimed that we were bragging, showing off, and they'd like to show the bride a real honeymoon.

I became scared for Tracy, and I couldn't just open the door and pretend I could take on a group of guys. I had thoughts of starting up and driving away fast, but decided to wait it out.

They never did go any further than words, and after twenty minutes of proving their ignorance, they ducked their drunken heads down and into their cars. This wasn't a wise maneuver either, but we no longer felt threatened. As we lay still and quiet in bed, we heard cars rolling past the back of the camper. Neither of us could breathe. One of the cars beeped twice in rapid succession as it passed.

It relieved us to hear them drive away, enabling us to settle down to sleep once again. Anyone who asked us if we had any trouble with people along the way received Tracy's answer that just outside of Phoenix we were subjected to a drive-by tooting.

October 31, 1992
Halloween

The five month mother-and-child reunion was greatly needed because Tracy kept asking what would be happening later that night, and my answer about kids in masks going door-to-door for candy was always inadequate. After the goings-on the previous night and such a rough travel day, I let Tracy sleep late as I enjoyed coffee outside next to a cactus, reading a newspaper. A man pulled up in a van, driving it slowly toward the camper, which remained by the curb. His left arm hung out the window, joined by his head once he stopped. "Ya sellin' that today?" I wasn't sure if I heard him right and asked for a repeat.

"I wanna know if you're sellin' the camper today?"

I began to tell him that we were only halfway through our journey. Molly nudged the back shade away from the window, poked her head between, then barked convulsively, but she wasn't looking his way. She was barking at the older dark-skinned man as he strutted past the van balancing coffee in a white Styrofoam cup.

He looked at the camper as well, actually walking up behind it and telling Molly to calm down. That only intensified her rage. He commented on the Beware of Dog sign in the matching window on the other side. Then he greeted the man in the van. These two guys knew each other, and the lanky man parked the van and helped us form a circle.

Tracy made four when she heard some deep discussions about traveling. Mr. Van seemed only interested in our camper for a down payment on his mobile home, but the other guy turned out to be quite a character. He was a weathered, sixty-three year old Indian with a bandanna around his head. He spoke like a sage, believing in what he said and feeling it. After thoroughly living for six months, our new philosophy on life was somewhat demonstrated in the life of this Indian.

He spoke about his life of freedom after asking and hearing about ours. I saw the darkness in the cup now halfway. He no longer had to balance, so his right-hand movements as he spoke could be sudden and sharp without spilling.

"What do you really need in life? As long as you can fill your belly and get the essentials, that's what's important. You don't need more than that in order to live. I travel always, and get odd jobs when I need to, but in the meantime I can live my life. What more is needed? People tell me I'm lucky to be able to live this way. I'm not lucky. They can do it too."

The nearly incensed Indian went on to explain that he was a POW of Life because of the white man, but refuses that lot, staying true to his free spirit. He couldn't comprehend how we could sleep in the city. His preference is the country, where coyotes run free.

"You missed the coyotes howling up a storm last night. What a beautiful thing." His aged eyes crinkled as he spoke.

Adamant in his philosophy, he wanted to know what was essential in life, and incorporated God into his findings.

"God is here and now—in everyone and everything. God's in the birds and the trees and everything else so beautifully placed on this earth. So you have to enjoy life now by enjoying these things before you, not waiting for your day to meet Him. People don't appreciate God now, and you have to in order to live life now."

This Native American Indian sounded convinced that his happiness could not be sustained if he surrendered to the American way of life. He could not and would not do it. He was happy. He was traveling. He was a participant in his tribal beliefs. He was living, alive, and vibrant, and his joy was contagious.

Then the van man interrupted with details about his mobile home, beautifully set in the mountains, and how he wanted to do what we were doing. He wanted our camper as a down payment. To keep him happy, I took some information from him just in case we decided that we wanted to settle down, but it was unlikely after what his friend just told us.

When the Indian disappeared, leaving only footprints and words of wisdom behind, his impression weighed heavily upon our minds. He thoroughly convinced us that we had made the right move in breaking away from what American people believe to be essential in order to appreciate what Native American Indians believe to be sacred. The old camper of ours had whisked up to people and places we no longer had to dream about. We'd sacrificed our future for the present and would have it no other way.

After encircling Sky Harbor International Airport three times, we found and merged into an appropriate parking lot for RVs. As it was Halloween, we put our traveling hats on and Tracy carried a plastic pail of candy. We entered the airport dressed as travelers with traveling hats and a pail of candy. Only these costumes fit into our budget, but they worked for us.

Tracy placed the pail of candy on the conveyor belt, watching it pass through the hanging black flaps and disappear into the metal detector. When it reappeared, Tracy offered a piece of candy to the women checking, who accepted a Tootsie Roll with a hell of a big smile.

A slight delay of the flight from Hartford to Phoenix forced us into the café sipping sodas. A middle-aged lady with shoulder-length, curly black hair sat at the table beside us and began conversing with us before her seat hit the seat.

She hailed from Manchester, New Hampshire, and told us that she would love to travel the country some day. "I've been to four or five different states, but all the states are the same anyway, so what difference does it make?"

I couldn't let it go. Last year, I may have nodded in agreement, but not now. I felt like I had to defend my country.

"All the same? We've been to twenty-seven states, and they're all strikingly different." Tracy smiled, shaking her head, and I knew that I spoke for her too. The lady easily gave in to our findings, saying that maybe they are kind of different, and now I'm sure that she'll go around saying that the states are different. She had based her findings on four or five states, assuming that all fifty were similar. Yet, Tracy and I had found no two alike. Some parts of states resembled each other, usually from the interstate, but the comparison by no means extended further.

After we scooped up Judi at the airport, she began telling us that she had heard that there existed a place in Arizona that is known as the spiritual center of the universe. Moving through stores in and around Phoenix, we happened upon one in which a lady helped us. I carefully asked where the energy or spiritual center was located. Sedona was the center. We went into further discussions of where we were from, then heard her story of living in five different states. Since she always ends up in Arizona, she thought it was meant to be.

This lady kept referring to an experience of hers, but never elaborated on the exact experience. Finally, Judi drummed up the courage to delve into this experience a bit further. "Could you tell us a little more about what that experience was?"

"Sure," she responded in the same nonchalant way, her eyes surveying the other couple of customers in the store busy holding shirts up to their shoulders. "I was driving down a road close to here...when I saw a spaceship. I thought it was a dream and didn't tell anyone for years."

Since I stood in back, I saw Judi and Tracy firmly entranced, unwilling or unable to move their heads. Wanting to know more, I quickly thought of anything to ask, and shot questions her way.

"What did you do when you saw it?"

"I was not afraid. I was communicating with them; all thirty of them. My grandson once saw a ship, but no spacemen."

"What do they look like?"

"Just like us."

"All of them?"

"Some of them. Some are very different."

I wanted to whip my head back and forth like a dog shaking dry, and then see if this lady still stood before us telling her story. I could not believe what we heard, and I knew I wasn't alone. She slowly revealed the experience in the calmest of ways, as if she was telling us of a trip to the store for milk.

The way she related the story had a soothing effect, even though the content of her story should have transformed our minds into unidentified flying objects. Her innermost thoughts, dominating her life for many years, were now deposited in our bank. It wasn't until she had met her husband that she was encouraged to discuss her experience. Then she met people who had similar experiences, and no longer felt alone.

Judi shot a glance back my way, then Tracy followed, and their eyes ended up back at the lady and the story.

"It wasn't a plane...it wasn't a glider...it wasn't a kite. I really believe that you will have an experience too, because you're open to it with your travels. You're going to see it." She paused to nod her head. "I know you are." She paused again, nodding slowly. "There's nothing to be afraid of. I don't tell many people about this, but I really believe that you people have that special energy within you." She nodded up and down again for a few seconds after her conclusion. No laugh. No smile. Nothing.

This lady handed over her business card and told us to let her know when we had an experience, not if we did, which made me wonder. Leaving the store a tad spaced out, we thoroughly examined everything that soared through the air.

Tracy and I were elated that someone else had accompanied us for a firsthand account of what we had been running into during our travels. It's unique, and you can only explain so much in regards to travel. It's living it and feeling it and breathing it, which really is the only way to receive a thorough understanding.

If we had been asked at that very moment what we were most sure about, the answer would have been that we were out west. That response would have even preceded what we had come upon while tucked away in a red rock canyon in Sedona for the evening.

Judi had originally planned to sleep in a motel every night while we parked our camper in front or shared the room. However, the atmosphere seems to change people. What had been a set plan now became so flexible that she agreed to sleep in the camper surrounded by this red rock.

Darkness accompanied us down Interstate 17 into Sedona. Riding a stretch north of Phoenix through the high concentration of Cacti to both sides, it plainly felt like a perfect night for a spaceship. I wouldn't discount the possibility that spaceships and

222

spacemen exist, and maybe my open mind led me to strain my eyes during the entire drive. The lady had sure convinced me when she kept repeating that we'd see one. Tracy insisted that she too had been convinced of this phenomenon, and we all wondered when it would come.

For a spell, Tracy and Judi sneaked a catnap while I pushed through the desert before dusk and headlights. I felt kind of silly driving a camper alone with that wedding message on the back and even more so when Molly insisted on sitting in the passenger's seat and looking out through the windshield. People enjoyed this entertainment while passing the camper. My evidence included twisted mouths and crinkled foreheads when they looked back.

When we reunited in the cab, the free campground book directed us to Sedona. We ventured down a slow moving dirt road, which rocked the camper and its occupants until we stopped to eye a spur road with no outlet. We paused to view a couple of campers parked along the circle. The site was a round dirt parking lot, but since we'd learned that anything can be what you make of it, I shut the engine off and we gave it a shot.

When the engine quieted, we could hear singing; the sound of the Blues sneaking around the corner of bushes. Unsure if this area permitted overnight parking, we agreed to follow the tune to see who sang, while covering up our true intentions by asking about parking.

As we rounded the corner, two guys sat in complete darkness, playing music with only a harmonica. Their vocals became much louder, even evil . The three of us exchanged looks of uncertainty. Then we noticed two couples sitting on a picnic table by a campfire strumming guitars to softer music in a section adjacent to the two guys. We huddled inconspicuously, whispering our thoughts on which path to follow. The three of us voted alike.

We opted for the campfire songs, slowly altering our path, easing our way over. When we got close enough, we noticed that they belted out tunes in a foreign language. We huddled again, determining that we probably wouldn't have a lot to discuss, so our footsteps retreated to the Blues brothers.

Again we went unnoticed, like three ghosts. It was more eerie not being able to see their faces even while standing immediately before them. They were so wrapped up in song that the short round of applause we afforded them when the music concluded took them by surprise. We still could not determine if our actions were apropos, but something drove us to find out about these two guys.

The man singing his heart out sat up in a lawn chair inches from the ground. His friend sat about two feet higher, while playing harmonica with one hand and firmly slapping his other hand on his leg. Both men tapped their feet up and down on the earth.

Unsure, but committed, the three of us waited for their awareness as the scent of beer permeated the air before us. When the applause died down, they greeted us, thanked us, and advised us that we had chosen a beautiful red rock canyon to visit. Although it was too dark for us to appreciate, we agreed nonetheless. The chill in the evening air forced our hands inside of our winter jackets. Had we learned a foreign language quickly, we could have been warm.

Craig was a rough-sounding forty-eight year old Buddhist, his face mysteriously tucked inside the darkness of the snorkel on his jacket. Eric was an enigma within a small baseball cap, forty years old himself, but soft-spoken. Once we got a feel for each other, the conversation opened up, but an underlying uncertainty tormented us all.

They praised us for our travels, and when I asked them if they were traveling, Eric laughed and reached over to slap Craig's arm. This made a popping sound on his jacket. "This one is the traveling man," said Eric of Craig.

"Have you seen all of the states?" I asked.

"Yes," he said, and again they laughed.

Craig and Eric claimed to have been gypsies for twenty years and acquaintances for merely one week. The way they joked back and forth, sometimes hitting each other softly, gave us the impression that they had a long history together. That wasn't the case. They were living hand-to-mouth, working only when necessary. They eliminated the amenities of life and were living their lives to the fullest in these natural surroundings.

Craig admitted to having taken more drugs than most people live to tell about, which raised interesting questions from Tracy.

"What's the correlation between spirituality and drugs? Why do you need drugs if you have spirituality?"

Craig paused before answering that drugs increase his spirituality, but he never adequately answered the questions. The contradiction was obvious. If his spirituality consisted solely of becoming one with nature, then why escape through drugs? Nonetheless, he spoke of the freedom, beauty, and reality of travel. It was what the Indian had preached in Apache Junction almost verbatim.

Eric, the quieter of the two, was reduced to sobs while discussing his life as a gypsy. He began at age seventeen, when he couldn't hold a job. None of us were sure if his tears were real, so we did not react. Eric continued as soon as he was able to compose himself.

We just stood there, caught between the cold evening and the hot fire, finally convinced of the sincerity of his sobbing. This only increased our anxiety because now his depression was mixed with alcohol and possibly drugs. Sure, we feared for our lives, but we couldn't let them know. We played it cool, keeping our distance.

Eric would sometimes get lonely, and his sister could never get herself to be supportive of his decision to live this way. They had once been close, but now no longer were. They had become so different. She was very materialistic, which was exactly what Eric had adamantly rebelled against.

Craig, the son of a multi-millionaire, claimed to have given up everything for nothing in order to satisfy his life on his own. He gave up the chance to float through life with anything he could possibly desire. He could have had everything, but that wasn't what he wanted out of life. He wanted happiness and freedom without the root of all evil, so he gave up the fortune only to become enriched by nature.

Both of them sat beside their vans, which served as their home and transportation. At one point, Judi walked behind Tracy and hugged her for warmth. Eric got up, walked to the van, and draped a blanket over them when he returned.

Everything took place under the cloak of blackness, as each side had to paint faces on the other through voice interpretations. After a couple of hours of deep discussions, we requested a closing song to remember them by, and Craig struggled with a spontaneous lyrical message about our traveling.

Eric played his harmonica with one hand, slapped his leg with the other, and tapped his foot in conjunction with Craig's. They told us to make music with life, and after handshakes, we parted as faceless friends.

November 1, 1992

This time when we ran into Craig and Eric, they had faces. Both were clean-cut and intelligent, but more importantly, the mysteriousness of not seeing a face ended for us all. Craig looked all of his forty-eight years, but that wasn't a bad thing. His black and graying beard, together with his red beret, gave him a distinguished appearance. Eric looked about thirty of his forty years with a light brown start to his beard, neatly trimmed hair, and a white baseball cap.

Molly sniffed them out, becoming a little too boisterous and ending up in Tracy's hands. The dog looked a little more suspicious of them now that they had devoured the eggs they had scrambled over the fire. When Craig went to pet the dog, Molly snapped at his hand and drew blood. Craig shook it back and forth, then stuck the wounded finger in his mouth rather than using our first-aid kit. That's how we left the two gypsies, moving on to further spirituality.

A Hopi Indian named Big Bear invited us into the back of a warehouse, then into a small room that he called his home. It was time for our Tarot card reading in Sedona. This tall bald Indian wore a bandanna around his head. We followed him into a very small room. He then instructed us to sit on two bare mattresses with our backs against the wall.

Looking around the congested and informal room, again wondering what we were doing and why, I watched Big Bear shuffling his cards in preparation for his readings. He spread the cards in piles in the shape of a clock, then put the remaining cards in the center. The silence of the room was interrupted only when he asked a question and received an answer.

Big Bear told me to slow down in order to fully appreciate life around me. He then told Tracy that she would become a channeler and that she would find her calling in life within the next six months. He told Judi that she had to stop worrying. He kept the readings focused around these main individual concerns.

Three readings and three hours later, we left this basement mentally exhausted. However, his philosophy paralleled the philosophy of everyone else in Arizona. Judi could not believe what had filled her life in just two days out west, but she cherished it and craved more. She had started the trip with an open mind, a point in her favor, so she was able to enjoy everything that passed her way.

The fact that people out west really take the time to talk impressed her the most. People out here think nothing of leisurely conversing with strangers. The land is very much like the philosophy because both are so open.

A constant flow of information drifted toward us from all angles. The basic motto is to be at peace with oneself. Also, you should do what you desire in order to be happy with life, and not waste that precious life toiling away in a job you despise. Be yourself and live your life, and have fun with it because it is possible. When you hear something enough, you start to believe it.

November 4, 1992

We had to squeeze in Bryce Canyon and Zion National Parks before moving Judi to Las Vegas, where she would fly back to Hartford. She asked to see as much as possible in ten days, so we motored along as we normally did, and our plans did not have to be altered in doing so.

Entering Utah through Kanab, we had no idea that we were approaching our favorite attraction in all of these United States. Thinking that the Grand Canyon would take the honor, we found the hole too grandiose to deeply appreciate. But to get to the awesome display in Utah, we rode through the Dixie National Forest and Red Canyon. Through back-to-back tunnels, precisely carved through the red rock mountain covering the road, we entered Bryce Canyon National Park. This landmark fit perfectly into southern Utah, a land unmatched.

Our first and only stop in the park came at Sunset Point. We pulled aside for an overview of a sea of glowing, reddish-brown, towering and eroded rock structures contained within a canyon. Somehow these rocks balanced on the earth. We were instantly taken in, drawn to these pointy, needle-like towers of rock. A path descended to the base of this natural city. We eyed each other, mouths agape, nodded, and moved down the path. We then took part in what turned into a strenuous ninety minute hike on Navajo Trail.

The temperature chilled us through our winter coats while at the top, but by the time we had descended to the bottom, the sun warmed our coats away. Walking down steep switchbacks, every step became so picturesque that Tracy and Judi both snapped a roll of film before even reaching the bottom. But they had feared that might happen, so they had stocked up on film before descending.

Eventually we became dwarfed at the base of these needles, feeling insignificant, yet content. We agreed whole-heartedly with the Indian, the gypsies, and the tarot card reader, because a feeling overcame us that was as if nothing could go wrong. There's no comparison to being high on life. So many times we'd been subjected to it because we were living meaningfully with the earth, and not just on it.

Our traveling hats came in handy as erosion in progress rained pebbles down upon us, so at least two-thirds of our group entered this canyon well prepared. Further down the trail, we experienced windows, bridges, arches, and serenity within this unworldly fascination, all the more striking against the dark blue-hued sky. The position of the sun determined the shades of brown at any particular moment. If you stared long enough, you could see the shades change.

But it seemed difficult to stare. My eyes constantly scanned this sea of rock, not so much to appreciate it than to believe it. Striped rock surrounded us. Appreciation automatically kicked in. Judi stopped in her tracks, snapping pictures of awesome beauty. But we wanted to make sure she returned home with many experiences, so we motored along.

Zion held its own, undaunted by our experiences at Bryce. Large hills of sheer rock barraged us, soaring overhead for our entire drive through the park. A mile-long tunnel through the mountainside became a tight squeeze, forcing me to drive on the yellow line because the sides of the tunnel's interior hung too low.

Fortunately, since we arrived later in the day, few cars visited this road. We slowly made our way toward the light at the end of the tunnel. A couple of times, I had to move over as far as I could, then stop the camper to allow a car to pass. If we came upon another camper, then one of us would have had to backtrack.

A couple of arched windows cut out of the side of the tunnel enabled us to peek into the canyon below and helped to light the inside. The other side of the tunnel showed us yet another world. Judi instantly gave up the passenger's seat for the pillow between the two seats. She became dizzy while viewing the steep descent via switchbacks into the canyon. She also became nervous, unable to see the side of the road through the passenger's window. The dizzying view from the top showed where the road would take us.

The winding switchbacks did nothing for Judi, and our sounds of contentment made no difference to her. She sat down with the serious stare of a sick person. If she looked at the beauty before her, then she would pass out. Once through the canyon, we needed to camp in the park at a campground surrounded by massive rock, next to the surging Virgin River. Dusk forced this move.

A couple of hikes along the giant rocks the next afternoon teased our appetites. After our jaunt, we rolled on to the city of St. George in search of a picnic along the way. A grocery store at the end of the main strip stocked our picnic basket. Across the street from the parking lot, a private drive crept up the side of a mountain.

We felt a little adventurous. Besides, we had no place to drop a blanket. The urge to find out about the mountaintop excited us far more than moving on to a park, and the overlook looked quite enticing.

After a unanimous vote, the camper chugged to the top of the mountain, where sat a private airport. I parked the camper on the edge of the lot so our dining room window would overlook the entire city of St. George. Our cookout attached us to this surrounding like Velcro. It became our home for the night.

Darkness converted St. George into a city of lights below us. The next morning, we witnessed the city lights being replaced by the emergence of the sun showing itself from the mountaintop. We wanted to stay put, but we had something else planned, which would be a large part of our trip. This slow, soothing transformation inspired us to prepare for Las Vegas. We pushed through the northwest corner of Arizona into Nevada, the three of us hooting and howling our way into the Pacific Time zone.

Welcome to Nevada: 125 Years of Vision. The colorful sign containing a wizard greeted us on Interstate 15, but Route 69 along

Lake Mead was our entrance to Las Vegas, arriving before the true city of lights glittered. If we ever remember an arid picture of the desert, this moment would come to the surface of our minds. Mounds rolled us around cacti as the temperature warmed and our mouths shriveled.

The strip of casinos buzzed with people, instantly putting us in the mood, but Tracy and I argued about setting a limit. Although it sounded as if an auction was being conducted within the camper, we finally settled on twenty dollars each for the first night.

The best bargain led us to the Excalibur Hotel, but it must have been too good because the rooms were booked solid for two weeks. The parking lot looked more than attractive to Tracy and me though, and that's where we stayed. We could not remove ourselves from the camper quickly enough, bumping into each other along the exit.

Thirty-five dollars evaporated quickly and effortlessly for Tracy and me, quarter after quarter sliding gently into the slots with no million dollar payoff. It wasn't the ideal beginning, but with the free parking and the All-You-Can-Eat-Buffet, I think we came darn close to breaking even.

Waking up in the back parking lot of the Excalibur, which gave me the impression of Disneyland with the colorful castle features, we prepared for what would be the craziest day of the trip. The three of us rode a crowded bus down the strip. The rude driver warned that if everyone didn't migrate to the back of the bus, he'd have to pop a wheelie. He never smiled during or after his lovely comment.

After being safely deposited onto a sidewalk, the Silver City Casino started our day, but nickels replaced our quarters. We'd have to hang it up before noon if we resumed gambling with quarters to start the day.

Free fanny packs drew us over to Circus Circus, but we ended up being lured into the El Morocco Motel by a guy dressed in a bear suit. He handed out free passes to see a four show performance highlighted by an Elvis Presley impersonator. The bear looked like he deserved a hard time, so we stood around providing just that.

A microphone sticking through the mouth of his costume rang out information about a free show to passersby on the street, but it also enabled him to announce, "Folks...these people are harassing Homey the Bear!"

Homey promised to buy back our drinks if we thought the show unworthy, so the three of us gave this two-drink minimum a shot. This may have been a mistake, because Tracy wasn't much of a drinker until this night, when she became silly and awfully bold. After hearing Elvis inform the crowd that he was also a reverend, Tracy jumped up to talk to a black man named René, who was sitting at the bar. He too had been handing out passes, but on the other side of the street. Tracy asked him if he could help us get our wedding vows renewed onstage.

Before I knew what was happening, and with music blocking any chance of my hearing, René rose to his feet and brought Tracy to Elvis' manager. The manager couldn't promise anything, but told her he would talk to Elvis on his break. Judi and I could see them discussing this backstage from where we sat off to the side. She buzzed and rolled along as never before.

"I'm gonna continue being bold," she said upon returning.

She walked up to Terry Presley, who is the cousin of the real Elvis Presley, while he sat at the bar. She wanted his autograph for her friend back in Connecticut who is also an Elvis impersonator.

Tracy received it, and then the manager presented her with the Elvis impersonator as she returned to our table. The manager pointed Tracy out, introducing Elvis to the three of us. Elvis had stopped renewing vows on stage, and began lecturing us as to what matters most, which was for us to be together.

"But could you still renew our vows?" Tracy blurted out.

Elvis hesitated before answering with carefully chosen words. "Yeah...I could."

"For free?" Tracy shot back.

Elvis hesitated again as he leaned over the round table, his hands holding on so he could be low enough to hear over the music. "For free?" He thought some more, but could not compete with Tracy's determination, nor could he refuse her big smile.

"For love," she tried, and he surrendered.

"For love? Yeah...I could do it for love. But the chapel costs forty dollars."

"We don't need a chapel if you can do it in our camper," Tracy shot back.

Elvis paused again before he agreed, then left for a brief moment to get us his phone number for the next day's reunion. He returned with his phone number written on a large photograph of himself as the King, for which he charged everyone else five dollars. Judi and I looked at each other across the table in disbelief, wondering what had gotten into her daughter. Was it Vegas Fever?

Before the show ended, we had to leave because we had a wedding to prepare for the next day. We had to clean the camper. We also needed people to stand in for us. Judi was an obvious selection for the Maid of Honor, but who would be Best Man?

We ran into the answer upon our exit, reuniting with Homey the Bear, who still had that microphone stuck in his mask. He announced to the street, "Come on in to see the Elvis show. Look at these happy people, who just came out of the show."

Homey peeled off his mask. "You guys are walking billboards," he said. We told him our business, and he told us that he would be honored to stand in as Best Bear.

Across the street stood René. He wasn't in his costume, but he was performing the same task to the swarm of people. He became insurance if Homey couldn't attend. He told us that he was from Storrs, Connecticut, where Tracy and I attended the University of Connecticut. René, a struggling musician, was trying out his fourth large city for size. He broke out with a verse from Mighty Mouse: I've come to save the dayyyyyyyyyyyyy!

He was soon swept away by a large crowd coming toward him, but his pitch could still be heard while we walked a fair distance away. René followed people down the sidewalk while singing at the top of his lungs about this free pass. That is entertainment at its best in Las Vegas. We didn't have to spend the big bucks on a show. Entertainment was offered for free by a struggling musician with true talent, who handed out passes while awaiting his big break.

We made a final stop at Circus Circus to pick up our free fanny packs, but we didn't want our day, our momentum, or our adrenaline to end. A little old lady with a nametag reading Bertha stood behind the merchandise booth waiting to hand three pink fanny packs over to us. With delirium intact, I asked Bertha if she could autograph the three fanny packs.

233

"What do you want my autograph for?" asked Bertha, who laughed during the agreement and the actual signing of her first name on all three. We walked off with our autographed Bertha packs, and I turned around to see her still laughing away at her moment of fame.

Into the nearest bathroom went Tracy and Judi. Shortly thereafter, out of the bathroom walked a couple of laughing ladies. Tracy and Judi soon came out laughing and looking at me like they were going to bust a gut if they didn't tell me what had just occurred. Tracy had apparently lined up a couple of female photographers for our wedding, asking for the favor under the stalls.

On Judi's last day with us, we had a wedding to plan. We cleaned the camper. We cleaned ourselves. We all suffered from nervous amusement, wondering how we got into this predicament. However, between Elvis, the bear, and the beer, our times somehow got crossed and the wedding never happened.

We took Judi through it all, but she was a true sport and a happy camper by the trail's end. She slept at truck stops, traveled dirt roads, and bathed in our small bathroom using a dishpan and cups of water poured over her head. She adjusted well, learning our daily survival techniques, and any doubts that she had harbored about our journey had been eliminated.

The Excalibur became our home even after Judi flew out of Las Vegas, and we ended up completing one week in the same spot. However, our search for temporary employment in Las Vegas ceased. This city wasn't camper-friendly when it came to a dump station or water, so we moved on to California.

November 14, 1992

The California Border Patrol stops all traffic entering the state to ask if there is fruit in the car, and if so, they'll take it. An insect in the core of some fruit means that all fruit is confiscated and thrown in a dumpster.

I was immediately shot back in time to when we stopped in Ashland, Oregon to see a former Glastonbury resident named Carole. As this retired family friend drove us into northern California to show us Mount Shasta and Yrica, she told us an incredible story about the capabilities of human beings being faced with hardship. When Carole first crossed into California and discovered the fruit patrol, she became enraged. Having just purchased four shiny, red apples, she backed her car up and ate every last one of them.

"I wasn't going to let them take my apples," she protested vehemently. "I just bought them."

We threw all of our bad fruit in a plastic grocery bag and placed it on the floor between our seats for when the border patrol stopped us. However, they had to conduct a search underneath the camper for gypsy moth eggs since we hailed from Connecticut, so we had to pull the camper aside anyway.

The search conductor let us know that he would be underneath the camper, and I mentioned that while he was down there we'd appreciate if he checked for any leaks. He never really responded with more than a snicker, but when he popped his head up afterwards, he told us about a leak in the master cylinder of the brakes. He asked me to lift the hood, then proceeded to examine the brake fluid, which was fine, but advised us to keep a watchful eye on it.

We had visited the town of Tracy in Minnesota, and Maynard in Massachusetts, so it would only be fair for us to pop over to Glenn in California. Population 280. Elevation 95. In the post office, the postal worker stamped the back of my hand, then Tracy took pictures of me gloating under the town sign. Once I got my fill, we drove toward the coast.

November 18, 1992

Redwoods stunned us even before we reached the park, and when we finally arrived, the enormity of these trees left a lasting impression on us. It fascinated us to walk up, touch, and stand beside something so massive, and we reserved time to do so at a leisurely pace. We didn't reach the visitor's center until the end of the day, but we managed to slip through the doors before closing. A ranger looked at us as if awaiting a question, so I shot one his way from across the room.

"Where are the campgrounds around here?

"Developed campgrounds?" He responded.

"Free campgrounds," I shot back.

He advised us that campers are always lined up along a stretch on the Pacific Ocean because of the free parking. That worked in the most wonderful way for us, sliding right into our plans. We had passed these campers on the way up to the park, but a sign prohibiting camping on the other side of the road gave us the impression that it was a Day Use area.

The dining room window overlooked the ocean, and the open windows enticed the explosion of smashing waves right through the air and into the camper. This fierce crashing made it seem as if the waves would be visiting us, perhaps toppling the camper. They were more threatening after the sun sank below the ocean.

We ate dinner, looking out at the ocean. We looked out at the ocean until we could no longer see it. This was the life, and we never wanted it to end.

By the time the sun had wrapped around to the other side of the sky, we motored down the coast. Eureka: Yes, through that city we drove, en route to the real coastal drive on Route 1. The camper struggled up these twisting, turning roads. They proved to be too much for a tractor-trailer, which had missed a sharp turn coming down. The wheels stuck up from a ditch, and the rescue team looked as though the hard part was over. Up higher we drove, even more cautiously than before.

Our climb to the top became a thing of the past when the sky opened up, and the coast arched before us. Now we could verify the many reported concerns we had heard regarding our motorhome and moving down the coast. I soon learned my fears had been unfounded, or else my practice in the many mountains had strengthened my craft.

The coastal drive on Route 1 proceeded through monstrous mounds and hills. Seals spoke to us from an inlet in Fort Brag and occasionally emerged for a quick lap on the surface and a little sunning. Ridiculous gas prices soaked drivers along the coast. Gigantic rocks sat isolated in the ocean with no ties to land. Roads wound up and down the mountains, but I safely managed to look from the road to the coast to the road. Then we started humming the theme to Hawaii Five-O.

We spent the night thirty miles north of San Francisco in the solitude of a fishing access area.

"We're in California," I said as we both nestled into our armchair pillows in our corner of the camper.

"We're in California," Tracy echoed. "This is my dream, but it probably won't hit me until we leave. So far, it's everything I envisioned."

Our weary bodies drifted from one dream into another.

Although we got off to a late start the following morning, we edged our way to the big city hoping for a truck stop and a day off. San Francisco had a layer of fog, which rose over the entire city. International orange approached us before we knew it. Up and over the bay we drove, over the Golden Gate Bridge. This gave us a panoramic view of the city jutting out over the water, then down we moved into San Francisco. The graded Route 101 into the city offered even steeper side streets. Our choices were up or down, with houses piled on top of each other in this bustling city. The extensive bridge impressed us, and although we had been forced over it, we drove willingly.

The second day in the city, while trying to find a parking spot for a motorhome on the street, we ended up locating the best spot in the United States. The meter had a one-hour limit, and it cost one quarter per twenty minutes, so I began with the coins. I deposited quarter number one, but didn't hear it drop into other coins when I turned the lever. The dull thud sounded like coin against metal.

On the other side of the parking meter, the coin door was missing. My lonely coin sat on the bottom waiting for me to rescue it before someone else did. Back on the other side of the meter, I noticed a twenty minute reading. I reinserted the quarter, twisted, rebated, reinserted, twisted, rebated, smiled, and we went on our way with one hour to spare.

The series of steep rolling hills making up San Francisco proved difficult to climb in a large vehicle, so our walk to Chinatown became an uphill battle on the sidewalks with steps. The cars parked side-by-side nearly perpendicular to the sidewalk looked as though they would topple. We didn't want anything to do with this city during rush hour or after dark, so we departed after a morning and early afternoon on the town.

The following day, we pushed further down the coast, ending up in San Luis Obispo, and parking on a dead end side street across from a restaurant. Again, too tired to move on, our standards became atrocious. However, another car and trailer parked behind us, so this mix worked.

Then came a knock on our camper door, which was the second knock in many days. Before I could look to see who knocked, Tracy began discussing our need for a doorbell. Through the window I saw the lady from the trailer, so I opened the door to hear her request for mayonnaise.

She began speaking at length about what a cruel world in which we live. Her paranoia became apparent from the beginning, speaking of the evils of traveling at night and her inability to trust a soul on this planet.

The trailer parked behind our camper represented her home on the road, literally, which she had shared with her daughter ever since her RV had been stolen from an RV park. On and on she preached about how this is such a miserable world. She hated California, especially this town of San Luis Obispo, yet remained here even though her home had wheels. We didn't bother making the connection for her.

Mrs. Paranoia knew of a man in town who had sixteen thousand dollars of her life savings, and told us she wanted to hire a hit man if she didn't get it returned. We showed her the Pepperguard defense spray that was our insurance against perpetrators, which we'd yet to use. I then offered to spray the man for half the cost of a hit man.

She did not respond, but we scooped the mayonnaise into a plastic cup and tried to shake her loose. When our dinner smelled ready, the tone of my voice changed to indicate someone would be leaving, and it worked. Our neighbors kept to themselves for the remainder of the evening.

Following our peaceful night's sleep, the camper rolled us further down the coast to Carpinteria, where we looked for Santa Claus Lane to take pictures that we'd put on our Christmas cards. We afforded a day to snap pictures of us on the beach. Tracy cradled Molly in her arms, and before the automatic timer snapped off at the tripod, we had to advise Molly to look at the camera. It was quite difficult calling the dog to look straight ahead when she only owns the brain capacity to look at the messenger of the command.

November 26, 1992
Thanksgiving

Our first major holiday found us waking up on the side of the road with a long string of other campers. The ocean was pounding against the beach just over a cement wall. Across the street lay railroad tracks, and we walked the difficult rocky incline to where they rested. The other side of the tracks fell sharply into grass leading to prickly brush.

Needing to snap off a roll of pictures for Christmas, Tracy set the tripod on the elevated tracks and I sat on one rail in order for her to properly focus. We saw no danger because we could see far down in both directions of the track. However, as she finished preparations, red lights began to flash, and a white headlight came at us a great distance away. These stories are all too frequent. We didn't want to be another statistic which people wonder how the hell that could happen, or what the hell went through our minds other than a train?

Instead of descending the rough terrain back to the street, we figured that we'd head for the brush, allowing a twenty foot separation from the tracks. Then when the train whistled past, we'd continue with our session. However, things didn't work as planned. The slow-moving train made it to us after about five minutes. The engineer waved, then eased the train to a stop, trapping us between the train and the brush.

The length of this train appeared too great to walk around, and we couldn't see either end anyway. While trapped, waiting for the train to move on, we could vaguely see passengers on the two levels looking down at us through tinted windows. The train left after fifteen long minutes. We could then resume our shots, which surely contained at least one thousand words.

As the time came for us to enjoy Thanksgiving Day with full hookups, we set off for Santa Paula, parking in front of the office before registering. Mountain View Campground cost twenty dollars, but Thanksgiving Day deserved it. Since the lady running the grounds had prepared to pig out on turkey, she told us to pick a site and we'd settle the finances later.

Back at the camper, our ailing starter informed us, in the only way a starter knows how, that it had expired. So Thanksgiving for us began by pushing our twenty-two foot motorhome, packed with a year's supply of belongings, through the gravel roads of the campground and into the site.

As luck would surely dictate, these sites had been designed for campers to back in. Tracy stood outside, pushing the steering wheel with her right hand and the driver's door with her left. I pushed from behind, digging my sneakers in for support, and the camper sailed along at speeds exceeding two inches per minute. Our destination was slightly inclined, so sometimes we moved two inches forward and four inches back before Tracy could find and apply the brakes.

A gray-haired businessman from New York hopped out of his trailer to assist us with this arduous task. Amazingly enough we doubled our speed, huffing, puffing, and pushing the camper down the road. Then we backed it into the site until the hookups for water, sewer, and electric could be met.

As we neared the site, gritting our teeth just to keep the slow, budging pace, Tracy poked her smiling head out the door and said, "Let me know when you want me to take my foot off the brake." Soon after that, I huffed and puffed our gratitude toward this Good Samaritan as he too keeled over and tried to recapture his breath.

We dined on our Thanksgiving chicken later that evening with thoughts of repair bills dancing in our heads. We did experience a much quieter holiday than the normal gathering of our families, outside of the overanxious dog who wouldn't settle for a mere pinch of a dinner roll. We tried our best to have a wonderful holiday on the road, but a high tide of problems made us wonder if we could keep our heads above water.

The day after Thanksgiving, as I sat up at the dinette sipping caffeine and writing down my thoughts, I felt the camper gently swaying back and forth. This type of movement is normally the result of wind, or whenever Tracy or I move, but I looked to see her sleeping on this calm morning. I asked her if she had moved, but she declined. I continued writing, and the memory vanished with the morning.

When Tracy popped the television on at noon, we heard the top news story of an earthquake east of Los Angeles at Big Bear Lake. This aftershock from a June tremor registered as a 5.4 on the Richter scale. I quickly fetched the map to figure out our distance to be one hundred miles from the epicenter.

"Didn't you ask me if I was moving around this morning?" asked Tracy.

"Yes," I said, having formed no association after the passing of a few hours. Then I became motionless in thought once I realized the connection. "We felt that earthquake!" I said in disbelief, staring ahead, remembering the movement of the camper. "We were in an earthquake!"

I was excited, yet relieved that one of my worse fears passed by nearly unnoticed. However, scientists note that this high desert region had experienced forty thousand related quakes during the previous eight months. Tracy summed it up well when she said that every day is an earthquake in the camper.

With the planet still, I squeezed one more start out of the starter and drove to a garage for repairs. The sympathetic campground owner had recommended the garage and eased the sting of the repair bill by knocking twenty dollars off the twenty dollar campground fee. Then she handed me a bag of tangerines that would have gone bad if she didn't give them away.

Continuing down the coast through Malibu, Hollywood, and Beverly Hills, our starter landed us at Newport Beach a few days later. Tracy wanted to be able to say that she had gone swimming in the Pacific Ocean, and the late fall season did not deter bragging rights. Even dipping our toes in the water felt suicidal, but Tracy convinced me that I'd get used to it. I painstakingly made it to my waist without suffering a heart attack, but completely submerging myself was out of the question.

Tracy dunked as far as her shoulders twice, claiming that she was the only one who went swimming. The ensuing debate wasn't worth my breath because she held firm to her findings, and we quickly walked out of the ocean and back to the camper. Iced tea and iced Pacific Ocean gave me an artificial second wind, enough to push further down the coast. Tijuana, Mexico stepped up to the plate.

November 30, 1992

We tossed ideas around a bit, and then decided to just pursue Mexico, because our plan included the forty-eight states, Canada and Mexico. Otherwise, an important ingredient would be missing. Trying to avoid the parking fee, we pulled into a factory outlet on the United States side, and made like customers. This might be the oldest trick in the book, but our visit would be brief.

After parking and preparing for this new country, I heard a commotion outside. I looked out through the windshield to see a Mexican frantically bending a license plate up and down with both hands in an attempt to remove it from a car. He tossed it in the car after succeeding in his mission.

Another Mexican performed the same task two spots over. Looking around, I noticed a few more doing the same thing, so I exited the camper to make sure that our plate was intact. When I made my way to the back of the camper, I noticed yet another Mexican sneaking about with the word "GUILTY" tattooed across his forehead. He tried extracting a plate from the back of a van parked one spot over from the camper. It was against Tracy's wishes that I go outside. The Mexican looked up at me and stopped working. "Do you huv a sacrew driva?"

I walked over for a closer look at his work. "What are you doing?"

Although very uncertain about the situation, I puffed up my chest and kept my shoulders back, acting confidently unconcerned, like a bad John Wayne movie. He sounded as if he needed the tool urgently, but I denied the loan without knowledge of his true intentions. His words came rapidly, and his nervousness prevented a complete sentence.

His actions reeked of paranoia; each movement associated with a quick survey of his surroundings. He pointed to a temporary pass from Mexico, taped to the inside of the back window, claiming to no longer be an American. When I asked why everyone was taking plates off cars, he claimed ownership of the car he worked on, and reiterated that he was now a Mexican, like the others.

They all jumped into their respective automobiles, tearing out of the parking lot and vanishing. Another Mexican greeted me with a fistful of CD's before I could return to Tracy, asking if I wanted to buy any. I looked him straight in the eye and told him that we didn't have a CD player, and he too vanished.

After crossing through the gates, we entered into Mexico, country number three. It was that easy. Nobody checked us or questioned us, which seemed rather strange when crossing a border into another country. It seemed wrong, almost criminal, but in no time, we found ourselves walking past booth after booth of insistent craftsmen. They went as far as chasing us down for a sale, and it became obnoxious real fast.

One Mexican insisted that we take home a hooded cape for Tracy for thirty-eight dollars. We had no desire for this cape.

"I only have twenty dollars," I said.

"I'll let you have it for thirty."

"I said that I only have twenty."

"Oh, then how about twenty-five?"

"I only have twenty," I reminded him, and we walked.

"Okay!" he screamed down the street. "Twenty."

But we continued on, past a little girl with a dirty face waving a cup in our faces, and then past two nurses holding cups, though this was not as shocking. Tracy and I walked along in each other's arms, and she kept whispering to me that she didn't want to be in

Mexico any longer. It wasn't as bad as when she had visited as a kid, but she still felt uncomfortable.

Back then, she had seen kids selling meat. She had seen a kid drop a piece of meat, pick it up, brush it off with his hand, and return it to the table. She saw flies swarming over the meat, and children who looked dirty and neglected. It had frightened this child.

We never saw that, but we never made it more than one hundred steps into Mexico before our annoyance with these craftsmen proved too great to continue. We couldn't walk past a single booth without being harassed. It felt like a used car salesman's convention. We shook them away, one after another, then agreed that we had officially been to Mexico, for the record.

We had certainly seen enough, and with concerns for the camper and the dog, we agreed on an early exit. Back at the gates, we witnessed an attempted escape of Mexicans over a wall to America. Three males converged to form a vertical chain, standing on each other's shoulders, while the top Mexican reached up about a foot shy of the top. He anxiously stretched to the sky, hoping to grow, and growing for hope.

Below them stood a Mexican girl acting as the lookout as a dozen or so Americans passed by. They then went through the legal passageway to the states. People strolled past them every which way as if nothing out of the ordinary was taking place.

Back in America, this time being questioned, we made it back to the camper. We pushed our way north, having decided to persevere up to Sequoia, then into Death Valley before leaping out of California. About an hour or so after pulling away from Mexico, an officer stopped us at a blockade on Route 5.

"What are you doing?" he asked.

"Traveling around," I answered.

"Oh," he said, and knocked twice on the top of my door. "Have a nice trip."

December 4, 1992

There appeared to be a city glimmering like a great ball of fire in the desert evening. I drove on, confused, because the map indicated that nothing should be there. I called Tracy up to the front to help me solve this mystery. Closing in on this mystery city, we discovered that it was no city after all. We had reached the Nevada State line, which welcomes visitors with dozens of casinos.

Driving into the fireball and pulling into a casino parking lot, we had to decide to either spend the night or move on. It was a place to stay, but could we knock off some more miles toward Phoenix? We thought it best to persevere.

After brewing coffee, we sipped our way to Laughlin, Nevada, an eighty mile stretch through dark desert. The night drive blackened mysteriously as we passed between groves of Joshua trees. We kept closing in on small birds flying away from the road at the final second as if playing Chicken. Stars twinkled overhead, and snow spotted the roadside and the mountain. A car that came up from behind shattered this serenity, so I pulled onto the shoulder for its passing pleasure.

When the car refused to pass, I returned to the lane. Blue and red lights soon invaded the once-pleasant setting, and an obnoxious spotlight enveloped the camper. My heart pounded as it descended to my stomach. I pulled over during this confusion, but was well aware that the camper wasn't speeding. Tracy instantly began gathering the vehicle papers.

The policeman took a minute or two before appearing by my window, asking for the important papers. All that pandemonium had begun with a burned out taillight. Tracy reached under her seat and handed me the dust-covered black leather folder containing insurance and registration. The officer carefully watched as I quickly brushed the dust off with two sweeps of my hand, creating a large cloud.

"Obviously we don't get pulled over often," I said, hoping to earn some points.

I did, since we were just passing through Nevada. He didn't even bother writing up a work order because they'd have no way to verify whether or not we fixed the light. I re-entered the roadway and drove below the speed limit until the police car passed our camper.

We pulled into a Laughlin casino for the night, and the parking lot looked like a fine hotel. The more miles we conquered in a day, the more attractive a parking area could be, and this particular one felt like top-of-the-line.

To rekindle the spirit of the casino, we spent the following morning looking at flashing buffet and hotel signs. It didn't hurt to look, but...could that be eighteen dollars per night? Yes, but that wasn't what hooked us. The complimentary second night nailed down our decision. We couldn't afford to stay in the camper at that price, so Tracy turned to Molly and explained that she loved her a lot. She then apologized for having to keep her out in the camper for a spell.

Inside the hotel, we acted like two uncivilized people who had never seen simple luxuries before. We marveled, almost becoming dizzy from the flushing toilet. It had been a while. Furthermore, our room had a shower, bed, running water from the faucet, cable television, and a phone. What had been our necessities became our luxuries.

Tracy was so excited about having a phone that she ran to a payphone in the casino to call people at home with our new number. The service charge deterred our calling from the room. Before she even returned to the room, a ringing phone interrupted my television viewing, nearly knocking me off the bed. It was Tracy's cousin in Florida, and I began to wonder if an answering machine would have been a wise investment.

For two days we lazed, making sure that the hotel would not lure us in with cheap rent then suck us dry at their casino. We behaved with utmost caution. In Las Vegas, we saw emotionless people sitting between two slot machines, mechanically feeding them both silver dollars, and never even looking to see if they won or how much. Money did not seem to be an issue, and it no longer was a game.

On a stroll through the casino to our room, we passed the clinking of coins and ringing of bells. This had been part of the plan when they designed the building. I was adamant about reaching our room with the same amount of money that we had when we began our journey from the other side of the casino. Tracy seemed torn, and her eyes kept glancing at the machines. I waited for her to ask nicely, and then...boom, the room's paid for.

I couldn't and wouldn't allow it, because it's so easy to get sucked in. Then it happened. I reached into my pocket and handed a nickel over to Tracy, whose eye continued to wander. I told her to go and lose it so she could get it out of her system.

Walking alongside the machines, she randomly slowed, but without breaking stride, stuck the nickel in the slot. She pulled...lost. Surprise, surprise. But that was it, and while continuing through another room of casinos, we stopped by a series of payphones lined up against the wall, and it wasn't for a credit extension.

While Tracy talked on the phone, I waited for her to finish, leaning against the wall. As I dropped my eyes to the floor, I found something that pushed us over the top. I found a dime, and we found ourselves a nickel ahead of the game. More importantly, we left Laughlin casinos ahead.

December 8, 1992

Over the Colorado River and through the woods...to Mountain Time we go. The two hundred mile trek to Phoenix reintroduced those famous stately cacti, standing at attention, resembling uneven forks. We returned to Arizona. California had been state number twenty-nine, and the count would hold at twenty-nine for some time.

We now became serious about getting jobs; desperately concerned. Our trip fund was insufficient to bring us around to the remaining nineteen states. It overwhelmed us that nineteen states remained, even though most of America's land had been covered. Since winter neared, we had no choice but to call Phoenix our home for a couple of months.

The low mountains around the dry desert of cacti and sagebrush provided the dusty backdrop to our ten dollar campground north of Phoenix and west of Carefree. Besides the small private airport with occasional glider rides, there wasn't a whole lot there, which soothed us. Day after day, I kept handing the owner ten dollars until finally our determination awoke. We had rested enough to pick up and start into Phoenix for employment. But the owner held us up by saying that if we stayed a sixth night then the seventh was free, and we did just that.

251

In our time there, coyotes ruled the land at night, howling up a storm, which the owner attributed to the killing of rabbits. The rabbit population dwindled as a result of the coyotes. They make the kill in the desert at night, and the entire pack of coyotes howl as they run into and away from the kill.

One bright, sunny afternoon, a coyote slowly and calmly strutted into the campground, sniffing around garbage pails for food. It resembled a dog, but then I learned that a coyote walked through the campground on a daily basis, so we had to be careful with Molly. She might eat the coyote for lunch.

For our new task of searching for a job, Tracy thinned my hair outside of the camper, maintaining the length, which hadn't been touched since we left. Since my hair becomes thick faster than it becomes long, this needed to be performed every month or two, depending on how much rain fell.

Aside from hair, we had to worry about apparel, and work anxiety had already begun to set in. Our first try came through temporary agencies in Phoenix. We had to sign up for light industrial work since we had no professional attire for clerical duties. I've pushed mail carts with a suit and tie before, so office work would not do.

Our mouths sagged when we heard that the industrial jobs paid $4.30 per hour. We knew wages would be lower out here, but we weren't prepared for ridiculous. We next tried north of Phoenix in the towns of Carefree and Cave Creek, tourist towns with several restaurants.

We found ourselves on the corner of Easy Street and Ho Hum Boulevard, believing our task would be a breeze. It wasn't, and we became more desperate. Although the Ho-Hum pace was what our hearts desired, the Carefree opportunities wouldn't allow such a thing, forcing us to drop down again into northern Phoenix. We had been in these parts before, so we knew that it wasn't as hectic or dangerous as downtown. But our success depended on sacrifices.

We accepted a three-day assignment through the temporary agency at a law firm. For $5.50 an hour, which was probably lower than the wages of the lawyers, we had to worry about professional attire. The wage was actually very good for these parts, so we jumped on it for the couple hundred dollars it would bring in, and we sure needed that.

Once we agreed to take the job, which would begin the following day, life became tumultuous. I felt compelled to scurry around to every restaurant that crossed our path to find something better. For several reasons, I had this overwhelming sense of despair antagonistically blended with anticipation. The assignment would be in downtown Phoenix, an unsafe place for a camper, especially during rush hour. Then the worry of finding a parking lot would be tremendous.

Public transportation? Well, it was late afternoon, and we had no time to look into that, and hardly cared to. We needed at least three sets of professional attire each, an iron, ties, panty hose...

This pervaded our minds as we continued through town looking for something else. Finally, we decided that it just wasn't worth it, and called the agency back late in the day to cancel. This eased our minds greatly, even though we desperately needed work.

We moved to Maricopa County, the familiar and busier section of northern Phoenix, where Tracy suggested we commit ourselves to a campground for a month. Employers seemed to demand an address and phone number. What high expectations they had.

Phoenix Metro RV Park, mostly a retirement community, but the cleanest and safest around, convinced us that this should be our home. It cost a little more than neighboring parks. Right off the highway, it provided easy access to Phoenix.

It was an exhilarating feeling for us to wake up at home. We were living in Phoenix, perhaps for a month or two. We had a mailbox, telephone message board, showers, and the security of knowing where we'd be sleeping at night for the first time in seven months.

Our financial situation looked so bleak that I even contemplated the use of rest areas during our spell of employment. This was the toughest check we had ever penned, extracting over two hundred dollars from the mere six hundred dollars remaining in our account.

The feeling that first morning produced was beyond secure, even though we faced poverty. On a disturbing note, however, we ruled out Mardi Gras due to winter and lack of funds. We simply could not attend the party, which disturbed us, since that was the only deadline for the entire trip. Phoenix became home. Even though mornings and evenings chilled us to the bone, daytime would sometimes reach seventy degrees.

Searching for work took much longer than we anticipated. Five weeks elapsed, and another monthly campground fee forced us deeper into poverty. We feared that we would not find work, and we had no other available resource.

Every day, we frantically walked around malls, filling out applications and needing employment together. Running around hoping for minimum wage jobs at any fast food restaurant or grocery store, we learned what desperation can do to people. But we continued to choose this lot over the corporate world, somehow maintaining control over our lives. We were extremely limited from the start.

After greeting our retired neighbors from Canada, their lengthy motorhome with Alberta plates parked right next to ours, the couple visited our site for a chat. When the man told us that we could borrow his tools at any time, Tracy advised him that I wouldn't know what to do with the tools if I had them. He produced a Canadian chuckle, but the offer still stood.

As time passed, each temporary agency sounding so hopeful, nothing resulted. Some agencies blamed it on the holidays, and others blamed it on the excessive rainfall. While plummeting to a net worth of four hundred dollars, we felt the world falling apart around us. However, the very thought of being lured back into the corporate life seemed the greater of the evils. It seemed possible, almost likely, that we would be stranded without a dollar to our name. Although a consideration when we left, we never seriously thought it would happen.

It wasn't until we were as down and out as a couple could be when my car at home finally sold for thirteen hundred dollars, which made us breathe a lot easier. Our net worth had more than tripled.

Christmas Day

Packages containing our mail began to drift in during the last couple of days. This would be our Christmas on the road, but it would be just as exciting, if not more. We enjoyed listening to Christmas music under the cover of dim candlelight while opening lots of mail. Presents from home were sprinkled into the equation.

Then came the clincher: Christmas dinner of roast beef, potatoes, corn, salad, and rolls. Homemade chocolate cream pie would follow. We could never normally eat this way because it's a very small camper to cook in, and we never really knew when the dinner bell would ring prior to finding a place to park for the night. And the refrigerator wasn't exactly a walk-in.

The roast should have been done before we realized that the potatoes and vegetables weren't even started. Tracy and I cringed when the back burner wouldn't light. All we could think of was being out of propane.

Quickly opening the oven, we saw that the pilot light was out, which verified our fear. We pulled the roast to see if we could cut off cooked ends and go without potatoes. It wasn't to be. The propane must have been long gone because the roast still had a pulse.

I went berserk. I was incensed, confused, trying to imagine a place that could feed us propane at nine o'clock Christmas night. I steamed. Tracy laughed. I wanted to give up. She wanted me to calm down. The amusing part of it all could certainly be extracted, but not while living through it. Definitely not while living through it.

Outside the camper I jumped, adrenaline flying. I unhooked all attachments while Tracy worked at finding a place for all of the food. I jumped into the driver's seat to warm the engine, but when I turned the key, I heard no sound. The battery was as dead as it could be, more lifeless than the roast, drained from Christmas music.

After successfully jumping ourselves with cables and scattering Christmas dinner around the camper, we readied for take-off. With the refrigerator stuffed, we placed the bowls of salad and plates with shelled hard-boiled eggs on the bed. The roast remained in the oven, where it slid around with each cautious turn.

Feeling hopeless and helpless, we set out in search of propane. Tracy continued to smile, while I continued to frown. It wasn't until our fifth attempt that we pulled a groundsman from his trailer at a mobile home park. He reopened the propane in order for us to attain our dream of this roast beef dinner. It was truly a miracle, and we again believed in Santa Claus.

By the time we returned, we had to cook the stone cold roast all over again. This two hour mission put us back at the dinner table after eleven o'clock, and we had to devour our food in order to still eat it on December twenty-fifth. It wasn't a bad meal, but it could have been better, and only after dinner could Tracy make me find the humor of it all.

1993

The New Year came and went, and we still had no jobs. We wondered if our plan to work would ever be fulfilled. It was so easy for us to fall in love with the low surrounding mountains and cacti-filled desert, but it wasn't paying the bills, especially that second monthly campground fee. Coyotes frequented the desert, and we could hear them howling at night right from our home, but they didn't pay the bills either.

Meanwhile, Arizona declared a State of Emergency. The rain had no end in sight. Cars, bridges, people, and even a landfill washed downstream. People died attempting to drive or walk through water over the road, unaware of its depth or that it could suck them under.

The rain found a leak, which soaked our bed, and at one time water poured in from the camper door. We tried towels and a hair dryer for the bed, but nonetheless had a tough night's sleep. Both of us fought over who would get the wet spot.

We also had a couple of instances when a helicopter circled or hovered above the campground, shining a spotlight down, searching for escapees from the nearby detention center or prison. The second time this happened, we double-checked the locks on the doors. Then I slid my head between the window and the shade to watch the helicopter and look for suspicious activity.

My heart plummeted to my stomach when I heard a knock and Tracy saying, "Who's that?" My head escaped from the shade. I wondered what I would do, or how I would handle it. My mind spun a web of thoughts, blocking any solution. I looked into Tracy's worried eyes, and knew I had to protect her.

I hoped the rumbling helicopter above us would be able to land in time to apprehend the suspect. Ridiculous. I thought of the baseball bat, or the spray, but would I open the door? Of course not. Only in the movies would they do that. Maybe I should lift the shade first and take a peek. I could roll open the window to communicate. How many of them? I certainly wasn't going to open the door. Could I swing a bat at anything other than a baseball?

All of these thoughts raced through my mind in about five seconds flat. Then Tracy stepped up to the plate and admitted that she had knocked on the window for a little prank. I was much too pissed off to enjoy the laugh she shared with herself.

January 25, 1993

After pounding the pavement for six weeks, we finally got a break when I called one of the four temporary agencies. They sent us out to work in production lines together for $4.30 an hour. We jumped on the assignment without much thought, working within the hour.

Making one small nickel above minimum wage, we worked harder than ever before in our lives. They handed us white hairnets, and we stood in fast and furious production lines. We began tightening caps on lotions and creams, bagging containers, boxing the containers, and stacking heavy boxes, which absolutely destroyed both of us.

We worked with a guy who went by the initials JD, a thirty-one-year-old former trucker from Pennsylvania. He would join us for lunch out in the camper in the parking lot, instantly connecting with us and becoming a friend of ours.

After that second day, we limped back to the camper, thinking only of going home and soaking our aching bodies in the ninety degree pool. However, that never happened. On this day, the pool was under construction, so we had to settle for a sponge bath. This reduced Tracy to tears because of her brutally unforgiving pain, and by evening she couldn't lift a limb. All that work for minimum wage.

I gave her a complete rubdown, but she really wanted another job. So did I, but we had killed ourselves for six weeks until we landed this one, and were too desperate to let it go. We had to hold onto what we had no matter what the cost until we found another job to replace it. Chances of that happening were slim due to our demands, which this job amazingly met.

JD and I worked together much of our time there, while a manager pulled Tracy aside to run one of the most important lines in the company. JD, between jobs, abhorred this demeaning work as much as we did, but thought it was at least good for a laugh. Every day that went by, he threatened to quit. He made no secret of his intentions, even in front of management. However, he turned out to be the hardest and fastest worker there, so I'm sure they didn't want to see him go.

Weekends meant something to us for the first time in a long time, but we couldn't continue this for long. JD did quit after two weeks, and we seriously considered it. Our friend actually installed front brakes on our camper one night after work as his wife prepared a spaghetti dinner. The brakes ran us $12.75, plus the labor charge...a postcard from Mardi Gras.

That's right. This cruel job would have pushed us ahead about twenty dollars after an extra month, extracting another month's rent. We decided that it wasn't worth it to stay and work beyond the third week. Having previously discounted Mardi Gras, we decided to reconsider.

Temperatures had been climbing into the seventy degree range as February approached, but we still opted for Mardi Gras and winter over production lines and warmth. The weather didn't frighten us anymore, and we felt the need for a vacation. The last time we quit our jobs, we traveled through twenty-nine states, but this time we only sought nineteen.

We did have our work cut out for us though, because we only had eight days to get to New Orleans. The managers hated to see us leave, and asked what it would take for us to stay. The owner of the company popped in and saw Tracy running the whole line. He told the plant manager that he wanted to keep her, but she said that we had to finish the trip, and they probably couldn't pay us enough.

Although we had worked for only three weeks, they ran around worrying because Glenn and Tracy were leaving, and they needed replacements to work on the big line. We felt deep down that it was time to pull up anchor and continue on. We became restless, seeking more adventure, and following our gut feeling. We soared with adrenaline when we pulled out the maps to see if we could make Mardi Gras. There was no turning back. All signs pointed to the road, and the job meant so little, almost as little as the pay-checks.

America offered more, so we obliged. However, this meant rushing through the southern plains to get to Louisiana and abbreviating our time in the remaining states after that. With most of the highlights behind us, we could afford to follow such a rigid plan. Besides, our wedding date had been chosen by counting one week back per state to coincide with the festival.

We went for the gold. Smaller states, cheaper gas, and one thousand dollars accumulated with overtime all contributed to our confidence. The plan that I drew out turned into a two thousand mile route through New Mexico, Texas, Oklahoma, Arkansas, and landing in Louisiana. We did think we were being foolish, but we'd be back on the road, and foolishness could never compete with the feeling we got from the road.

Tracy actually quit the job for us both, without even informing me of her intentions to do so, before the end of the second week. When our final day of the third week ended, we felt happier than when we left our jobs in Connecticut. We weren't sorry that we stopped in Phoenix, however, even though the job wasn't exactly ideal. It became an experience. We had met JD, and it helped finance the Louisiana party.

February 13, 1993

By six in the morning, under the disguise of darkness, our headlights provided passage away from our Phoenix home. We were back on the road for a tough agenda. I warned Tracy that the next week would be grueling, but the thought of Mardi Gras drove her to accept the challenge as well.

It would definitely steal sleep, but I was the one who could recoup losses in that category with a five minute nap. Tracy couldn't, but she agreed to handle my pace even if it meant my hauling along through the desert while she slept in the bedroom.

Out of the RV Park we pulled, and through Phoenix we drove, onto Interstate 10 for the fastest way to cut through this path. The city we once called home appeared further and further away from us, then ducked completely out of view. We were heading back east.

We pierced the dry and dreary desert through Tucson, and rolled right out of Arizona, which carried us right into our thirtieth state of New Mexico. The desert continued, except for forked cacti. The plants became even more rugged, having to withstand such brutal heat. Our first destination on the journey had us heading for Carlsbad Caverns, but we had to slash Texas via El Paso, then head east through Guadeloupe National Park.

Thirteen hours after departure, mostly in drive, we found a rest area in the Guadeloupe Mountains, a few miles shy of New Mexico. The entire region was so dry that Molly injured her paws when she went outside to do her duty. The dry grass mixed with thorns, and she wasn't able to sit properly until we removed the thorns from her paws. By the time we shut the engine down for the evening, we had destroyed our previous mileage record for one day with a five hundred sixty-seven mile performance.

That was fine, because Arizona owned quite a bit of the drive, and we'd be fools to believe that we cut the state short by just driving through. We never remembered resting our heads on the pillow or how we slept, but when we woke up, it was both Valentine's Day and Tracy's twenty-sixth birthday.

Valentine's Day

Before we started out to Tracy's birthday present of Carlsbad Caverns, my treat, she opened the birthday gifts that had been sent to her at the RV Park from family and friends. For the week that the presents had been hidden under the dinette, Tracy kept insisting that it wouldn't hurt to open one. She acted like a little kid at Christmas, and I kept catching her eyeing the gifts under the table.

When I let her loose on her birthday, she wasted no time digging the presents out and ripping them open. She wore a grin throughout. Her Valentine birthday happened to come at a bad time since it interfered with our push, but at least we had Carlsbad Caverns. At least we shared the day away from the road.

Without the benefit of three hundred thousand Mexican Free-tail bats dramatically escaping from the natural opening of the cave, we still marveled at the enormity and sculptures of the caverns. Mammoth Cave hadn't tainted this new cave experience like we thought it would. We were sorry about missing the bats, but we'd be back...sometime. We would see them.

The conclusion of the cave tour coincided with the conclusion of New Mexico. Weather prevented us from traveling north to Albuquerque because of the elevation and snow. Again, we headed east with the feeling that home was fast approaching.

We cherished our great find when Hobbs, New Mexico offered us a rest area prior to our invasion of Texas. However, we reached state number thirty-one easily the next day. There may be thousands of reasons to love a large state like Texas, but we didn't seem to find them. The people were very friendly on the roadway, and we were reintroduced to Central Time, but all we saw and smelled was oil field after oil field.

It became the dreariest of drives, nothing en route to Dallas through Abilene and Fort Worth. Oil fields, and more oil fields, or else dry barren land. The biting cold accompanied very windy conditions. We gladly moved on, hoping for much warmer conditions ahead.

Having the road to myself all day long, I was insulted when cars wanted me to share it upon reaching Fort Worth during rush hour. Every Texan on those back roads waved, but here they all did the city thing. They cut us off, not allowing us to move over, and shifted into different lanes in an attempt to weave through traffic to arrive eleven seconds sooner. I yelled for my co-pilot, and Tracy rushed to the front to help me through the mayhem. Sometimes I just needed her presence in the passenger's seat with such a large vehicle.

After speaking to natives in the Fort Worth area, we agreed that we shouldn't park in Forth Worth overnight or even consider taking the camper into Dallas. Tracy and I decided that it would be best if we just got the hell out, and a northern path took us away from the metropolis in favor of a truck stop in Denton.

We froze at the gas pumps, where the canopy rocked violently back and forth. I made sure the gas hose snuggled into my tank just in case I had to bail out. The constant wind gusts persisted through the night; the cold, dark, windy, and ugly night. Even with savagely gusting winds, our weariness turned the jolting camper into a rocking cradle, and we had no trouble sleeping.

February 16, 1993

I had plans to wake Tracy for the new state, but until then I pushed through forty miles of land with the help of coffee. Although the wind had abated, we still froze. Our thoughts were with the temperatures we had deserted in Phoenix and with our decision to leave. But we weren't deterred from knowing we had done the right thing. Nonetheless, we had to deal with thirty-four degrees with a nine degree chill.

Tracy walked up front before I had to call her. She too saw the bridge over the Red River and our journey into state thirty-two. Oklahoma welcomed us, and we welcomed a dramatic drop in the price of gas. We had thought that $1.12 was great in Phoenix, but even that went up three cents before we uprooted. Ninety-five cents, the norm throughout Texas and Oklahoma, was OK with us. I filled the tank once again, but for the first time ever at the Happy Hog Express gas station. We filled up even though we already had three-quarters of a tank, unsure if the price of gas would increase.

The friendliness of Texas carried over into Oklahoma, where even a police officer waved. I was almost relieved that it was frigid because the lethal combination of heat and Oklahoma just wouldn't do it for me.

All I ever hear is that another funnel appeared in good old Oklahoma. We swiftly cut across the southeast corner through Durant, McAlester, and Eufaula, sharply turning east on Route 9 about fifty miles south of Tulsa.

Aside from the fact that I wouldn't live here for the world, the portion of Oklahoma that we saw from Texas to Arkansas was strikingly beautiful. The entire path shot between glittering golden fields of grass; golden and dry, yet flowing, waving, and stunning. We barely touched Oklahoma on this crisp day, but we really had nothing planned except to drive through it to reach Arkansas.

We had to plow through this portion of the country like a steamroller, and still had to move down the boot-like shape of Louisiana all the way to the toes of New Orleans. If it got any colder, we planned on screaming. These places weren't supposed to have winter, yet here it was gripping us like we never knew it could. We learned quickly where heat escapes from the camper.

In the throes of warmer weather, we rejoiced while pushing south into our thirty-third state of Arkansas, which made no secret about the state's product of President Bill Clinton. What Arkansas had in common with its neighbor to the west was small abandoned houses ready to topple, but left to rot to the ground.

We saw abandonment often, but sometimes these deteriorating houses were occupied. People had strewn trash all along the road. Route 10 took us all the way down to Hot Springs National Park, but the road was littered more than we'd seen in our lives, much less our travels.

Although we noticed many dead dogs scattered around the south, Arkansas took the prize. We saw dogs on the road, to the side of the road, and we even saw one knocked against a cement bridge sidewalk. As if that wasn't bad enough, many dogs roamed the streets, awaiting their fate. By the looks of things, their time would come.

But Arkansas, looking beyond the shanties, the pet neglect, and litter, was one of the most beautiful states we'd seen. The west to southwest region through the Ouachita Mountains on Route 7 brought us up and down steep hills with valley overlooks abounding.

We pulled into a picnic area within the Ouachita Mountains and forests at dusk, about thirty miles from Hot Springs. This circle drive had designated sites. It was dark and secluded, but it was legal. The note on the bulletin board indicated that it was legal as long as we refrained from staying longer than fourteen days and did not run around nude.

The swift, soothing stream, which ran through our heads as we drifted off to sleep, resounded when we regained consciousness at sunup. The blackness we were thrust into upon shutting the lights off did not go unnoticed. We had been used to a large light at the campground shining over our camper. It had never been entirely dark at night, so this turned into an eerie experience. We could have slept with our eyes open.

Inside Hot Springs National Park, which is located in the town of Hot Springs, the bathhouses that lined the main drag awaited our money. We decided that eight dollars for a mineral bath wasn't drastic, even though we really shouldn't be spending. When we finally decided to take a bath, we discovered that our bank account was much weaker than we had imagined. Our cash advance only permitted a drawing of twenty-four dollars.

Tracy called the bank from a phone in the middle of town, near a round cement mineral fountain with ten faucets for public use. The water came out of the ground at one hundred forty-three degrees, but cooled to one hundred degrees by the time it reached the public.

Out of the camper we hopped with a couple of gallon jugs and a five gallon jug, but we met competition. A man had his car parked next to the fountain with an open trunk, which was filled with gallon milk containers. We took our own mineral bath with the preheated water since we couldn't afford to pay for one, but it was just as soothing.

After carrying the water jugs back to the camper, Tracy lifted her foot up to step inside. She cracked her knee directly into a metal piece jutting out from the side of the door opening. I heard her knee connect so crisply that I could actually feel the pain. She reacted as if she had smacked her funny bone. It hurt so much that tears began to well up in her eyes, but with no sounds accompanying them.

Before she lost her footing, I grabbed her and assisted her up the last step and into the camper, but she couldn't move her knee for a long while. Nothing could be done. The only remedy was to wait for the pain to go away because touching or rubbing only aggravated it. After our Hot Springs bath, and when Tracy's knee had recovered, we were off and running once again.

The excitement of moving into the state associated with Mardi Gras was quite satisfying, and not having that professional bath became that much more academic. Even having no money after filling up half the tank was unimportant. The only thing concerning us was moving as far as we could down Louisiana with the gas we had.

We hooted and cheered when entering this thirty-fourth state, shooting south into warmer temperatures and darkness. We had nine days to conquer two thousand miles. This path encompassed five states, but we completed the trek in six days. This left us time to ponder how we would go about making it into New Orleans with a camper. We moved down Louisiana with a diminishing supply of gas and one paper dollar, but with confidence that coins were scattered about the camper.

We welcomed any help, and that's why Tracy decided to call Gary in Baton Rouge. He is the son of her aunt's best friend, but we didn't know him. Although we were apprehensive at first, he was our only link to Mardi Gras. Tracy called, and Gary was more than accommodating, making his driveway our parking space. He told her that if we arrived early enough, we could accompany his family to our first Mardi Gras parade at LSU.

Our camper made its own boot out of Louisiana. We moved south down the middle through Alexandria, and into Lafayette, then completed the boot with eastward movement to Baton Rouge. We cringed at seeing so many more cats and dogs dead or roaming with that same fate awaiting. It seemed to be commonplace in the south.

Since we didn't own a bankcard from the bank where we stopped, we couldn't get a cash advance. Fumes landed us safely in Gary's driveway. Gary and his wife, Diane, were preparing for the pre-parade cookout when we arrived, and their two children were gearing up as well. Our Mardi Gras began here.

February 18, 1993

Mardi Gras means "Fat Tuesday" in French, a term that resulted from parading a fat ox through Paris on the Tuesday before Ash Wednesday, the last day before Lent. However, the carnival represents an ancient Roman custom of merrymaking before a period of fast.

French colonists introduced this legal holiday to America in the early 1700s. It originated in Europe, where the kings of France, riding through the masked crowds, threw gold doubloons or commemorative coins to the poor people on Fat Tuesday. The event began with people masquerading through the streets, before the addition of parades in the 1830's.

The masked carnival organizers aboard the floats continue this tradition today. They throw trinkets or "throws" into the sometimes masked crowds who still yell, "throw me something, mister!" They've been yelling that since the tradition started a long time before my birth.

The holiday season officially begins on January sixth. The week prior to Ash Wednesday is when the hype begins with parades, while crowds progressively grow until the final showdown.

The king cake is to Mardi Gras as the chocolate bunny is to Easter. The King cake is a large round cake of pastry, danish, or coffeecake dough with no center, which dons the official Mardi Gras colors of purple, green, and gold icing. A small plastic baby doll is hidden inside this cake, and the person who gets the piece with the baby doll must buy the next King cake or throw the next party. Long ago, a bean was hidden in the cake, but the young children too poor to buy the next cake would swallow the bean.

There are more than sixty parades in the greater New Orleans area alone. Tracy and I took in two parades in New Orleans, two in Baton Rouge, and one in Metarie. We amassed over two hundred fifty bead necklaces, seventeen plastic Mardi Gras cups, forty-one doubloons, six Frisbees, candy, cheap sunglasses, and many other assorted trinkets.

As part of the crowd, we felt the obsession with trying to maximize trinkets. People jump into the air, dive, run to the street to fetch what fell short, and scramble to the ground to fetch what slipped through the sea of hands.

The crowds were sometimes ten people deep as far down the street as our eyes could see. We always made it a point of arriving early enough to finagle front row positioning. As the procession approached, police cleansed the littered streets of people to prepare for the passing of "The Greatest Free Show on Earth."

Although the Peterson's had considered our first Mardi Gras parade a low-key event, it was the best parade we'd ever set eyes on. Tracy and I only had pockets to fill, which did not take long. The krewe members launched "throws" overboard their floats in great numbers.

We had known about trinkets being thrown overboard, but we never imagined that our pockets would not provide enough room for our stash. Each krewe member stuck both hands into a bucket of trinkets, then came up and heaved them overboard. Moderation had no place in this parade.

Before putting our first parade behind us, which would slowly build us up for the bigger ones, we put our first King cake behind us during the Peterson's cookout at the parade. Cookouts spread throughout the metro area. The strong aroma of steaks, burgers, and hot dogs had permeated every step of the parade.

Parades moved up and down streets through town, and we joined the Peterson's group, learning fast how to follow the parade along and sometimes cutting through yards to maximize trinkets.

Only when the parade stopped moving did the fever dissipate. We gathered up the kids and headed for home, wound up, but ready for more.

February 20, 1993

Our early morning drive to a mall parking lot in Metarie enabled us to take a bus into N'awlins, both of us having been clobbered over the head with the feel of the season after two parades. The natives rubbed their holiday joy all over us; so contagious it had become.

Into New Orleans we trampled, where the tombstones sat above ground. People cannot be buried below the earth because of swamps; digging one foot down would turn up water. We hoped to survive Mardi Gras without ending up six feet over.

After stepping off the bus and into the chaos, we followed the crowd, hoping they'd pull us to where we wanted to be. We didn't know the where, but neither did anyone we asked. Since most people walked in one direction, we followed along.

By the time the Iris parade reached our front row positioning behind a thick, twisted wire running alongside the street, ninety minutes had passed. The street quickly cleared, and the parade owned the crowd.

Krewes seemed to love the hysteria they created, and sometimes they'd reach into their buckets and heave handful after handful of necklaces overboard. A tug-of-war would ensue by the commoners until all the beads were taken.

Serious struggles arose over these cheap plastic beads, sometimes resulting in injury, but it seemed worth any possible injury at the time. There's nothing like that moment during a Mardi Gras parade. Nothing else really matters.

The mania turned adults into children, while children only stood a chance if they were on their parents' shoulders. Tracy admitted that she had become a victim of greed, but only once gave in to a struggle for beads against a child. She felt so terrible while reflecting on what Mardi Gras does to people and what it had done to us. However, I'd be lying if I said that we didn't enjoy a teary-eyed chuckle from these childish reflections.

During the second parade of the day, which had long gaps in the procession, the restrooms called so loudly that we had to call it quits. The line for relief at McDonald's led out of the restaurant and never moved, so we had no alternative. We returned to the bus stop slowly and painfully, making it back to Metarie in the late afternoon hours. All this had to happen because of a ridiculous restroom shortage.

Veteran's Boulevard in Metarie had a parade starting thirty minutes after our return. This ignited us, making us hopeful at the prospect of more trinkets, but only after using the precious bathroom in the camper. We didn't care that we already had four bagfuls of trinkets. We wanted one more parade to satisfy our Mardi Gras appetite. After all, we did travel two thousand miles.

As if we weren't feverish already, we stood on the boulevard median because the parade would be marching up one side of the street, then turning and moving down the other. At points, we timed the floats so that we could nab trinkets thrown in the air from both sides. I pondered counseling for this sickness of ours.

Two bead necklaces that were slowly lofted into the air had my name on them. They were the only things I could see in the entire world around me. I timed my leap for a successful catch, flicking my wrist for assurance. I believed them to be in my sole possession until feeling the pull of competition. Some lady who looked to be in her forties had grabbed the same necklace with equal vigor and determination.

During our airborne moment, a tug-of-war forced the beads to the ground. As our feet landed, my greater height forced my elbow to slam down upon her head.

274

This poor lady saw one necklace land and quickly scooped it up before comforting her head with her hands. I shot a grimace her way during my frantic moment, then managed to find the second necklace, and we both returned to our original position. She never looked to see who owned the elbow. There was only time to regain composure enough to start all over again with the next passing float.

Tracy held the trinket bag, catching what krewe members threw at her, hoping that I would do the majority of the fighting. At one point, when we became too wrapped up in the chaos, we decided to take a step back and passively observe.

The screaming and hungry crowd held their hands in the air, looking like chicks waiting to be fed by a mother hen. The parade ruled over the people like a king, controlling their every move. It magnetized them. It was a baseball in a crowd. Although it interested us to see adults acting like children without knowing it, we felt lonely and edgy as nonparticipants, and so rejoined our fellow players.

When Mardi Gras came to a close, we sat back in the camper, truly content, and more than satisfied with what our two thousand mile journey offered. We looked around the camper at our Mardi Gras collection. This was the proof that we had attended: hundreds of necklaces, dozens of plastic cups, Frisbees, flags, candy kisses, and smiles.

We felt genuinely excited about our accomplishments. Although the time came for us to pack it in and set off on the road for more America, we had gotten our fill here in N'awlins. We moved on, wondering if we were technically on our way home.

February 21, 1993

Past swamps, marshes, and bayous we moved, away from Louisiana, parish after parish, until reaching the twenty-four mile causeway spanning Lake Pontchartrain. A musty smell drifted across the road for the entire drive.

The lake takes on the appearance of an ocean, especially at the midway point, when land disappears either way. The season disappeared for us as well, but what a pleasurable stop. Mardi Gras is a feeling, and so is Louisiana, because of Mardi Gras. Both seemed as large as the lake.

The trip almost seemed complete now, but we still had fourteen states left to go. How could that be? Where could they possibly be? All that remained for us was wrapping around the southeast and moving up the East Coast. Even counting these states on the map did nothing to solve the mystery.

Mississippi became our thirty-fifth state, and it pleased the hell out of us with the cost of gasoline at only $.89 per gallon. Maybe we could get back home to Connecticut. Along the Gulf of Mexico we ventured, past white, sandy beaches and antebellum mansions from Bay Saint Louis to Gulfport.

We were rushed, but still felt compelled to stop for a few minutes. We got out to dip our toes in the very fine sand, rinsing them in the dirty brown water. Watching the beach arc east and west, we stood with the small gulf waves breaking against our ankles. The gulf breeze was flapping flags and pushing the sun west. We just wanted a small piece of the coast before heading north, and the cold water helped to make that push.

We shot north through Hattiesburg, Jackson, taking a few driving days to do so. If anything, we were formally introduced to Mississippi living. It's difficult, I would imagine, to be more laid back than the residents of Mississippi that we happened upon.

A black man came out of a service station after I went in requesting propane. He was an older man of about sixty years or more, and he limped up to the camper, which we had parked next to the propane tank. He asked me if I would hook the hose to my tank. The last thing I wanted to do was fool with propane gas because I know what it can do, but we wondered about this man in charge.

Eventually, he got to one knee and hooked the hose to the tank. However, after finishing the job, he asked me to put the gas cap back on my tank. We were stunned by the man's brass, but just followed orders. We wondered if this was an extreme version of self-service. Perhaps he also wanted me to put the money in the register.

Before moving to our next chore, I asked the man if he could point us to an oil change. Since we had had trouble finding propane in this state, we assumed that nothing was common. The man gave us directions to a tire center "down yonder," so down yonder we went. On and on we bounced, but nobody could fit the tall motorhome into their bay.

Then BP came along, the first garage to figure out that they could work in the parking lot. The first man I spoke with admitted that they had never worked on a motorhome, but would give it a try. Since that was the best response we had had all day, we let them give it a try on ours. The job lasted about ten minutes, and we moved on.

Once reaching Kosciusko, we aimed northwest where cotton fields abounded. Although the sticks had been recently combed, little marshmallow-sized balls of cotton remained on the knee-high trees.

Glenn Maynard

Now we felt the Deep South around us, but this land of Dixie was behind us after about a week. This allowed us enough time to slowly meander from the bottom of the Mississippi to the top, which became a series of short drives instead of one long one. Even Tracy and I took it easy in Mississippi, but the sinking temperatures would alter our pace.

February 26, 1993

Tennessee marked a cold thirty-sixth state, but we still hooted and cheered at the welcome sign. The only thing Tennessee could offer us within driving distance was Graceland. This being the case, we bought tickets for the tour, our only expense for the state.

While waiting for the bus from the visitor's center, which would tote us across the street to the mansion, we agreed that no other time on the trip was colder. The cold stung us even through winter jackets, but the tickets were in our hands, so we couldn't change our minds.

Little snowflakes, barely identifiable, began releasing themselves from the cloud cover. That peninsula that separates the Gulf of Mexico from the Atlantic Ocean, better known as Florida, began toying with our emotions.

The following morning plastered frost on our windshield and forced me out of bed before the light of day. Once again, the battery was drained from the constant use of the heater. The ensuing cold was unbearable even with all the blankets on the bed and thick white socks pulled over our feet.

I started the engine to build up the auxiliary battery. It took about thirty minutes for me to brew coffee using the inverter, and all we really wanted to do was to cut Alabama down the middle and get our chilly asses to Florida.

After giving up on the weather, I retrieved the leveling blocks. I then discovered icicles jutting almost one foot down from the little water tap connected to the side of the camper. More icicles had formed underneath. We had to avoid the cold before our water pipes broke and real problems began.

Route 64 moved us far east, all the way to Route 65, one digit away. The interstate carried us into our twenty-seventh state of Alabama, but we would only be seeing the state from the roadway. The cold weather began mapping out our journey for us.

Shooting between Huntsville and Decatur, we dropped down into Birmingham, a hilly drive with steep grades through the city. We dropped as fast as the temperature, realizing that we wouldn't be happy until we reached Florida. We ended the day's drive at a truck stop in Pelham. Our dream would be realized the next day.

That day came. In the capital, Montgomery, we hooked up with Route 231, which ran southeast through Dothan. Florida neared, and we braced for what would soon come. We were ready. It would be the first true warmth since Phoenix, even though we had had some relief in N'awlins and Mississippi. I'm sure the camper would have thanked us if it could.

Boom! Here it was...Florida: state number thirty-eight, while just ten remained. Piercing that long-awaited border, we screamed with delight at the prospect of warmer weather. Having conquered eight states in sixteen days, we were plenty exhausted as we rolled out on our twenty-nine thousandth trip-mile.

Crossing into the Eastern Time zone meant another milestone for us. We hadn't been there since Michigan, but it didn't happen until halfway through the panhandle of Florida. Since we had pushed far ahead of schedule because of cold weather, and winter had hardly relinquished control of the East Coast, we decided to call Florida home for about a month.

West Palm was the home of Tracy's cousin, Mark, who invited us to stay at his mobile home for as long as we desired. His mobile home was much larger than our camper, and we needed time to recover from the mad rush east. We decided we would see the West Coast of Florida, then accept his offer.

March 1, 1993

March signified spring, the same season in which our journey began. Next month would mark our anniversary. By now, thoughts of returning home prevailed, and Tracy and I seemed to be discussing it more often. The camper still held up, but we wondered for how long, hoping that it would have the energy to return to Connecticut.

Pounding on through Tampa and stopping in Clearwater Beach for a couple of hours of warm sun, we cherished our decision to take Florida by storm. The brilliant, white sand was enjoyed by many spring breakers, but the enormous beach offered plenty of room for all.

Palm trees waved to us, and pelicans with their beaks tucked into their chests flew overhead continuously. Seagulls made fervent attempts to steal sandwiches from the family in front of us who had visions of a bird-free lunch on a beach blanket.

The sun threw seventy-five degrees our way, and it was hard to imagine that just a couple of days ago we had had icicles and twenty degree temperatures. We had been deeply mistaken in thinking that these warm, sandy moments would occur often on this trip.

As this was only our third time to the beach, we looked forward to a break from travel. However, the only concern of ours at this moment was sinking into the sand and soaking up an afternoon of solar energy in hopes of thawing our bodies. The sun absorbed our cold to the point where nothing else mattered.

That saltwater scent hit us early in Florida. Salt permeated the warm, dry air, and we tasted it with each breath we took. We wanted to bottle the weather for our trip up the East Coast, but staying here instead was a prescription that Tracy and I could deal with.

We had loved Florida during our previous one week vacation, and we loved it this time as well. The thought of being here for one full month filled us with exuberance. We felt time had finally teamed up with us, and we relaxed.

We spent the following day trying to reach Everglades National Park, but a gigantic problem prevented us from arriving anytime soon. It felt like a hurricane. The wind created impossible driving conditions, and it only intensified.

This familiar battle had me gripping the wheel fervently, gritting my teeth, and intermittently shaking my hands up and down one at a time to rid them of their pins and needles. Shaking them simultaneously was out of the question.

Since the wind gusted in different directions, I could not favor the wheel to either side. It twisted, swirled, and just plain barreled us over. I held tight and straight and negotiated the wind blow by blow. Tracy and I decided that it wasn't worth it to rush, so we paid for a campground with hookups. The low-hanging sky began to turn an eerie gray.

We set up camp in Bonita Springs. As we watched the tube, constantly peeking out the window to see trees that had been bent over and fast clouds, a message flashed across the screen. "The National Weather Service has issued a tornado watch until 2:00 A.M. for the entire listening audience."

I remember watching the comedy awards and not laughing, and the volume seemed like it had been muted after the warning because I couldn't hear anything. The volume was on, but my mind drifted elsewhere.

I stared at the television as if interested, but could only hear my own panic. I became lost in fear. The intensity of the winds continued. I could not hear what Tracy said because I was too wrapped up in thoughts of the camper going for a ride through the air. I was busy planning what to do if that happened. I even jumped to my feet to make sure all of the cabinets were secure in case the inevitable happened, as if a falling box of Corn Flakes would be the end of us.

Tracy's eyes showed a little uncertainty, but she acted a little too nonchalant, which upset me. I felt as though she'd rather watch the end of the show than seek shelter. For the whole year we'd heard warnings about getting out of mobile units, and you can only test Mother Nature so many times.

"Are you going to just sit there?" I said, with a mix of frustration and anger.

"What else can we do?" she asked, defensively and defiantly.

"Not stay here. There's a rec hall at this campground, but we can't stay here."

I went outside to feel the hurricane-force wind, eyeing the swaying trees with extreme caution, wondering when they would snap. What more would it take? Across from us was an older couple trying to strap down their awning, and it looked as if the project was being done urgently. I walked over and asked them if we should be taking shelter.

The man stopped to stare at me for a short time as if looking for a reply. With his hands tucked in his pants pockets and his belly taxing the straps of his overalls, he told me that it wasn't necessary. He said I could talk to the man over by the dumpster and followed up his statement with a finger pointing to the park manager, an older man with a pipe in his gray beard.

Tracy and I were being blown in that direction anyway, so we just stopped resisting. We saw two wide fence doors, used to close off the dumpster, flapping open and closed while the old man attempted to secure them. Even though the wind overpowered him while I asked about a solid structure, he only had this to say: "You gotta be kiddin.' This is just a breeze. Where you from?"

The pipe remained in his mouth, jiggling up and down as he spoke. He remained bent over his work. He head was tilted and turned to us. I told him where we hailed from, and he asked me if we had breezes in Connecticut.

I felt like kicking the pipe down his throat, but rather told him that this was no ordinary breeze. It was ludicrous, and I wanted out of it, but again, we had nowhere to go. What I would have done for a house, but even that wasn't safe. A basement would be like heaven.

I had had enough of Mr. Breezepipe, so I turned and walked away from him as he tried earnestly to secure the doors blowing in the breeze. As I neared the camper, Tracy opened the door and jumped out with Molly in one hand and Backgammon in the other.

"We're going to the rec room," she said.

I knew she had only done this for my sake. After turning off all the gas lines, we locked up and moved over to the small laundry room because the rec room was closed. The wind did not ease at all, but at least the walls weren't swaying anymore.

In our new, small, three-machine room with no doors, I kept leaping from the backgammon game, believing that a tornado was upon us when the noise of the wind picked up and howled louder than ever. Thunder and lightning forewarned us of the heavy rain expected. I decided we'd be better off in the camper, where we would have access to news updates on television. Tracy agreed to be where I needed to be, even if we moved around a lot.

Nothing ever became of the storm except this wind, which edged out the Dakotas, but this was merely a Gulf breeze. I awoke internally elated and relieved when I opened my eyes to the light of a new day. Everything that I had hoped for the night before appeared all around me now. Darkness turned to light, and the conditions had improved.

The worst part for me had been hearing the roar of the evil winds and not being able to see a thing. Daylight enabled me to look out the window and see. Tracy and I discussed our different reactions during this calm, and she suggested that my intense fear could be linked to my previous car accident: the feeling of helplessness, of being out of control, and the camper flipping over. The fear is so intense. It's so deep-rooted that I can't understand why she doesn't react the same way.

I seem to fear death so intensely that I would do absolutely anything to hold onto life. Death had come too close, so my reactions may be over-reactions, but I know inside that I'm doing all that I can to avoid this fate. Tracy figures that if it's going to happen, then it's going to happen, and she'd rather die than suffer, or feel the pain beforehand. What I saw as a potentially deadly situation, she saw as a tornado watch, and nothing more. Conditions were ominous, but it hadn't happened yet, so why worry?

Route 41 toted us to Everglades, and once again the road leading to a national park could easily be part of it. Alligators were stationed in the waterway, parallel to the side of the road. Another sideshow included roseate spoonbills, stick figured wood storks, osprey, ibis, and great white herons. Whether they slowly stalked a meal of fish, soared through the air, or just sunned themselves with their wings opened wide, their presence showed us all their secrets.

We traveled through Homestead, which is the gateway to the park and the town leveled by Hurricane Andrew. The storm had preceded us by six months, but the devastation left in its wake was still very much present. Our camper blew through town amongst piles on the sides of the streets about fifteen feet high and wide filled with trees, lumber, and furnishings.

Driving between these long piles and demolished buildings felt like driving through a war zone. Tiles and entire roofs had been ripped from houses and buildings. Windows were broken on all levels. It took us a while before this horrific scene lay behind us. We could escape it, but so many others did not.

Birds, birds everywhere, including Florida Bay, where pelicans and vultures happened to be hanging out. So suave those pelicans, flapping their wings gently and soaring overhead with that funny smirk, laughing at us.

When the sun began to fall, turning the wetland grasses into orange from the reflection of the sky, we felt the need to find the campground within the park. I would sleep safely tonight provided neither alligator nor wind knocked at the door.

March 5, 1993

Using Florida City as the gateway to the Florida Keys, we sank to the southernmost city in the United States: Key West. I wondered why they did not name the city Key South, figuring they probably would have had it been the westernmost city.

Early afternoon marked the beginning of this excursion on the one hundred thirteen mile Overseas Highway connecting the keys. Gas alone would be quite costly for the round trip just to see the sunset, but it sounded like a dream, so we followed it.

There was more to our excursion than the sunset, though, because this road between Florida Bay and the Straights of Florida offered views of these waterways simultaneously, but more so when we were on the bridges connecting the key islands. As we moved through Key Largo, Long Key, and Little Duck Key toward Key West, we entertained ourselves with new names...such as O'key-Dokey, Mon Key and Blang Key, and that's when we realized just how long the road really was.

The tropical waters were sparkling green on both sides. Pelicans dominated the air, land, and sea, commenting every so often. The warm weather secured our attachment to this land. Anything seemed better than the cold, but this was paradise. A slight breeze reminded us that we were in Florida, but nothing was threatening.

The closer we got to Key West, knowing that the sun was competing with us, the more awake we became.

After several stops along the way, we realized that the bright orange object had wrapped around the sky and continued heading west at a rapid clip. This sun soon shone below our visors, blinding us as we tried to get to the end of the islands. En route, we scoped out overnight parking opportunities, but signs posted throughout the keys listed fines for overnight parking at any roadside.

Upon reaching Key West, with the sun already below the buildings, we knew we had to hustle. The busy city streets increasingly narrowed, forcing me to sometimes back up or skip them altogether. The sun kept sinking, and our urgency to park became desperate. We had come all this way, and missing it would be disheartening.

One parking attendant sitting slumped on a stool offered directions to view the sunset three blocks away, and the race persisted. At the end of Key West, where land met the endless sea, the lone parking lot charged RVs fifteen dollars to park. That was out of the question, but the road in was too narrow to back up.

Cars behind forced us to drive right up to the attendant. I had to think fast because the sun was barely visible. I spoke in a voice mixing desperation with frustration, "We just want to see the sunset."

Without a moment's hesitation, the attendant blurted, "Go," waving us on with a right-handed fist full of dollars as his eyes shifted to the next car for money.

Into the gravel lot we pulled, smiling from ear to ear, but we had no time to think about our smiles, or even enjoy them, because we had a sun to catch. We saw it moments above the ocean.

Standing at a dock on the port, we marveled as the sun dipped into the ocean just a couple minutes after our arrival, and if we hadn't hurried even after getting into the lot, we would have missed it.

Our timing and luck was everything on this day. It only took a minute or two before the ocean swallowed the sun in the horizon. Just as it completed its disappearing act, leaving behind a brilliant orange-red sky, but no steam, about one hundred birds took flight over the water. They soared across the colorful backdrop as if a race began upon the setting of the sun, giving us a true natural high.

Sunset on Key West, Florida

As disappearing daylight brightened the sky even further, we decided that we shouldn't overstay our welcome. Our eyes teared up from wear and tear, and we were desperate for a fast place to park for the night. On and on we drove, heading through the Keys, checking out motel after motel in search of an inconspicuous spot. Nothing looked good, and we found ourselves far from Key West, crawling through many slow miles.

When Tracy began begging for a campground, I promised her that the lights at the end of the bridge ahead would provide the place for our night's sleep. Our bad luck continued on that Key, and nothing looked safe until we pulled into a crowded motel parking lot and hid behind a couple of trucks.

The warm sixty-five degree weather required us to open the windows to allow the Gulf breeze into the camper as we discussed how perfect this spot turned out to be. Slowly, the fluttering shades that blew into the camper, abruptly slapping back to the screen, began to lower their volume as we both drifted off to sleep.

Drifting, drifting, going, going...three sharp bangs lifted Tracy and me about a foot above the bed, startled because we were nearly gone. The knocks came from just above Tracy's pillow, below the side window. "Security! Wake up!"

Through the darkness, I scurried for my clothes to look presentable as I dreamed up an explanation, still in a daze. Again he knocked because of my inability to dress fast enough, so Tracy and I yelled in unison, "Just a minute!"

I eventually had to turn on a light because my clothes had gotten mixed in with the blankets on the carpet below the bed. Once clad, I moved to the front of the RV and lifted the curtain to verify that he was who he claimed to be. I saw a uniform, badge, and flashlight, so I rolled the passenger's side window down a bit to ask what he wanted.

"You can't park here," warned the uniformed man, "unless all the rooms are booked."

He asked for my license, and when he held it in his hand, he began talking into his burping walkie-talkie. We thought a ticket would be forthcoming, but instead we received confirmation that there was no vacancy.

"All right," he said. "You can park here."

"Thank you," I said. "We're much too tired to drive, and all the campgrounds are booked."

We had only checked one campground, but it was stuffed with campers. The officer went over the motel rules and pointed out the rest rooms.

"We'll be out of here bright and early," Tracy assured him.

The officer smiled back with some reassurance of his own.

"Oh, I'll make sure of it," he said, "by 6:00 A.M."

He made good on his promise, even giving us an extra twelve minutes.

"Gotta go."

Tracy and I opened our eyes to this and thanked him. Along we moved to another parking lot ten minutes away. It was ten feet from Florida Bay.

I shared a cup of coffee with a spectacular view of the vast green waters, trying to imagine how exactly we came to arrive here. It seemed that this life of ours, although rugged at times, seemed so natural that time had passed without our thinking about it; without comprehending what we were doing or why.

Then I thought of how our present location was the furthest south we'd be for the rest of the trip. Now our journey was only an East Coast away from completion, but the end wasn't real yet. At the time, I figured that the end would seem real when our stopover in Florida concluded, and the Sunshine State released us to head north through the remaining ten states.

Then again, I had thought it would seem like we were heading home once we left Phoenix, but it did not. Nor did it feel that way when we left Mardi Gras to move in on Mississippi. When would we be going home?

March 12, 1993

Tracy and I enjoyed a relaxing stopover at her cousin's mobile home in West Palm Beach. Mark understood that we desperately needed a break from our rugged lifestyle. We had experienced full-time traveling, seeking overnight parking, and additional uncertainties about the old camper. Now we could relax in a much larger home.

We didn't want sun. The beautiful days were not enough to lure us outdoors. We just needed a break. Our goal became kicking back, using this time to prepare for a mad dash home, and reflecting on the overwhelming year. Here we would wait and hope for a warming trend in the northeast.

Moving through Fort Lauderdale en route to West Palm, we reintroduced ourselves to the Atlantic Ocean for the first time since Maine in May. We cheered, we hooted, and we joined hands. The Atlantic Ocean was also where we had begun in Rhode Island, so now we felt a little closer, and home became a little more real.

A powerful storm was expected to assault the entire East Coast moving north, and it would begin in Florida, billed as the "Storm of the Century." And it wouldn't be a storm if a tornado watch wasn't incorporated into the equation, and that's exactly what happened when the weather reporters issued the watch to last from early evening to early morning.

Warnings for severe thunder and lightning continued until approximately 4:00 A.M., but the strong winds began to kick up early in the day. Mark and his girlfriend, Michele, decided to join us for the show in the mobile home, giving up her apartment to keep us company.

We all called it a night with gusty winds persisting outside, but we didn't think we'd see the light of the new day before being awakened by Mother Nature. At least that's what the Storm Center told the listening audience. This would be a dangerous storm.

My dream of "The Wizard of Oz" was interrupted at the exact time the weathermen indicated. One by one, the occupants of the mobile home wearily strolled into the living room and huddled around the television for updates. The buckling of the roof became louder and more frequent as thunder, lightning, rain, and wind assaulted us.

We could only brace ourselves and hope for the best, but I didn't believe we stood a chance, especially after hearing stern warnings from meteorologists to get out of mobile homes. It wasn't the ideal place for us to be, but it was better than our camper, and it was too late to change our location.

Vicious wind continuously made a thunderous noise, which Mark admitted was being caused by the wind swooping under and buckling the roof. This is the very reason mobile homes easily lose their roofs. I very likely could have gone without that tidbit, because now I searched the ceiling for telltale signs of disaster for the duration of the storm. This trapped feeling was eating away at me, and at Michele, but Tracy and Mark didn't let it bother them. I was convinced that it was something in the family bloodline.

The weather report updated the tornado watch to a warning when tornadoes were reported in the central and western part of Florida. Now they were being produced, and I continued to look up to the ceiling as it buckled, waiting for it to take off. My mind was consumed with pictures of being sucked out of the living room and into the sky. I also listened closely over the howling of the wind for that freight train noise that means a tornado is outside your door.

Molly trotted around the living room trying to hide under everyone. When she ran up to me as I sat on the floor, I noticed her shaking and giving me frightened glances. I could only pet her and explain that I wasn't the best choice for her. I expounded that I was probably more frightened than she and suggested she get comforted by one of the cousins.

We survived the onslaught, but sixty-eight people did not, and more were missing. Winds up to one hundred miles per hour spawned fifty tornadoes across the state. The statistics weren't divulged until the next day. When I told Mark about them, he stared in thought, then chuckled as he told us that we probably shouldn't have stayed in his mobile home. Although the storm rapidly and savagely moved up the coast to New England, strong winds continued to pummel Florida.

The winds finally died down by nightfall, but I was not exactly falling in love with the state of Florida. Winter remained up the East Coast, and even the southern states of Alabama and Georgia produced snow, using bulldozers to clear the roads because snow is foreign to those regions, and they have no snow plows.

During the three weeks that we spent in West Palm Beach, we received heavy downpours, thunder, lightning, and severe wind for two of them.

March 26, 1993

When our time in West Palm Beach had expired and Tracy's cousins had bid us farewell, they weren't sad to see us go because the sun had gone into hiding since our arrival. As we entered the camper for the first time in three weeks, well rested, but weather-beaten, we moved out of the area as the sun poked through the clouds.

We moved up the coast toward Jacksonville with our time in Florida coming to an end. One month remained of our journey, and I guess it seemed more realistic when we considered that we had traveled well over thirty thousand miles.

We next arrived at the very home in which we had concocted this plan to travel; Dave and Cindy had invited us over for the re-union. During our visit, Dave turned on the whirlpool, and twenty minutes later we tried to get into it. It was time for reminiscing, since it had been in this very pool that Tracy and I had picked up the real estate section and started brainstorming. We had come full circle.

It took me about fifteen minutes to completely submerge my body down to my head. When Tracy came out to the whirlpool, I warned her about the excruciating heat, but before I could finish my sentence she had sunk down to her neck with a relaxed grin.

We spent our last couple of Floridian days in Jacksonville, again being treated like a king and queen, which had been the case during all of our many visits throughout the country. Temperatures leaped up into the fifties north of here, which was a relief since the time had come for us to set out for our last hurrah.

March 28, 1993

Hello Georgia: state thirty-nine. Our one place of focus for the entire state meant a drive exceeding two hundred fifty miles upon leaving Jacksonville. We moved in on Camp Sumpter, otherwise known as the Andersonville Civil War prison for Union soldiers taken by the Confederate army.

The entire town of Andersonville is an historic landmark, and when we arrived later in the afternoon, we only had time to dash to the visitor's center. A very small and elderly lady with a southern accent watched us as we breezed through the door.

"How y'all doin' today? Where y'all from?" she asked. "Y'all make sure you sign our guest register."

Whenever a new group entered the center, we heard the pleasant old lady asking the same two questions followed by the request. When she spoke of an RV park with full hookups for ten dollars, we jumped on it because it was already late, our bodies were weary from the long haul, and the aroma emanating from our bathroom demanded a dump station.

Tracy and I walked a couple of blocks to a convenience store and engaged in conversation with the owner, and the RV park soon became the topic. When I inquired as to whether it included cable television, he seemed pretty certain that cable only ran to the permanent park residents.

As we discussed this topic, a friend of the owner entered the store, better qualified to answer our question because he was a permanent park resident. He confirmed that permanent residents have cable, and visitors do not. Then, without batting an eyelash, he invited us to park in the empty site next to his so we could hookup to his cable box.

After he gave us directions to his site, we started walking back to our camper. On the way, this resident pulled up to us in his red Mustang and called us over. He informed us that Channel two showed HBO and Channel four showed Cinemax, then continued on his way.

We not only had cable television, but we had two premium channels as well. This means more when television is a luxury. The stranger, if I may even call him that, didn't have to do what he did, but he did. Why? We did not know, but we were getting a pretty good impression of Georgia.

March 30, 1993

Having glided up and down roller coaster hills through Georgia's farm country in the central portion of the state, then pushing east through Savannah, we navigated Route 17 over an enormous harp-like bridge spanning the Savannah River.

On the other side of the river, at the end of the bridge, we discovered our fortieth state of South Carolina. Forty states and we still had a chunk ahead of us. However, we began to get antsy, and trouble with the motorhome still concerned us, though less and less so with each passing day.

We passed burning fields in our new state. The fires to the right of the road burned trees and grass, but this went on for many miles, and occasionally someone wearing an orange vest supervised these flames. After we drove from the bottom to the top of the state during the day, all that we needed in South Carolina was a garage so we could consult a mechanic about a loss of power.

It felt like the camper was running out of gas, so I took an exit to find a truck stop, where the mechanic advised us to add gas treatment to super unleaded. He hit it on the head when he thought the problem resulted from chips or dirt sucked into the fuel line. We always exhausted our auxiliary tank when gas prices soared, and our secondary gauge never worked. A couple of dollars solved our problem.

South Carolina disappeared in the blink of an eye, but not before we filled up with gas. At an Exxon station, I filled the tank while looking at a welcome sign for North Carolina. Our destination of Asheville would enable us to invade the Great Smoky Mountains, but the first truck stop we saw would be home for the night.

Everything changed when over the airwaves blared the Emergency Broadcast System alarm, indicating another tornado watch.

"Glenn...let's go home," Tracy protested.

My sentiments exactly. I had had enough, but that was the first indication that severe weather and traveling in an RV for a year didn't mix well for Tracy either. The radio updated the storm to a warning as a tornado reportedly touched down in Atlanta and headed toward us. Dark, gloomy clouds hung low all around, leaving the clear opening in the arched horizon, the perfect arena for a tornado.

The extremely eerie setting made us wonder about the next stage in our lives, and we scoped out the roadside as we traveled, looking for a ditch just in case. Further warnings indicated that the tornado had whipped through the land at a rapid pace and was heading to our present location, so we floored it toward Asheville.

We had reached our wit's end. Flood warnings then affected the Asheville area, so we had to choose between the lesser of the two evils, opting for the flood.

We flew along the roads in panic as the radio continued to update the storm, which had supposedly ushered in a very damaging tornado. People in the endangered counties should get out of mobile homes and trailers and immediately get in basements, whether their own or a neighbor's. We were told to jump into a ditch if that was the only option.

Tracy and I sweated it out as the map in her hand related the whereabouts and direction of the tornado, which spun too close for comfort. She scanned camp books for a campground with electricity so we could at least get television news updates.

Thunder, lightning, and hail accompanied mysterious blackened clouds hanging with destructive intentions, and our decision for a campground was upgraded to a motel as fast as the watch was upgraded to a warning.

Then we descended into a steep canyon, passing Lake Lure, which seemed level with the road. Safety seemed nonexistent. A tornado could destroy a motel just as easily as it could a camper. We drove through the area affected by the flood watch, the severe thunder and lightning warning, and the tornado watch. We saw a motel in Lake Lure. Well, not in the lake, but in the town about twenty miles southeast of Asheville, and our camper gladly pulled into the parking lot.

It was not a moment too soon, because a blinding rain began beating the wipers hands down as lightning struck close. I didn't even want to step out of the camper to register for a room. The thought crossed my mind that the motel could very well be in the lake before the clouds emptied.

We needed shelter, and we needed it now. Never have I witnessed such a driving rain, and before my foot made it down to the pavement of the parking lot, I was drenched, soaked, and dripping profusely as if standing under a waterfall.

Inside, any price sounded good, so I paid in the office with wet bills. They allowed dogs and had cable television so we could overindulge in the weather channel.

The night sky persisted in its ugliness, and an alarm that lasted for about ten minutes pierced our ears. Coming from just over the mountain, it sounded like an air raid. Later, we learned that the alarm notified residents about the tornado watch.

Our discomfort and nervousness heightened when the storm knocked out the cable for a couple of hours, and thunder and lightning blasted us with close-range activity. When the cable returned, we learned that our area had been upgraded to a tornado warning as one had touched down twenty miles away in Forest City. We had passed through Forest City to get to Lake Lure, relieved that we had passed through earlier.

A little while later, the storm weakened to the point where we could walk out of the motel and see some blue sections in the dark sky. We even noticed a couple of stars, and it wasn't so difficult trying to get to sleep.

April 1, 1993

No flooding, no twisters, and no fooling. We were still tucked into the little motel in the valley when morning came around. What started as a warm day in shorts turned cold as we climbed high into the Great Smoky Mountains. Temperatures plummeted, and we found ourselves digging into the closet for our winter jackets.

We met a cloud cover in the mountains, then saw a line of snow along the roadside as elevation directed us skyward. Further on, we passed snow banks left over from the Storm of the Century.

The camper kept moving up. Clingman's Dome is the highest point in the park, but was closed due to a late winter. We rose high enough to enjoy a dizzying view of the valley, even with an extra thick blue haze that exuded from the mountains.

Upon reaching Newfound Gap, the point where North Carolina hands off Great Smoky to Tennessee, we concluded our view of the valley within the blue haze. Since the cloudy day obstructed much of the distant view, and the snapping cold prevented us from leaving the camper for very long, we decided to cut east across the state.

The following morning, when we awoke at a truck stop just outside of Asheville, snowflakes fell gently from the cold, white sky. It looked like it could snow, and it felt like it could snow, and sure enough winter still lingered. It disconcerted us to think that the warming trend could have been a spoof to get us out of Florida hibernation.

Winter even closed off much of the Blue Ridge Parkway, so we hopped on Interstate 40, and plowed through Winston-Salem and Greensboro. From the East Coast of North Carolina, where flight began, we flew into a new state.

Virginia never presented a truck stop, forcing us into Front Royal for a campground, but at least we found the entrance to Shenandoah National Park. Into these mountainous hills of Western Virginia, we searched frantically for a campground in Front Royal, finally discovering something very similar on the Shenandoah River.

Upon pulling into the empty field, we saw one trailer and a mobile home further up. We couldn't confirm that they were open. The dark office looked deserted, but a man in the field yelled that we needed to see him, and he started toward us.

This tall, stocky man with short brown hair pushed to the side breathed heavily while he held a rake in his hand. His southern dialect related the story of the flood that covered the very field underfoot when the river had violated its banks by two feet.

The man had been fixing the damage with the help of another kid. The kid lived in the trailer on this guy's land in exchange for a helping hand. Since the season hadn't officially begun, he reduced our fee by one-third.

Having only one crisp twenty dollar bill, Mr. Flood told me that he would collect later when he got change from the store, then assisted us in backing the RV into a non-muddy site. Then we began chatting, and he couldn't say enough about what we'd accomplished. He said it was an American dream, then somehow moved on to the subject of beets. His face lit up as he spoke of his fondness of the vegetable.

"Ah luv bytes," he said. "Ahhh...luv 'em." He shook his head and smiled as he got lost in memories of his favorite vegetable. "Ah just ate too many ov' em, and the next day was passin' bleud through mah urine." An even bigger smile enveloped his face when he saw our surprised reaction upon hearing about his ever so personal problem.

Tracy and I didn't feel too out of place laughing hysterically, and he continued with his medical findings.

"Ah wen to the doctor and foun' there was no reasin' fer it. I wen home and mah wauf suggested it was from ayten all them bytes. Ah paid a hundreh and fifty dollas to fon out ah ayt too many bytes."

We stood out by the camper, talking and laughing and sharing stories with Mr. Flood until he had to get back to work, and he ended our discussion by saying, "Ah tell you whah. Anyone who 'as the courge to doowa you two are doin' desarve tah stay at mah campgroun fer free."

And that's what we did…with water, sewer, and electric hookups. From our positioning, we enjoyed the view of the sun setting below the bridge leading over the Shenandoah River to Shenandoah National Park and listening to trains rush along the other side of the river.

It had been a while since the trains joined us at a campground, and I missed them. I honestly missed them, almost as much as I missed the sound of tractor-trailers humming away at truck stops. I had gotten so used to the noise of the trucker's engines that it no longer annoyed me. Instead, it had evolved into the sound of safety. It was a place to park for the night, and the two combined to give me peace of mind.

We'd been living on the road for quite some time before stopping for a couple of months in Phoenix. The urgency to move on inflated us both until we felt ready to explode, which was probably the reason we had covered so many miles in such a short period of time.

After such a layoff, we yearned to become part of the road, to travel, and see new things. The feeling was so strong that we called it quits at the Phoenix factory without knowing if we had a sufficient cash flow to complete the trip. Included in this renewed spark was an appreciation for these truck stops as a place to park, and they came and went in phases as we needed them.

April 7, 1993

Shenandoah National Park was our final of twenty-three national parks. There are fifty of them, but we wanted to leave some for later. When we arose, the bridge helped us across the river and onto Skyline Drive, where right-side views of Shenandoah Valley made my eyes wander from the road longer than they should have. Tracy suggested on several occasions that I should watch the road and she'd take care of the country.

The Blue Ridge Mountains overlapped with the hazy mysteriousness of the Great Smoky Mountains. To our left was the eastern rolling piedmont country. The Piedmont, or rolling hills, are actually ancient eroded mountains. The multitude of deer cheered us up because we hadn't seen any since prior to Phoenix. As for groundhogs, we seriously wondered if they saw their shadows.

Reaching West Virginia was no easy task because of the dramatics of the Appalachian and Allegheny ranges. Although we had planned an all day driving affair, our goal wasn't fulfilled. However, the splendid drive made us carefree anyway.

About halfway through the combined drive on Routes 219, 55, and 250, Tracy and I decided that West Virginia held some of the most beautiful roads in America. This wasn't a very difficult decision, especially entering the state and driving through the mountains and valleys. It seemed as though we were driving on top of the state.

This drive took place as we turned thirty-two thousand trip miles over. Never did we drive on flat land; it was more like an endless roller coaster. The frequent vistas from mountains and hilltops had us looking down on treetops most of the way.

Further into the northern half of the state, we passed well-kept houses. Continuing on, the houses turned quite shabby. However, the properties resided between mountains, either in an enclosed valley or on the mountaintops.

Reaching a truck stop in Fairmont late at night was the biggest relief for us both. This all day drive refused to end. The drive was picturesque, but an earlier truck stop would have pleased us to no end. However, we never knew when truck stops would appear until we saw billboards. That's why we hooted, hollered, and sometimes did a high-five when we saw any indication of a truck stop. They meant that much to us.

Good Friday

One year ago on this day, I cleared my desk and tipped my hat to my former fellow employees, but this time around was much better for obvious reasons. Our plans had us traveling from Fairmont to Wheeling for the day, but we never took into consideration the gargantuan Appalachian Mountains. Therefore, the drive was much tougher and longer than we had ever anticipated.

This steep, curved path exceeded four hours before we finally landed in Wheeling. We couldn't tell what state we'd be sleeping in at the day's end. We just had to twist and turn our way to a decent resting spot.

The last battle of the American Revolution shot through Wheeling in 1782 when forty British and two hundred sixty Indians attacked Fort Henry before the news of peace reached the outpost.

The separation of West Virginia from Virginia also took place in Wheeling, which twice used to be the capital of West Virginia. The birth of West Virginia resulted when states aligned themselves north or south during the Civil War. Many of Virginia's counties wished to be associated with the slave-free North.

Tracy and I found ourselves strolling up to the West Virginia Independence Hall. We opened the restored one-ton, iron-trimmed steel doors and passed into the very courtroom where the actual separation took place.

I sat on a bench in the back of the lonely room as Tracy stood before a podium in the front. I suddenly rose to my feet and raised my right arm, accompanied with shaky maneuvers seen only in silent films. I spoke in a slow and choppy manner, like an ancient man asking for separation from Virginia.

Tracy raised her arm with somewhat equal vigor, maybe a bit more trembling, then sliced her arm through the air diagonally north to south, wearing a face of stone throughout. She shot down my request. "No," she flatly determined.

There wasn't much left after our debate, mostly because we couldn't control our laughter, so out of the courtroom we amicably strolled until a further session could be arranged.

April 15, 1993

By the time we reached our forty-fourth state of Pennsylvania, having only ten days left until the camper became a vehicle of our past, we were well-prepared to put an end to life on the road in a camper. We began to joke about living in a real house. We may have been joking, but only slightly.

We shared our excitement about having a house with a floor and walls in which three cannot be touched at one time (I then proved it could be done in the camper). The house wouldn't sway back and forth, viciously jolting us around inside, and we'd have a roof. The toilet would flush, we'd have a high-powered shower, and a glass of water would be easily attainable.

These things were now luxuries to us, and I think everyone should do without to see just what going without would do. Moving into Amish territory in Lancaster County wasn't too much of a stretch for us because of our denied modern conveniences.

Maybe life in the camper would have differed if violent weather patterns hadn't plagued us all year long, but that wasn't the case. I had feared for my life many times. Several times I remembered thinking that the trip would be interrupted by tragedy, and we wouldn't be able to share our adventures with each other or anyone else. My imagination often had us getting sucked into the sky or blown off a road and down a mountain.

Tracy's bravery had been worn down to metal, leaving her final weather-nerves exposed. My last weather-nerves had surrendered somewhere back in the Midwest. When a person is used to one weather pattern, they should expect an element of surprise when traveling through the plains, or anywhere else out west. No matter how many times you hear about strong sweeping winds off the plains, it won't mean anything until you feel them. I felt them, feared them, and wanted to run from them, and even the camper hated them. Molly could surely sympathize.

Home sounded great. We were anxious to reunite with family and friends, having last seen them waving goodbye as we pulled away and headed into America. In a couple of weeks they'd all be gathered around again, but this time to welcome us home from the journey that they had thought would never end.

Pennsylvania sounded so close to Connecticut that we began to feel the warmth of home, but still it wasn't possible yet. We were feeling emotional and homesick. We were going home in a couple of weeks, and the rest of the trip seemed academic.

One night, while in a campground in Amish country, Tracy and I sat in our usual corners of the camper reading in our armchair pillows. A blustery wind outside rocked the camper, which seemed to be the norm most of the year.

We discussed the camper and its problems, but the fact remained that it had whirled us around the entire country and back, and would bring us home. There were still a few ongoing problems, but for the most part we concentrated on the light at the end of the tunnel.

Our books now on our laps, we spoke of all that we'd accomplished, and how our weather-related problems had just been part of the package. It felt like the last day of school was approaching. The end seemed like it would never arrive, but when it finally did, we wondered how an entire year could have passed so quickly. That's the way life can be, but our memories would never vanish.

Traveling along the bottom of Pennsylvania, then highlighting our erratic east-to-west trail made our map look like a seismograph. Our camper moved from Civil War Gettysburg through

Amish country, Valley Forge, and back to Amish country in search of the community set back in time.

Side streets led to the backcountry, but the main road was just that. Tractor-trailers owned the roads here, but it still shocked us to see a truck stop within Amish country. The authenticity went right down the drain.

Semis whipped around the area, past horse-drawn buggies, and through the tourist areas. We weren't happy with this area on Route 30 because we didn't feel this was a true representation of the Amish. So we searched the back roads for answers.

Back roads throughout Intercourse meandered through neatly combed fields of freshly plowed soil, while horse-drawn plows kept tilling. These "plain" people did not look at much more than the ground when they walked since their bible dictates that it's sinful to have photos taken of themselves.

Still not getting our fill even after seeing this private life, we figured that a horse and buggy ride would satisfy us, so we strayed off to Route 896. Mr. Buggy, a fast talker who wore his brown hair short above his eyes, explained in earnest that his ride was a truly authentic one through back roads where the Amish reside.

He himself did not claim to be Amish, nor did the guides, but the Amish do not give tours, and he had to get permission from them to open the business. Mr. Buggy became enraged while speaking of his cheating competitor, who claimed to be Amish, but had his photo on his brochure.

"That right there tells you," he said, flailing his right hand in the air while making a point. "The old guy thinks he's fooling people with that white beard. He may look Amish, but everybody knows he is not. And nobody does anything about it."

As for the constant dangerous flow of traffic, he explained that the Amish are used to it, and that indeed there have been fatalities when horse-drawn buggies venture out at night. The tractor-trailers don't have the luxury of stopping on a dime, and the rest is history.

The law now states that the Amish must use safety reflectors, which, for obvious reasons, they abhor. Their peaceful living is becoming commercialized, and slowly but surely they're losing the battle.

A thin girl with blonde hair tucked in a ball under her cap sat down in the back of the buggy. Tracy and I spent these idle moments swatting gnat-sized insects that swarmed around the horse, which would shake its head whenever the insects violated its ears. The girl, once a milk farmer in this same area, loved her job. She pulled us through the back roads, blocking traffic until oncoming cars cleared. It amused us to see these tourists drive by, stretching their necks to the limit to get a glimpse inside our buggy.

A mid-sized car from Delaware packed six kids into it, who rolled a camcorder as they passed. Six heads turned to see us. We felt Amish, and they thought we were, but now we knew what it looks like from the Amish perspective when we do likewise.

The three mile path hardly brought us to an Amish person, and the connection to these people never materialized as advertised. The ride did nothing but give us sore behinds, but for some reason, while we stepped off the ride and Mr. Buggy asked our opinion, we did not tell him the truth by saying that the buggy ride sucked. But if we hadn't taken the ride, we would have wished we had. Now we can say we took the buggy ride and it sucked.

April 18, 1993

Pushing across our forty-fifth state of Maryland toward the capital of Annapolis wasn't too much of a chore for us because of its small size. Late at night, we reached a truck stop in this small capital city, parking and nearly collapsing from exhaustion after a full day in the nation's capital. The whiffs of gas that Tracy kept commenting on made me assume it to be the gas pumps.

However, when Tracy let Molly out, she followed the smell to a puddle of gas under the backside of the camper. Quickly jumping out of the camper, I stuck my finger in the puddle to verify gas, then noticed a steady drip from the gas tank. With a flashlight in hand, I saw that the leak came from a screw inside a rubber hose. I tried tightening it with a screwdriver, but it turned loosely with each revolution.

I turned off all pilot lights and shut off the propane gas tank as Tracy called for advice or road service. A representative told Tracy to call the Fire Department about the gas leak. Tracy shook it off and tried to get satisfaction from the Fire Department.

A fire truck with flashing lights but no sirens pulled into the parking lot and embarrassed the hell out of us as everyone in the truck stop peered out to see the commotion. The firemen looked at the puddle of gas under the RV, and one of them said that they couldn't do anything for us, wondering why we had even bothered to call. They advised us to park in back of the truck stop where the sand could soak up gas until the Texaco station could work on it in the morning. They also suggested that we rub soap over the leak to control it overnight.

Tracy called for road service again, and the same representative answered the phone and eventually agreed to send out a tow truck. When the truck arrived, the driver told us that he couldn't help because he had received word that we were a miscellaneous case, so he had no tools with him.

At least the lady had sent a friendly driver. Once an RV owner himself, he took a look underneath and seemed sure that the leak had been caused by the tank's breather hose due to an overfilled tank. This made sense because I had recently filled it to the brim. He explained that the screw acted as a plug to the hose to keep the gas in and should be there, but we should put a clamp over the hose to stop the leak.

"Do you know who you're talking to?" asked my under-confident wife.

The man looked at me and chuckled, but I thought it might be something I'd be able to handle.

We miraculously found one last clamp in the toolbox underneath the dinette bench and placed our plastic rug runner next to the leak. With clamp and screwdriver in hand, I struggled in a most awkward position on my back. I covered my hands with gas and grease as Tracy ran into the camper to grab the camcorder for those at home who wouldn't believe it.

After a twenty minute battle, I pulled myself from under the camper after strategically placing a piece of cardboard to check the leak in the morning.

I scrubbed gas from my black hands and clipped my black fingernails. At that point, I decided against opening a garage back in Connecticut. Although somewhat successful, the smell of gas permeating the camper would stay with us all night.

We had to keep the windows open through the frigid night, and we couldn't use propane, meaning that it would also be a cold, cold night. We wrapped our fully clad bodies in layers of blankets. We emphasized that seven days remained as we drifted off to sleep, though our faces were still frigid.

The next morning, I pulled a spotless piece of cardboard out from under what I discovered to be the auxiliary gas tank, then applauded myself. Our next mission was to run the auxiliary tank dry, then retire it.

Ridiculous oil change quotes forced us to give up on the idea. We knew that we weren't near the center of America anymore. Maryland wasn't overly kind to us. The state buzzed with commotion, but that all changed on the east side of the Chesapeake Bay when we reached the barren countryside of eastern Maryland.

We sorely needed this peace. Although it was prettier and much calmer, the serenity peaked as we crossed into our forty-sixth state of Delaware: The Small Wonder.

The accurate welcome sign took us into territory we sorely missed and that had been absent for quite some time. Whenever we spent any time in the chaos of a big city, experiencing the frenzied traffic and frenzied people, it made being in a laid-back countryside that much more appealing.

April 21, 1993

Delaware is so small. We drove south about five miles from its border with Maryland, then up the coast through Rehoboth Beach, shooting up to the top through the capital of Dover toward Wilmington in no time.

We hung out at a campground and thought about what life would be like back in Connecticut. We had readied ourselves to return, eager for the next stage of life with the last stage assured, and now it was only a matter of days.

En route to the top of the state, we had in mind a truck stop near Wilmington because of the late hour and approaching darkness. While getting gas, I asked the attendant clad in overalls if he knew of a truck stop around.

"About a mile and a half up the road," he advised, pointing to Route 13 and adding, "That's where the whores hang out."

I chuckled as if it was a joke, then proceeded there, pulling into the very back of the truck stop to ensure our privacy. While we sat back and read in the camper, I noticed a police cruiser through the side window, which had allowed my view of the gravel parking lot. The officer parked about fifty feet from the camper, facing it, and left the car idling as he communicated with police headquarters.

I moved to the front of the camper, lifted the dividing curtain, and waited for him to come over with his complaint. He never did, so I returned to my seat and kept an eye on him as I returned to my business.

When he finally got out of the cruiser, I returned to the front and rolled down the passenger window a couple of inches.

"What are you doing?" he asked.

"Just taking a break from traveling. We're heading to New Jersey."

"Roll that window down some more. I can barely hear you."

I rolled the window almost halfway down.

"Who are you with?"

"My wife."

"Oh," responded the officer in complete surprise. He even stumbled on his next sentence. "You're...you're with your wife? Well, this is just a bad spot. How long will you be here?"

"Well, since you put it that way, we're leaving now."

We were much too tired to move on through darkness, but we had no choice, and we were fortunate to have received that warning. As we headed out, we made the connection between what the gas station attendant had said and what the officer had said. The first comment regarding the whores, and the next about the bad section began to make sense. Plus the fact that the officer had been surprised to hear that I was with my wife.

We agreed that being back in the northeast proved more risky, and truck stops would no longer suffice. Into our forty-seventh state of New Jersey, where one book told us to "know your destination, do it and get out," we fought through yet another rainstorm while heading down to Cape May. These hazardous driving conditions brought us from campground to campground as the night grew late.

On Route 9, gates closed off most of the campgrounds, verifying our return to the northeast. Self-service and the "pick a site and pay in the morning" mentality were a thing of the past. None of that existed here, so we just moved along.

April 23, 1993

Our final days on the road threw very cold temperatures together with rain and severe wind gusts, which made it an easy decision to rule out Cape May, even though only twenty miles separated us from the southernmost part of town. Home was now very much on our minds, but our final stop put us in Atlantic City.

Never on the entire trip had we traversed worse roads than in New Jersey. It was like a bad roller-coaster ride because of the brutally bumpy roads and deep gouges, potholes, and unfinished construction. They'd give the Badlands a run for their money. Missing signs also helped to send us in circles.

When Atlantic City finally arrived, we decided that Las Vegas had probably spoiled us. The spread-out casinos couldn't create the excitement of Las Vegas Boulevard. We drove the narrow, crowded streets to the Taj Mahal, which we decided would represent Atlantic City.

The dirty city's Taj Mahal wasn't even better than the worst casino in Vegas. We took twenty-four dollars inside, lost it fast, and departed. Tracy wasn't even sold on going into the casino at all, asking if it was really worth it as we struggled for a parking spot, but it had been too tough of a drive to just cancel this attraction.

Wind gusts nearly blew us off the sidewalks while we attempted to walk back to the camper, but we ducked into the wind and maintained the sidewalk the best we could.

This final event on the trip gave us a couple of days to get home. However, nothing seemed to go as planned from the time we entered New Jersey, and this continued after Atlantic City. Every road was atrocious, we found no campgrounds, and the sweeping wind made it impossible to drive.

Moving north on Route 206 led us to Trenton. We hoped for a campground before my eyes completely shut. I looked up just in time to catch a glimpse of a red traffic light flowing horizontally from the right side of the street, but by the time I slammed on the brakes, we were in the middle of the intersection.

I hit the gas to make it through safely, but I was too shaken to continue on. I was nearly sweating, but thankful that no cars or trucks had sped through the intersection at the same time. I pulled into the first parking lot I saw, put the shifter in park, shut off the engine, and walked to the bed in back. Through a grin, Tracy asked if my pants were as wet as hers.

The roads, though we couldn't believe it ourselves, actually worsened. One exit ramp forced the camper to crawl cautiously at about five miles per hour through this rough sea. I had never seen nor felt anything like it, and wondered how they could leave it that way. The bumps and gouges were so severe that the camper moved high into the air, crashing to the ground even at a low speed.

The Garden State Parkway seemed like our last hope at getting our forty-eighth state spoon. My Uncle Roddy in Phoenix, Maryland, had not been far off when he warned us that on this parkway, once you get up to speed, you have to pay another toll.

Earlier in the day, we paid one dollar to drive over an extremely chewed up and damaged bridge. When I handed the kid four quarters, I asked him if this was going toward roadwork. He didn't quite get my point, answering my question in the affirmative, but maybe he was just used to it. We didn't want to be.

A rest area on the parkway became our final chance for a New Jersey spoon. They had them, but the store was cashing out with a gate closing the store off from the mini-mall. There was a two-hour limit in the parking lot, but if anyone asked, we were prepared to say that we were waiting to buy a spoon.

The fact that this turned into one of our worst days on the trip had us anxiety-ridden. We even agreed that we'd be heading home if it weren't for our homecoming party two days ahead of us. I awoke every couple of hours, until finally getting up for good by 6:00 A.M. We had a successful overnight, I grabbed the spoon, and we gladly left New Jersey and headed back to Connecticut.

April 24, 1993

Tomorrow would be the day. Tonight would be the last night to sleep in the camper, and we continually reminded ourselves of that. Skipping New York City, we gladly worked our way around, crossing the Hudson River at Newburgh, and pushing desperately through New York.

We closed in on Connecticut, and the moment we'd been waiting for soon came. As a sign welcomed us into our forty-eight[th] state of Connecticut, Tracy and I screamed in celebration, yelling things such as "State number forty-eight! We've made it! The forty-eight states, Canada and Mexico!"

It was not real for us. The moment hurt our cheeks with oversized smiles, and everything we said became a scream. Molly thought we were crazy, but at the moment we didn't care what Molly thought. Dark blue Connecticut license plates appeared all around us, and we wondered where the steep hills of northwest Connecticut had come from. We were exuberant, and it would only become more intense when the motor stopped.

After one year of experiencing this country, the Constitution State meant so much more to us. Seen in a new light, we noticed that the trees, the greenness, and the hills continued to roll. Life was beautiful as well. The ride to Winsted filled us with bliss as we rolled into a campground for the last night of the trip.

We backed into our last site. We hooked up electric and water for the last time. We noted and highlighted every last action. As tired as we were from the long drive, we still couldn't sleep as we kept talking about the next day. We'd be reuniting with family and friends, and the completion of an American Dream would be under our belts.

April 25, 1993

Although Tracy and I arose as anxiously as the sun and tried to kill time until morning grew old, we still managed to rush at the end, trying to get to the noon gathering in much the same way a late employee moves to get to work. The reunion would be held at a condominium clubhouse in New Britain, and family and friends would watch us pull in.

All that we talked about this morning was our emotions upon seeing everyone after one full year. The feelings at this time were too overwhelming to hold within, so the conversation never strayed to another subject.

We unhooked for the last time, and then used the dump station for the last time. We zeroed in on home, and our excitement multiplied as we passed over the town line. Everything looked different, yet familiar.

Then came the long road, which meandered through Judi's condominium units. As we took a right turn off the main road, we saw a bright pink fluorescent sign attached to a stick

in the ground that read, "WELCOME."

Every couple hundred feet stood another one word sign: HOME...HAPPY...ANNIVERSARY...TRACY...GLENN...AND ...MOLLY.

The long road spread out the message, which had us nearly jumping out of our skin to see what lay ahead. As we drove along, reading the words loudly and together, we found out what it's like to be in the most ecstatic mood ever. The morning weariness diminished, and our pulses quickened.

The camper slowly turned with the road. The clubhouse was nearly in sight. This happened so fast. We still couldn't see anything. Tracy told me to turn into a road hidden by trees, and I jerked the camper to make the turn.

At that very moment, what we saw further up made me jerk the camper back and continue on. We saw that the clubhouse parking lot began another fifty feet ahead. We could see people over the trees looking down on us from the balcony, and everyone apparently saw our camper take the wrong turn.

As we pulled into the homecoming party thirty-four thousand five hundred miles later, a multi-colored streamer ran across the entrance, attached to trees on either side. A sign in the middle read, "FINISH LINE!"

Slowly turning into the lot, hands waving us on, I drove the camper through the finish line, snapping the streamer and ending the trip. Our inspirational journey through America had come to an end, and the crowd seemed to have grown. The crowd was just that: a crowd. People looked down from the balcony. People closed in on us from the front yard, and the clubhouse kept emptying of people.

They moved in on the camper even more once I put it in park. We took a moment to look, to comprehend, to reflect, but it was too overwhelming to see any one face.

As Tracy and I slowly opened our doors, exhilarated beyond our wildest dreams, we separated for quite some time. Tracy walked out, leaving the door open, and began hugging her cousins, friends, her mother, her father, and whoever else stood in line.

I slowly, but anxiously, stepped down from the camper, leaving the door open, and saw people approaching left and right for hugs. I didn't know where to turn, and all that I honestly remember of this blurry moment is hugging one person, and moving on to the next, and the next.

I looked down to see little Matthew, my four-year-old nephew, and I bent down to hug him. I did remember seeing him. He had grown so much, and matured, but not enough to deter him from grabbing the traveling hat from my head and running away.

I let him run with it, then turned to see my pregnant sister, Gladie, and my other sisters, Karen and Lee. I saw my brother, Frank, my mother and father, and my next door neighbors. My fourth sister, Kathy, arrived later and introduced us to Kelly, our new niece.

When the smoke had cleared, I could talk to people. At one point, I looked at the camper from the balcony, sitting exactly where I had parked it in the middle of the parking lot. It looked like a champion, like a purple van with a monkey, having successfully completed the trip. One of the back tires was severely damaged. There were two deep slices on the sidewall, leaving it barely drivable. This was just a little something by which to remember New Jersey.

I spotted Tracy talking to a circle of people, and I drifted off as I reflected on how enriched our lives had become. Another vivid flash put me in Vegas, followed by one in Hungry Horse, Montana. The brilliant flashes made me feel like I was presently in those places even though I was home now. I loved that, and I also loved the fact that these places would be readily available for the rest of our lives upon simple reflection.

Even though we had unbuckled our seatbelts for the final time, these memories meant that we'd always be strapped into an American Dream, even after parting ways after five years of marriage. And, having shared what is a dream for most Americans, we believe our union had a purpose behind it. Thank you, America.

About the Author

Glenn Maynard has a Bachelor of Arts degree in English from the University of Connecticut, and a degree in Communications. After spending 4 years living in Denver, CO, he returned home to Connecticut, and now resides in Wethersfield, CT. He has a 9 year-old son named Andrew.

He was a travel correspondent for three newspapers while traveling through the United States, Canada and Mexico during his one-year journey. He had a total of twenty newspaper articles published. His story was captured on the evening newscast upon his return.

CPSIA information can be obtained
at www.ICGtesting.com
Printed in the USA
FFOW04n1122050116
19913FF